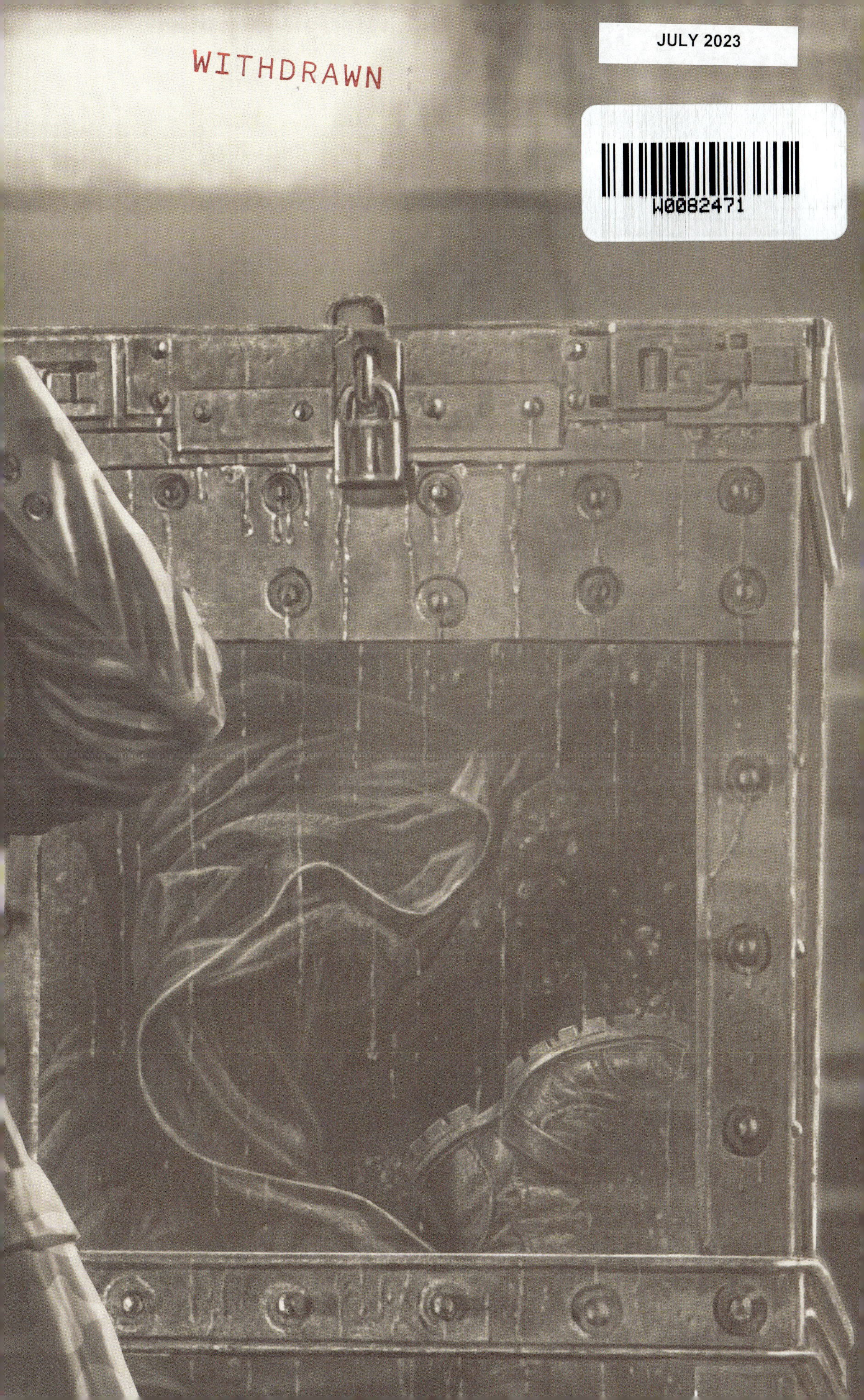

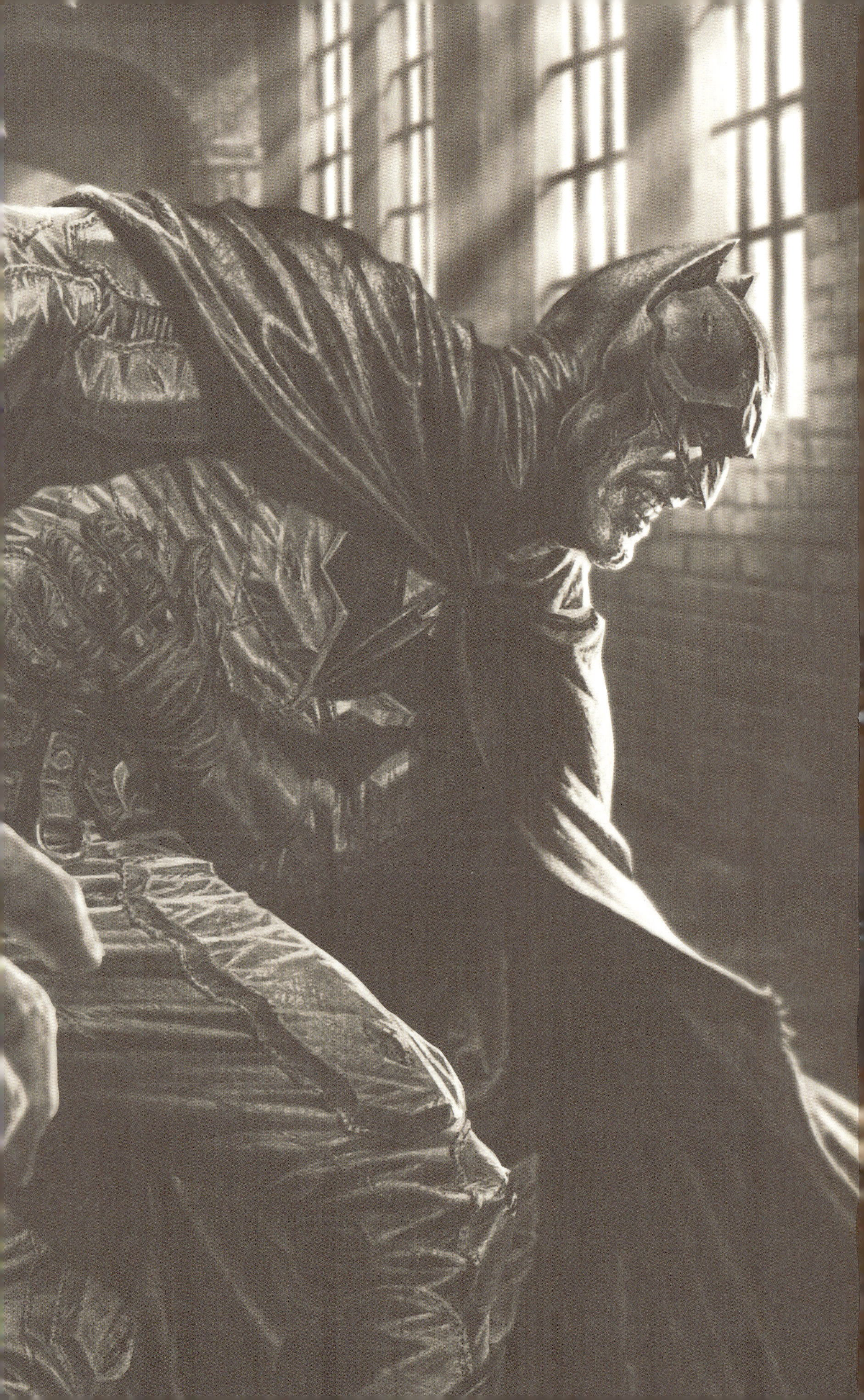

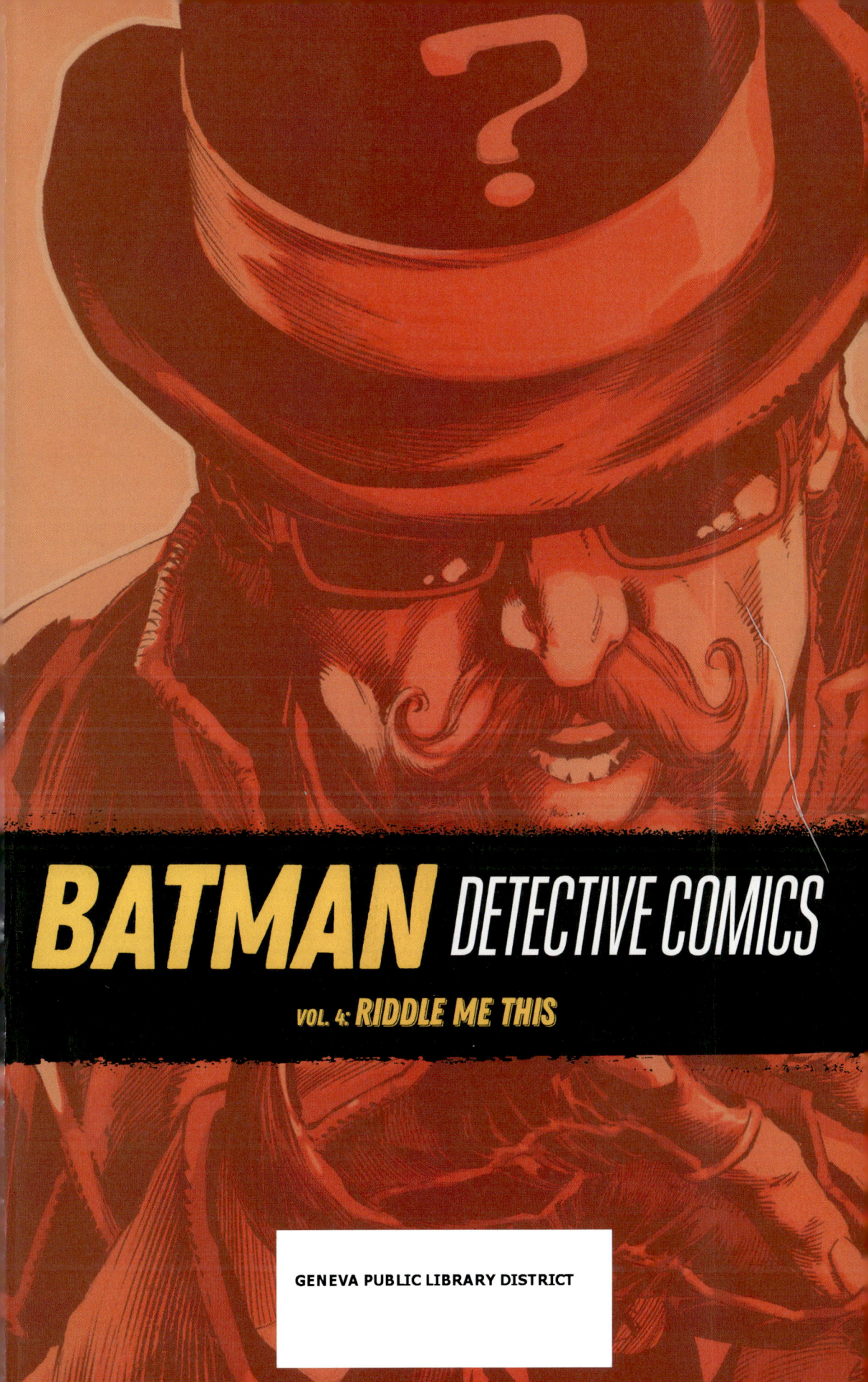

BATMAN DETECTIVE COMICS

VOL. 4: RIDDLE ME THIS

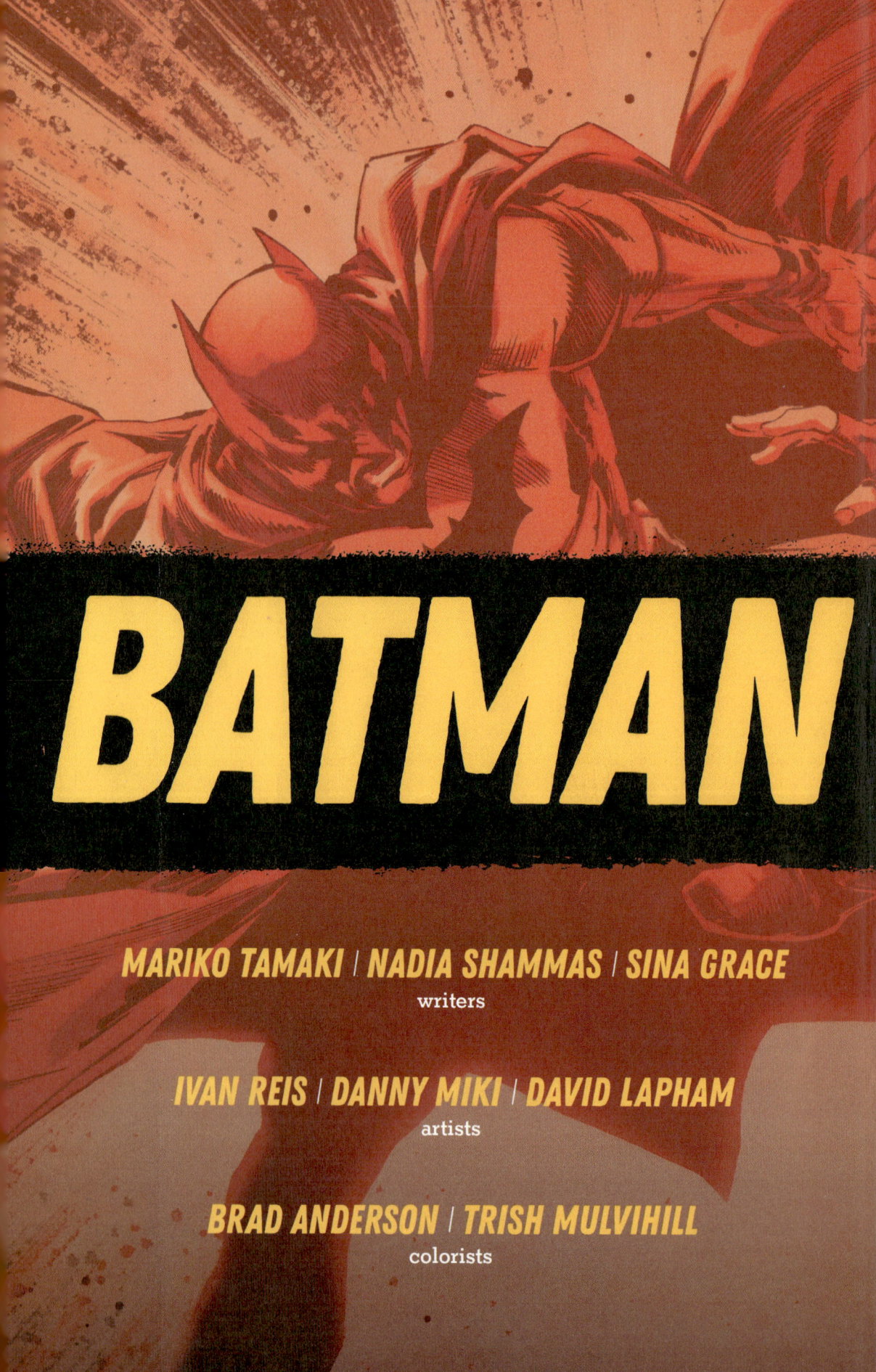

BATMAN

MARIKO TAMAKI / NADIA SHAMMAS / SINA GRACE
writers

IVAN REIS / DANNY MIKI / DAVID LAPHAM
artists

BRAD ANDERSON / TRISH MULVIHILL
colorists

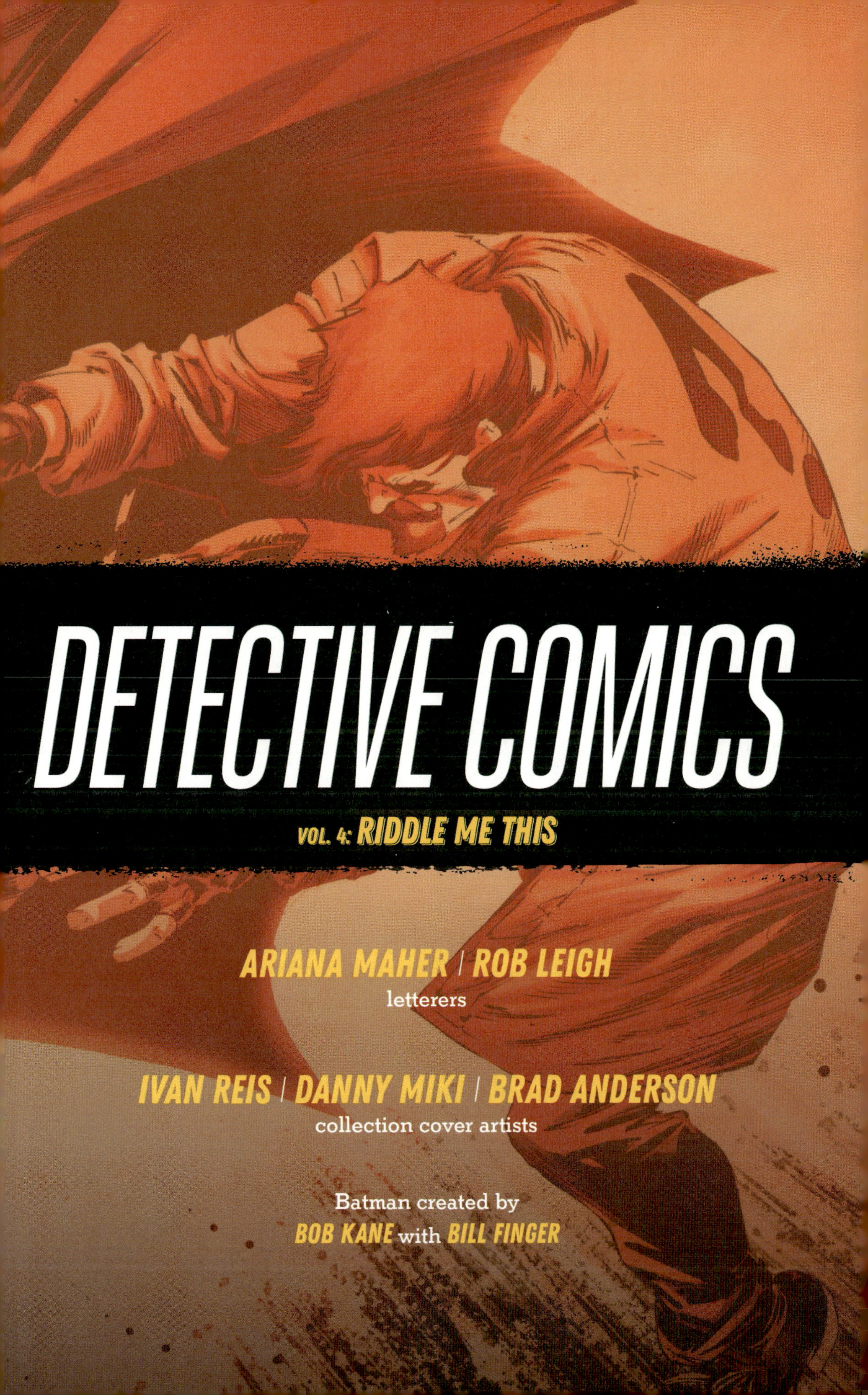

DETECTIVE COMICS

VOL. 4: RIDDLE ME THIS

ARIANA MAHER / ROB LEIGH
letterers

IVAN REIS / DANNY MIKI / BRAD ANDERSON
collection cover artists

Batman created by
BOB KANE with **BILL FINGER**

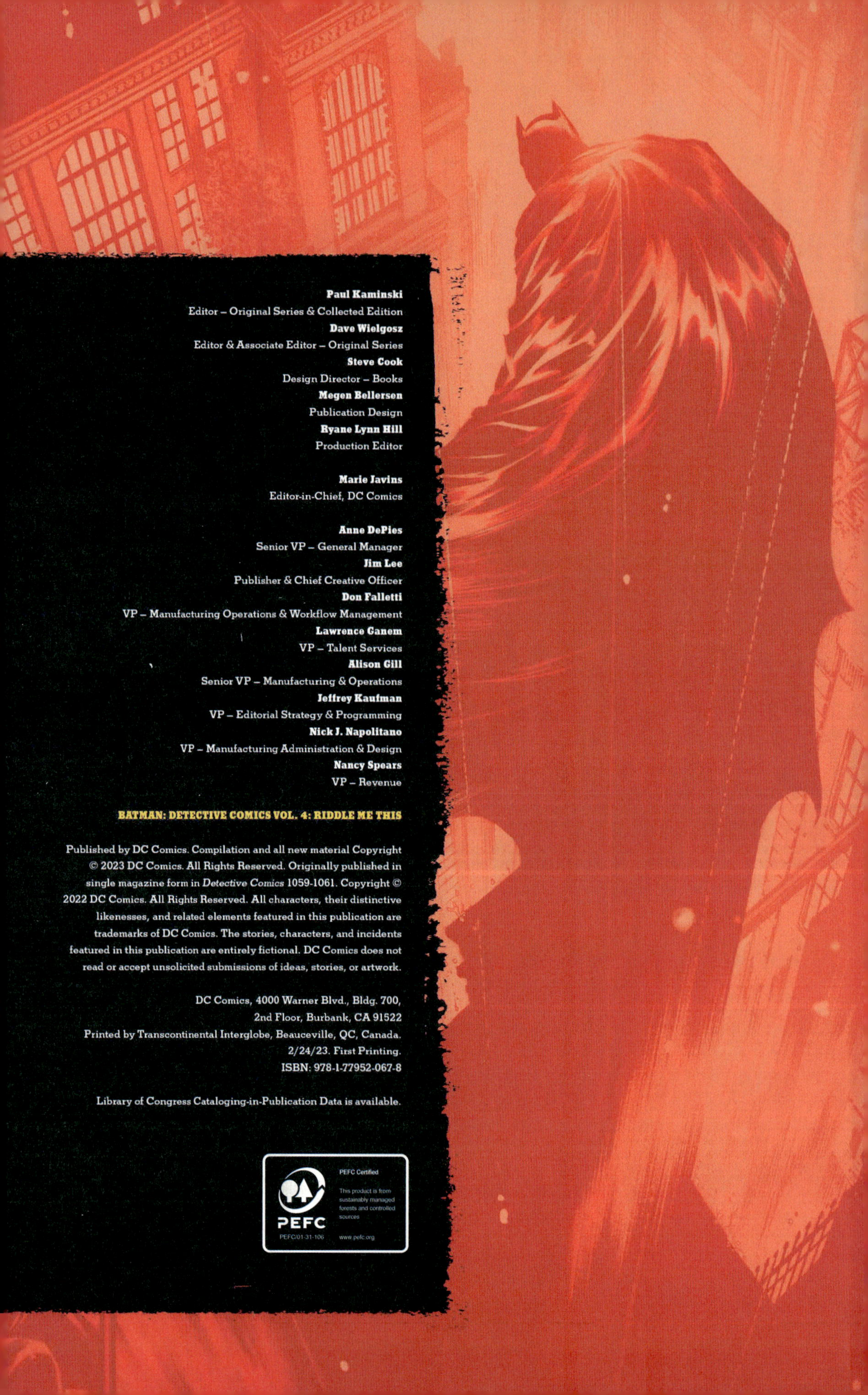

Paul Kaminski
Editor – Original Series & Collected Edition
Dave Wielgosz
Editor & Associate Editor – Original Series
Steve Cook
Design Director – Books
Megen Bellersen
Publication Design
Ryane Lynn Hill
Production Editor

Marie Javins
Editor-in-Chief, DC Comics

Anne DePies
Senior VP – General Manager
Jim Lee
Publisher & Chief Creative Officer
Don Falletti
VP – Manufacturing Operations & Workflow Management
Lawrence Ganem
VP – Talent Services
Alison Gill
Senior VP – Manufacturing & Operations
Jeffrey Kaufman
VP – Editorial Strategy & Programming
Nick J. Napolitano
VP – Manufacturing Administration & Design
Nancy Spears
VP – Revenue

BATMAN: DETECTIVE COMICS VOL. 4: RIDDLE ME THIS

DC Comics, 4000 Warner Blvd., Bldg. 700,
2nd Floor, Burbank, CA 91522
Printed by Transcontinental Interglobe, Beauceville, QC, Canada.
2/24/23. First Printing.
ISBN: 978-1-77952-067-8

Library of Congress Cataloging-in-Publication Data is available.

PEFC Certified
This product is from sustainably managed forests and controlled sources
PEFC/01-31-106
www.pefc.org

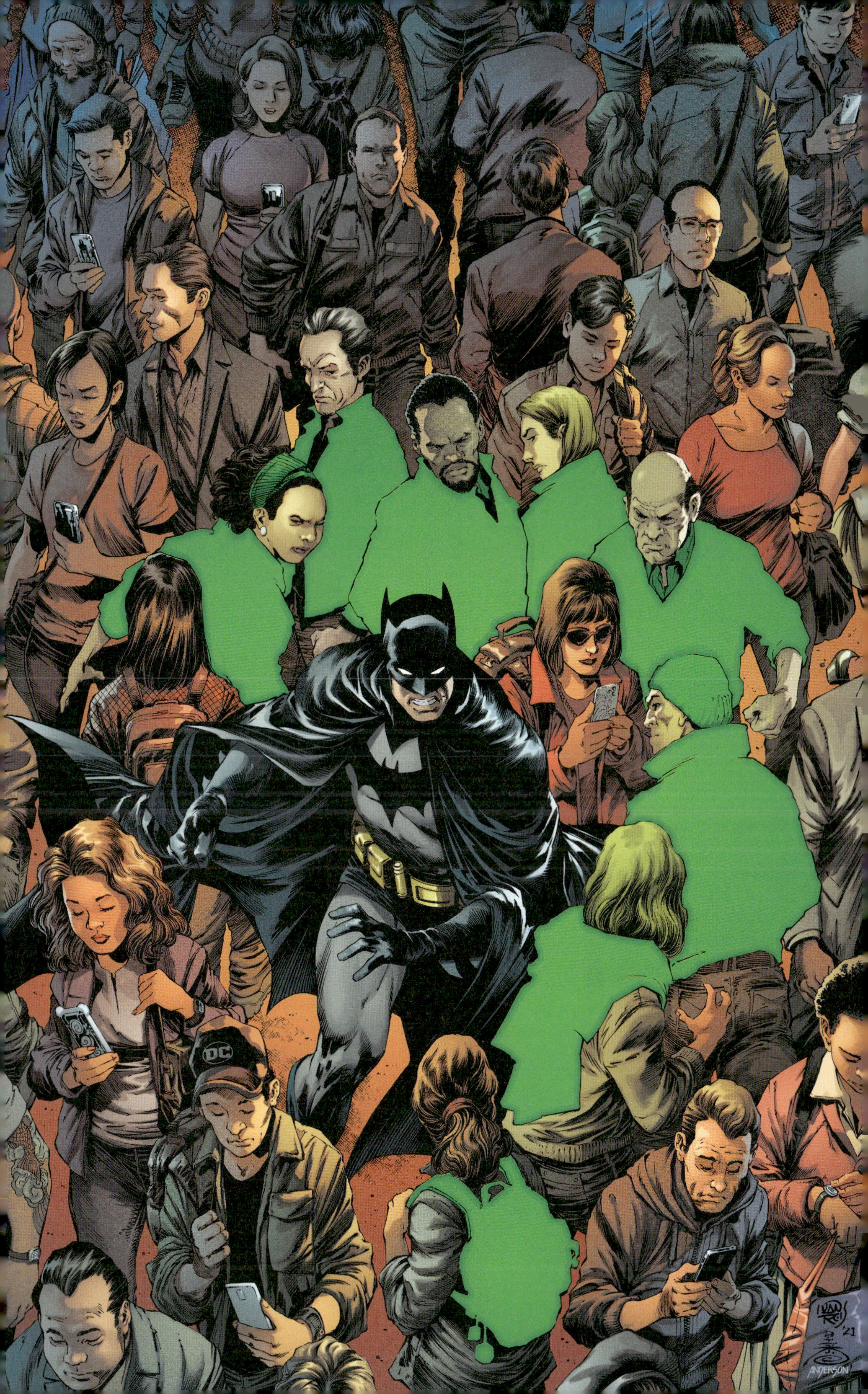

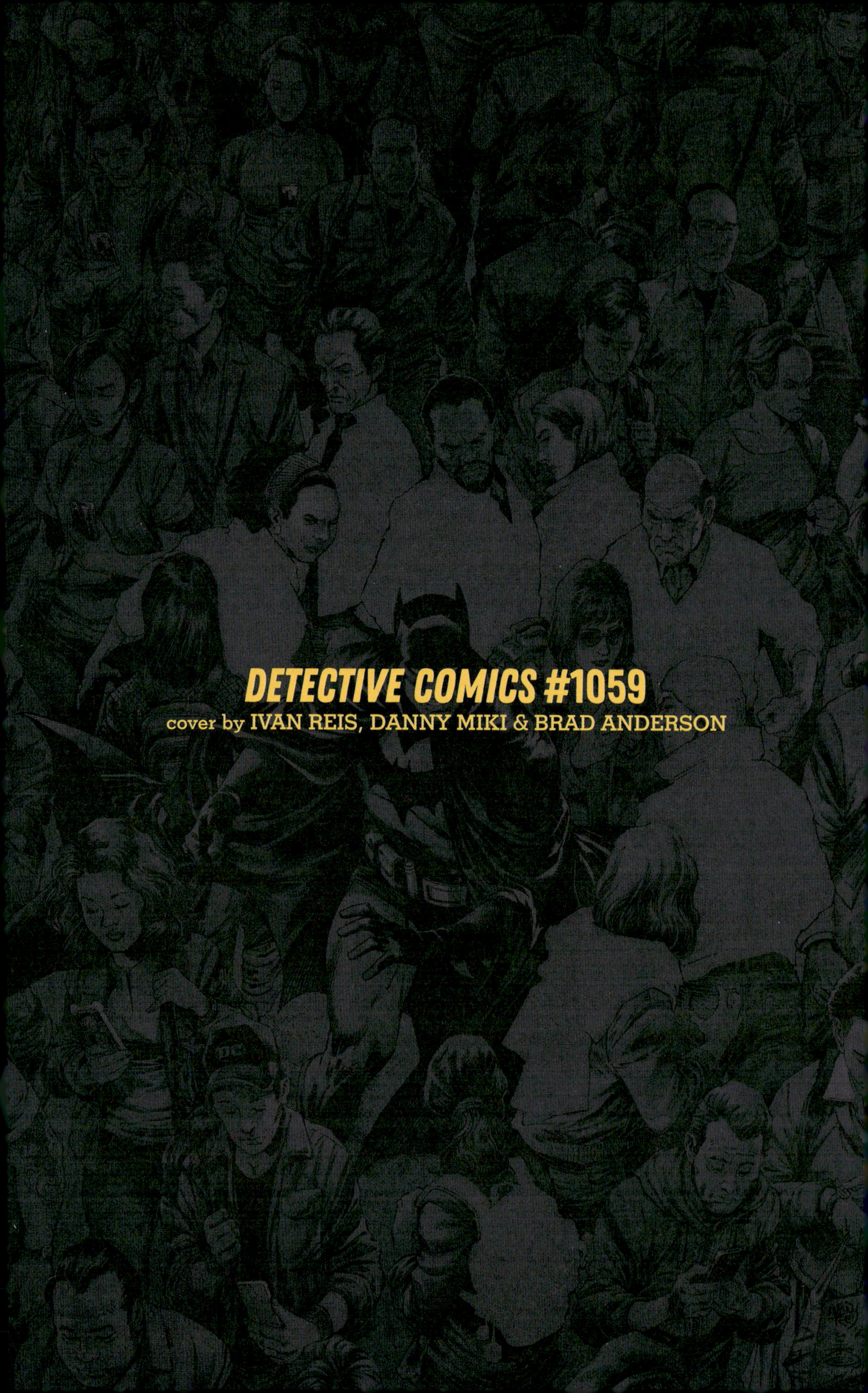

DETECTIVE COMICS #1059

cover by IVAN REIS, DANNY MIKI & BRAD ANDERSON

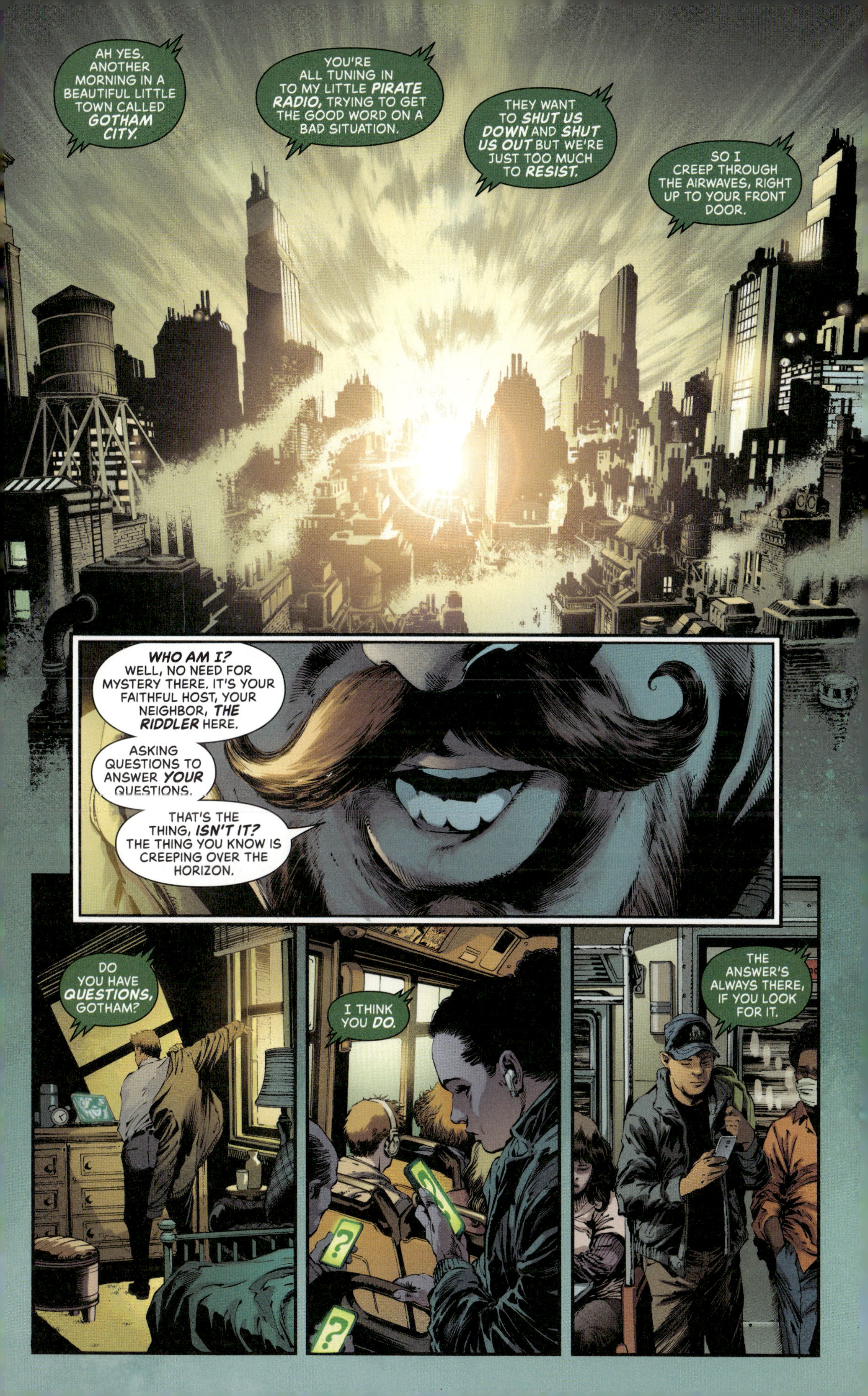
AH YES. ANOTHER MORNING IN A BEAUTIFUL LITTLE TOWN CALLED GOTHAM CITY.
YOU'RE ALL TUNING IN TO MY LITTLE PIRATE RADIO, TRYING TO GET THE GOOD WORD ON A BAD SITUATION.
THEY WANT TO SHUT US DOWN AND SHUT US OUT BUT WE'RE JUST TOO MUCH TO RESIST.
SO I CREEP THROUGH THE AIRWAVES, RIGHT UP TO YOUR FRONT DOOR.
WHO AM I? WELL, NO NEED FOR MYSTERY THERE. IT'S YOUR FAITHFUL HOST, YOUR NEIGHBOR, THE RIDDLER HERE.
ASKING QUESTIONS TO ANSWER YOUR QUESTIONS.
THAT'S THE THING, ISN'T IT? THE THING YOU KNOW IS CREEPING OVER THE HORIZON.
DO YOU HAVE QUESTIONS, GOTHAM?
I THINK YOU DO.
THE ANSWER'S ALWAYS THERE, IF YOU LOOK FOR IT.

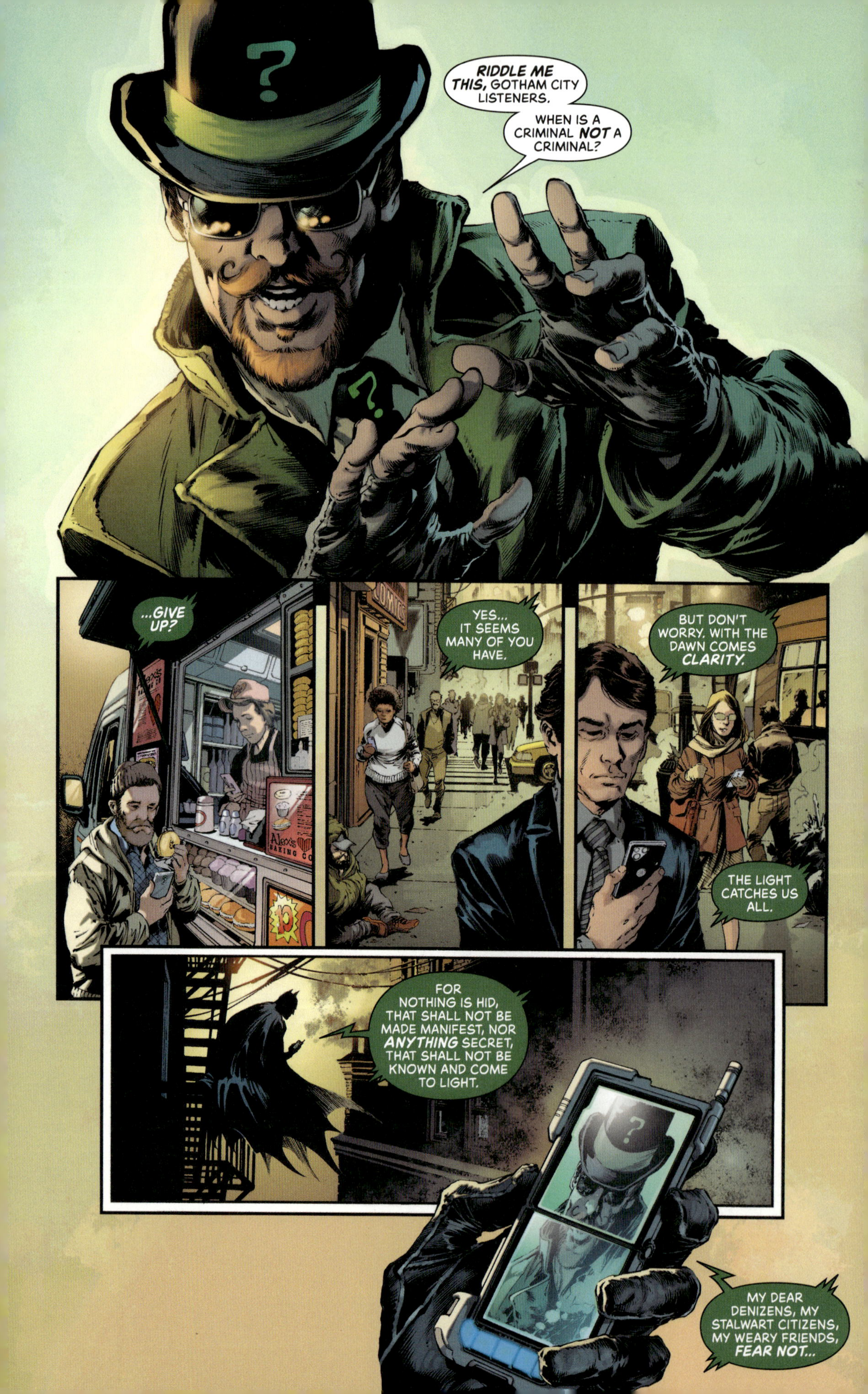
RIDDLE ME THIS, GOTHAM CITY LISTENERS.
WHEN IS A CRIMINAL NOT A CRIMINAL?
...GIVE UP?
YES... IT SEEMS MANY OF YOU HAVE.
BUT DON'T WORRY. WITH THE DAWN COMES CLARITY.
THE LIGHT CATCHES US ALL.
FOR NOTHING IS HID, THAT SHALL NOT BE MADE MANIFEST, NOR ANYTHING SECRET, THAT SHALL NOT BE KNOWN AND COME TO LIGHT.
MY DEAR DENIZENS, MY STALWART CITIZENS, MY WEARY FRIENDS, FEAR NOT...

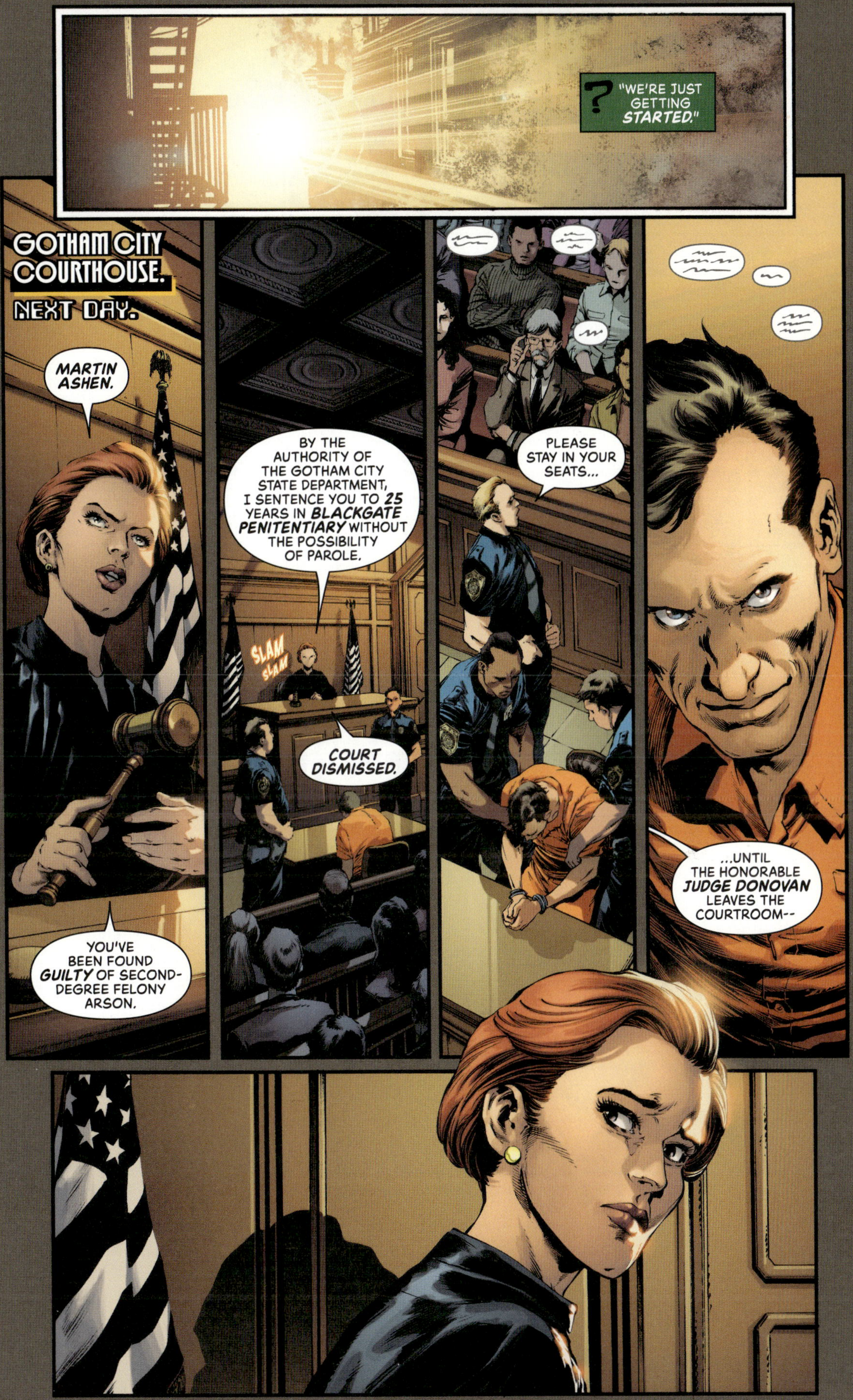
"WE'RE JUST GETTING STARTED."
GOTHAM CITY COURTHOUSE.
NEXT DAY.
MARTIN ASHEN.
YOU'VE BEEN FOUND GUILTY OF SECOND-DEGREE FELONY ARSON.
BY THE AUTHORITY OF THE GOTHAM CITY STATE DEPARTMENT, I SENTENCE YOU TO 25 YEARS IN BLACKGATE PENITENTIARY WITHOUT THE POSSIBILITY OF PAROLE.
SLAM SLAM
COURT DISMISSED.
PLEASE STAY IN YOUR SEATS...
...UNTIL THE HONORABLE JUDGE DONOVAN LEAVES THE COURTROOM--

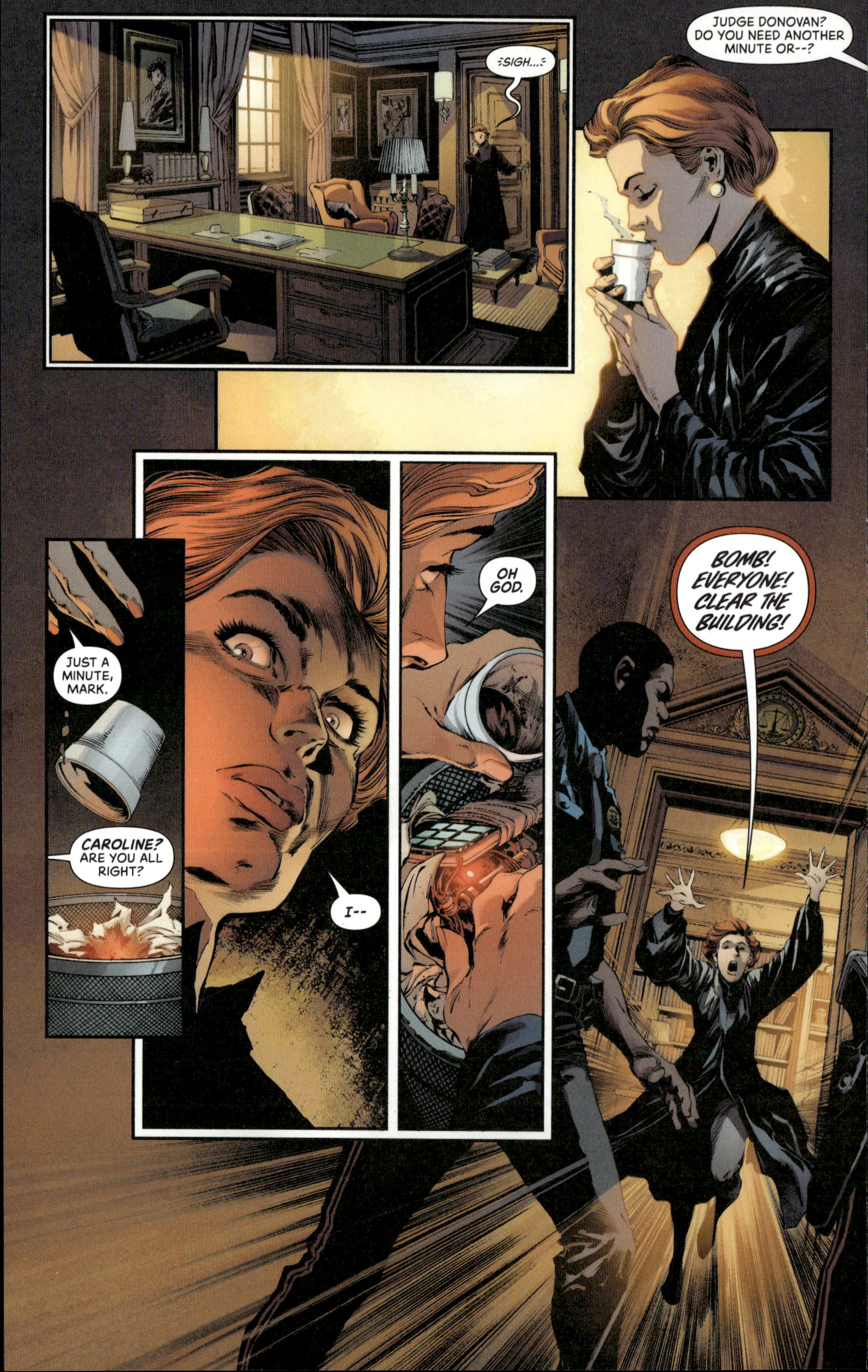

SIGH...
JUDGE DONOVAN? DO YOU NEED ANOTHER MINUTE OR--?
JUST A MINUTE, MARK.
CAROLINE? ARE YOU ALL RIGHT?
I--
OH GOD.
BOMB! EVERYONE! CLEAR THE BUILDING!

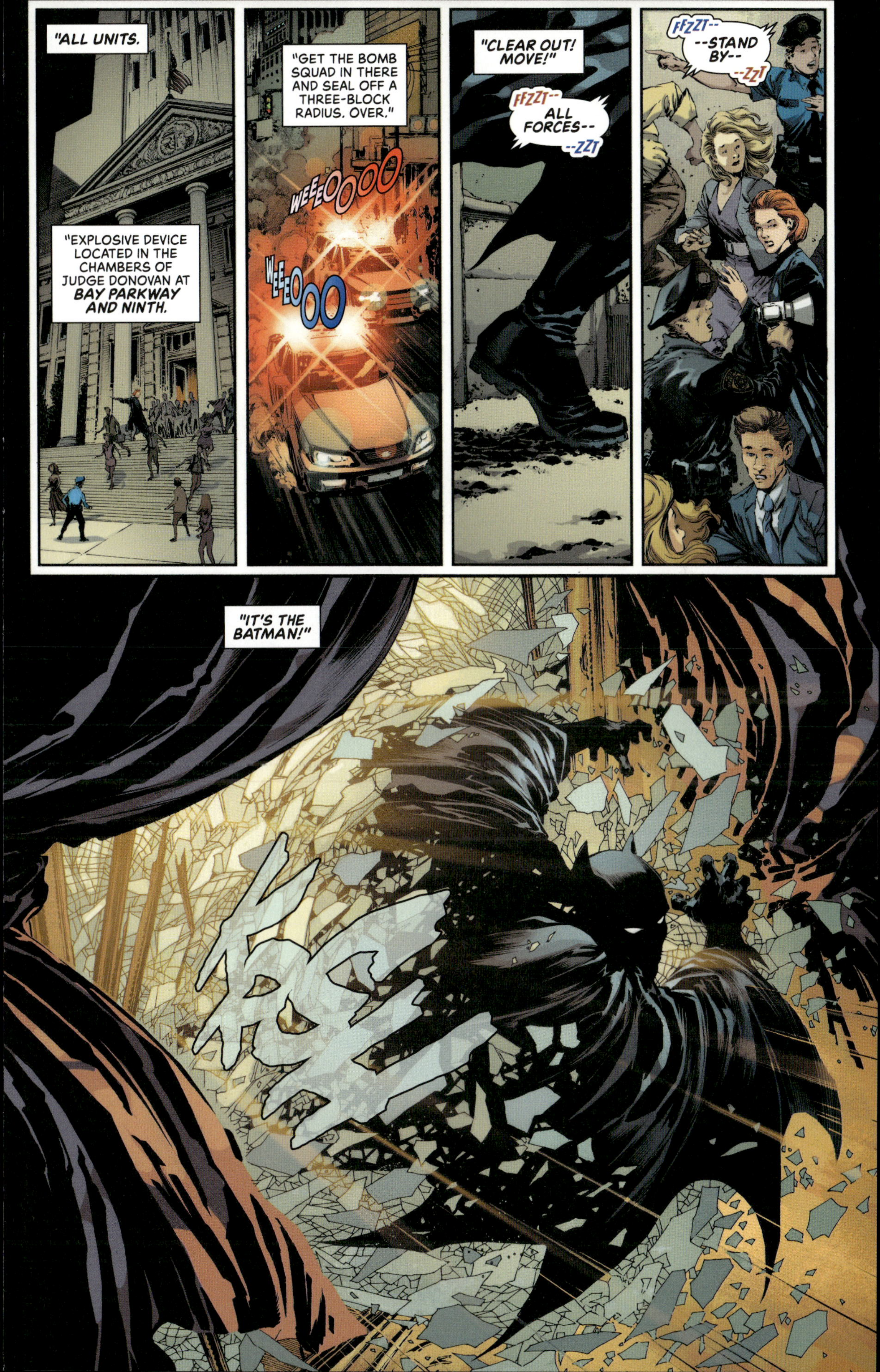
"ALL UNITS.
"EXPLOSIVE DEVICE LOCATED IN THE CHAMBERS OF JUDGE DONOVAN AT ***BAY PARKWAY AND NINTH.***
"GET THE BOMB SQUAD IN THERE AND SEAL OFF A THREE-BLOCK RADIUS. OVER."
WEEEOOOO
WEEEOOO
"CLEAR OUT! MOVE!"
FFZZT-- ALL FORCES-- --ZZT
FFZZT-- --STAND BY-- --ZZT
"IT'S THE BATMAN!"
KSSH

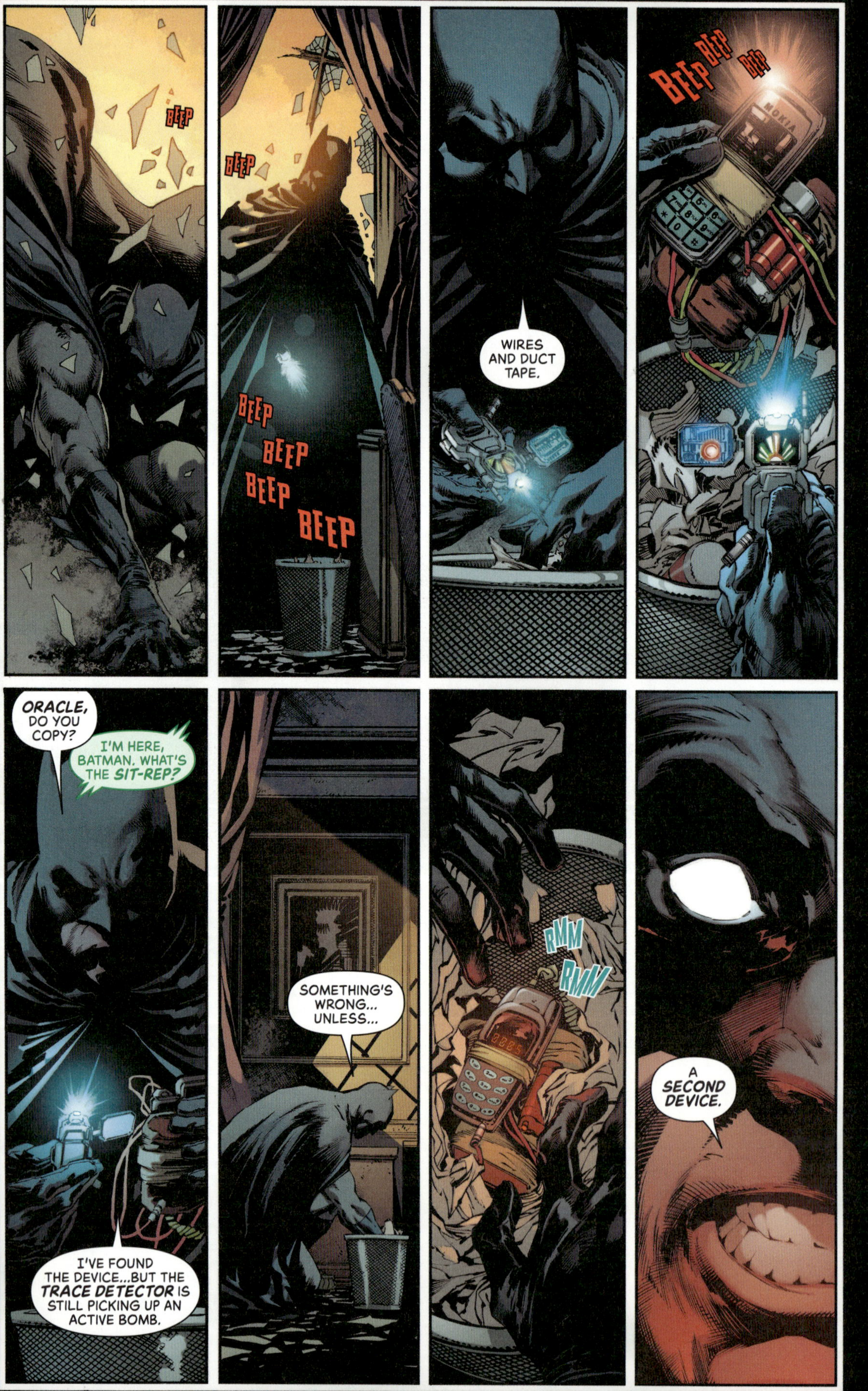
BEEP
BEEP
BEEP
BEEP
BEEP
BEEP
WIRES AND DUCT TAPE.
BEEP BEEP BEEP
NOKIA
ORACLE, DO YOU COPY?
I'M HERE, BATMAN. WHAT'S THE SIT-REP?
I'VE FOUND THE DEVICE...BUT THE TRACE DETECTOR IS STILL PICKING UP AN ACTIVE BOMB.
SOMETHING'S WRONG... UNLESS...
RMM
RMM
A SECOND DEVICE.

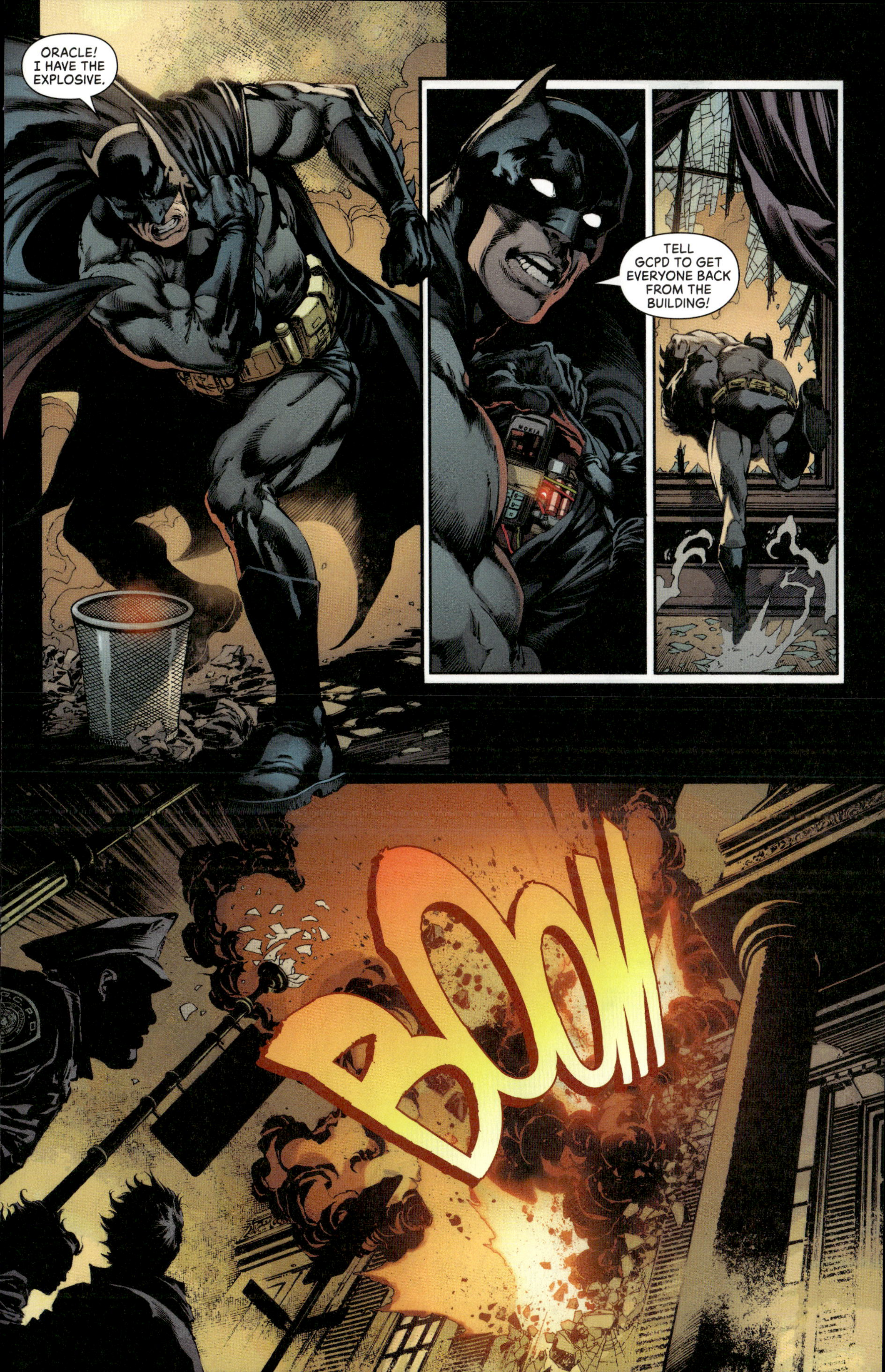
ORACLE! I HAVE THE EXPLOSIVE.
TELL GCPD TO GET EVERYONE BACK FROM THE BUILDING!
BOOM

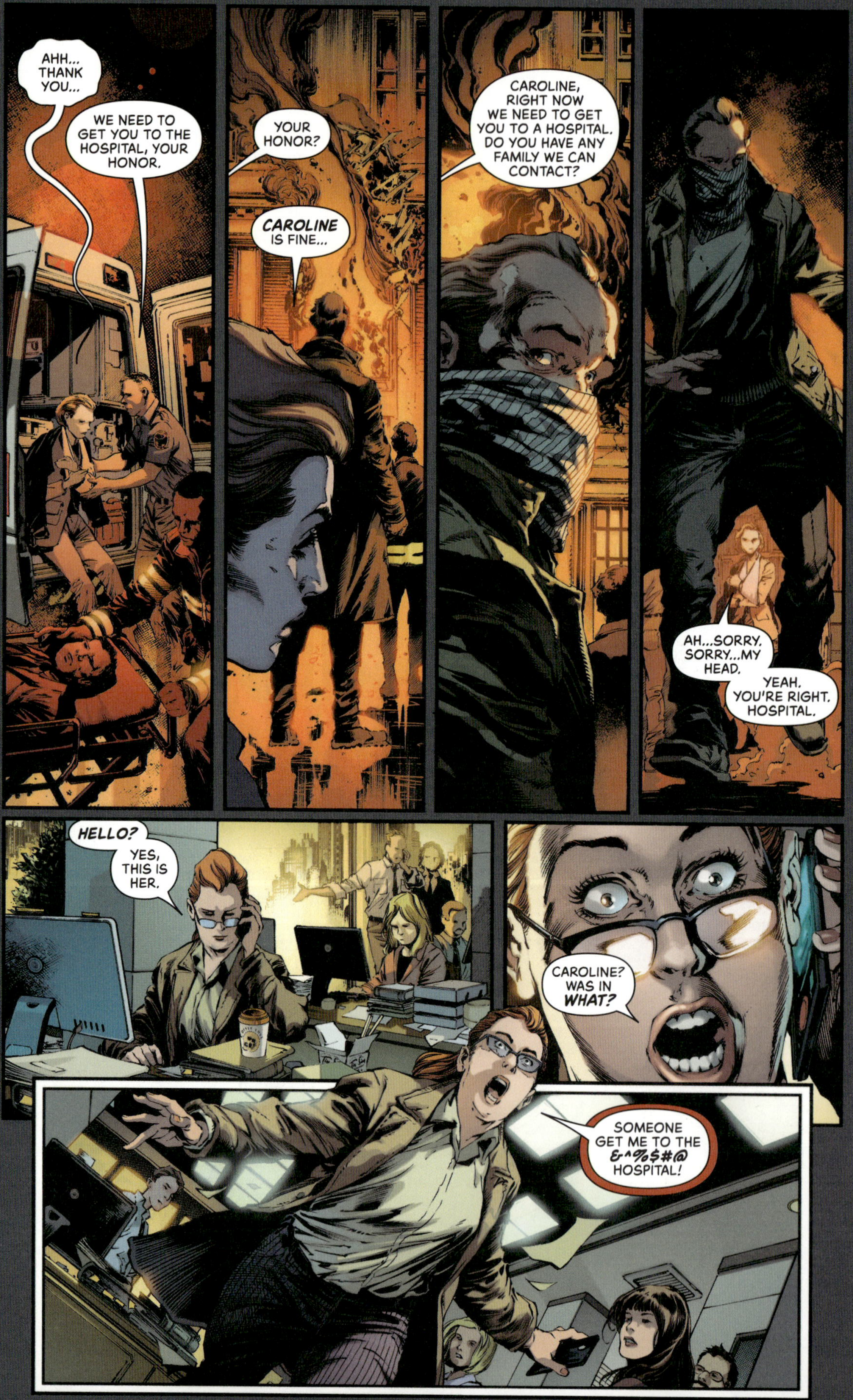
AHH... THANK YOU...
WE NEED TO GET YOU TO THE HOSPITAL, YOUR HONOR.
YOUR HONOR?
CAROLINE IS FINE...
CAROLINE, RIGHT NOW WE NEED TO GET YOU TO A HOSPITAL. DO YOU HAVE ANY FAMILY WE CAN CONTACT?
AH...SORRY. SORRY...MY HEAD.
YEAH. YOU'RE RIGHT. HOSPITAL.
HELLO?
YES, THIS IS HER.
CAROLINE? WAS IN WHAT?
SOMEONE GET ME TO THE &^%$#@ HOSPITAL!

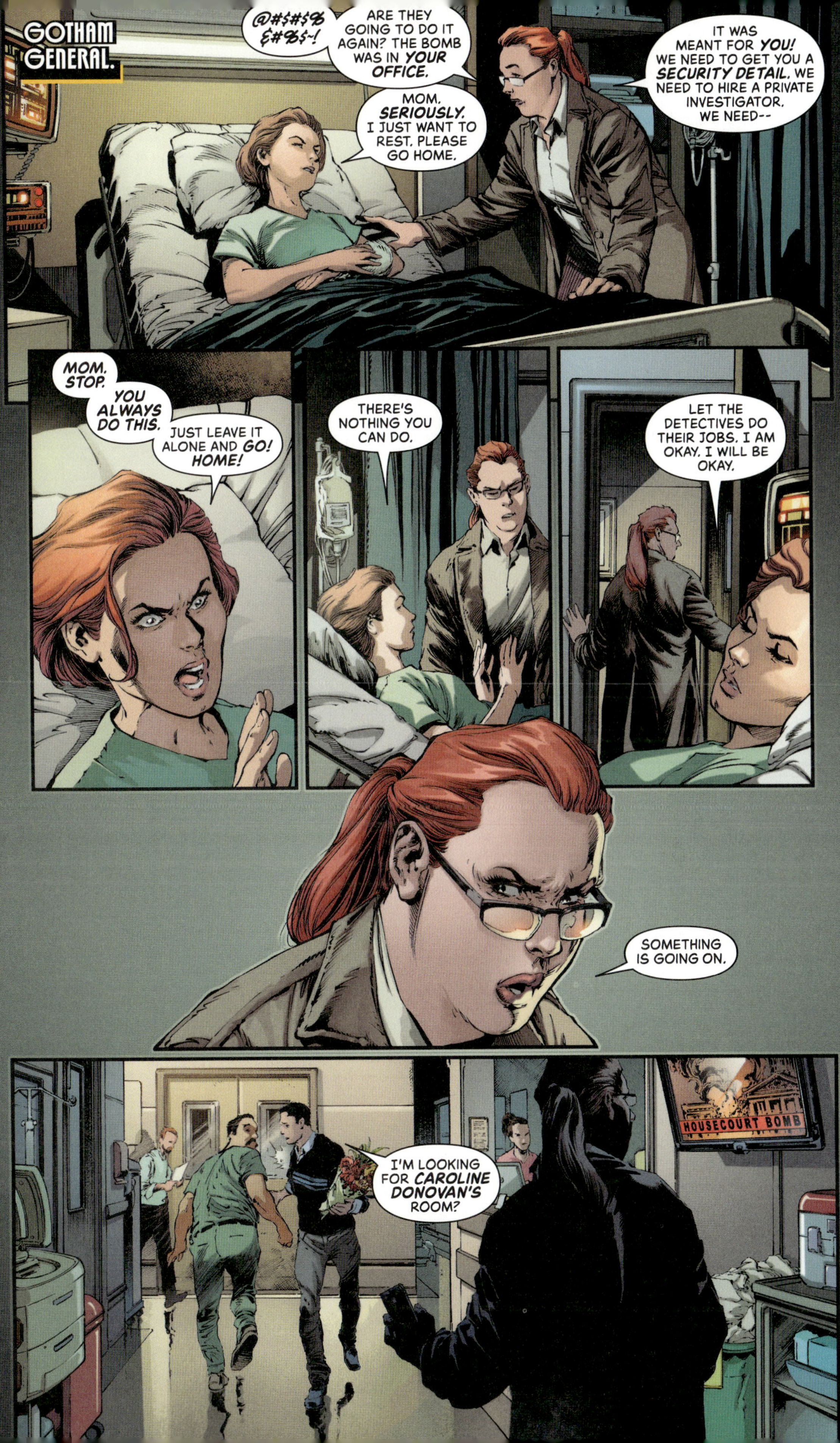
GOTHAM GENERAL.
@#$#$% &#%$-!
ARE THEY GOING TO DO IT AGAIN? THE BOMB WAS IN YOUR OFFICE.
MOM, SERIOUSLY. I JUST WANT TO REST. PLEASE GO HOME.
IT WAS MEANT FOR YOU! WE NEED TO GET YOU A SECURITY DETAIL. WE NEED TO HIRE A PRIVATE INVESTIGATOR. WE NEED--
MOM. STOP.
YOU ALWAYS DO THIS.
JUST LEAVE IT ALONE AND GO! HOME!
THERE'S NOTHING YOU CAN DO.
LET THE DETECTIVES DO THEIR JOBS. I AM OKAY. I WILL BE OKAY.
SOMETHING IS GOING ON.
HOUSECOURT BOMB
I'M LOOKING FOR CAROLINE DONOVAN'S ROOM?

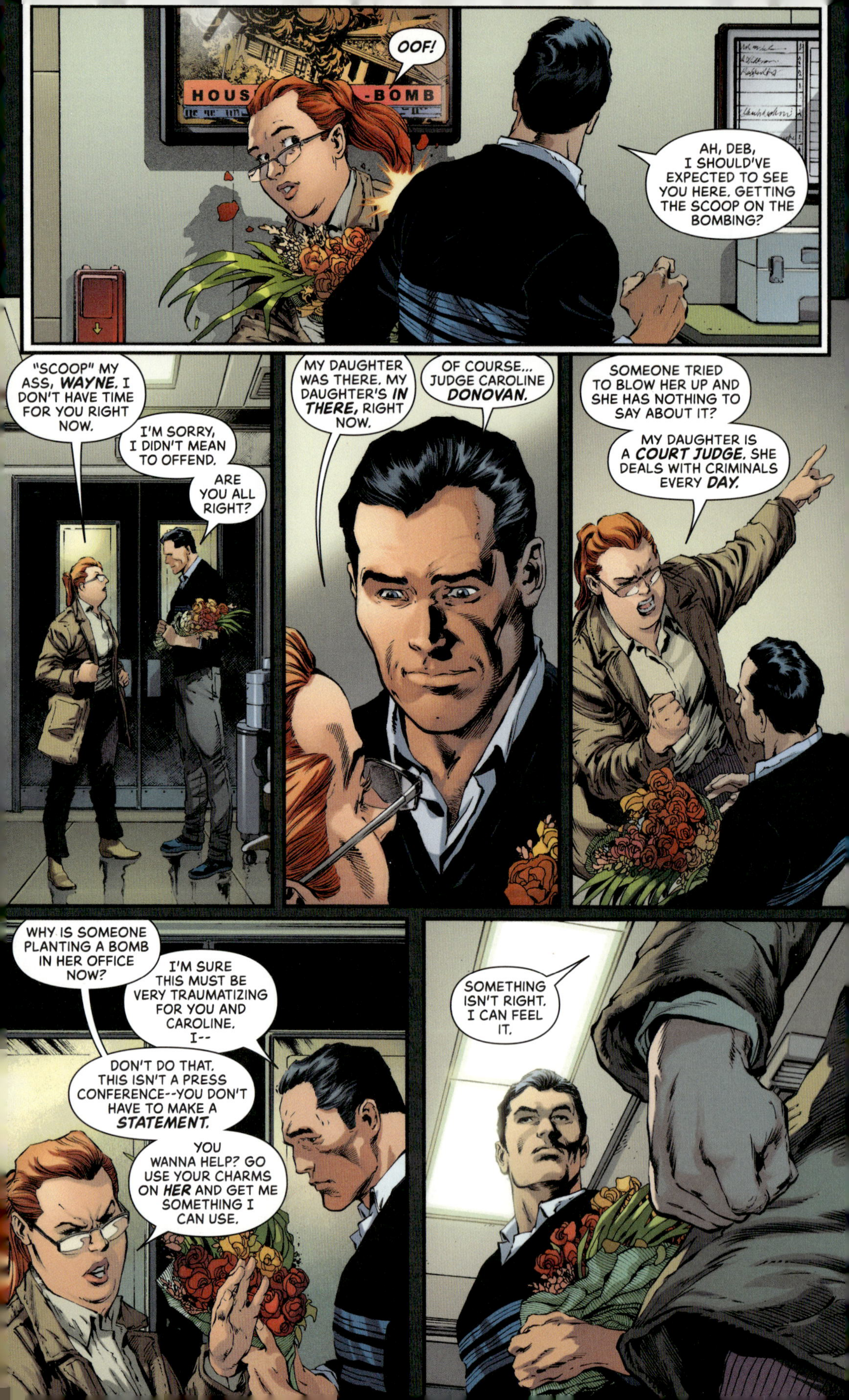
HOUS -BOMB
OOF!
AH, DEB, I SHOULD'VE EXPECTED TO SEE YOU HERE. GETTING THE SCOOP ON THE BOMBING?
"SCOOP" MY ASS, WAYNE. I DON'T HAVE TIME FOR YOU RIGHT NOW.
I'M SORRY, I DIDN'T MEAN TO OFFEND.
ARE YOU ALL RIGHT?
MY DAUGHTER WAS THERE. MY DAUGHTER'S IN THERE, RIGHT NOW.
OF COURSE... JUDGE CAROLINE DONOVAN.
SOMEONE TRIED TO BLOW HER UP AND SHE HAS NOTHING TO SAY ABOUT IT?
MY DAUGHTER IS A COURT JUDGE. SHE DEALS WITH CRIMINALS EVERY DAY.
WHY IS SOMEONE PLANTING A BOMB IN HER OFFICE NOW?
I'M SURE THIS MUST BE VERY TRAUMATIZING FOR YOU AND CAROLINE. I--
DON'T DO THAT. THIS ISN'T A PRESS CONFERENCE--YOU DON'T HAVE TO MAKE A STATEMENT.
YOU WANNA HELP? GO USE YOUR CHARMS ON HER AND GET ME SOMETHING I CAN USE.
SOMETHING ISN'T RIGHT. I CAN FEEL IT.

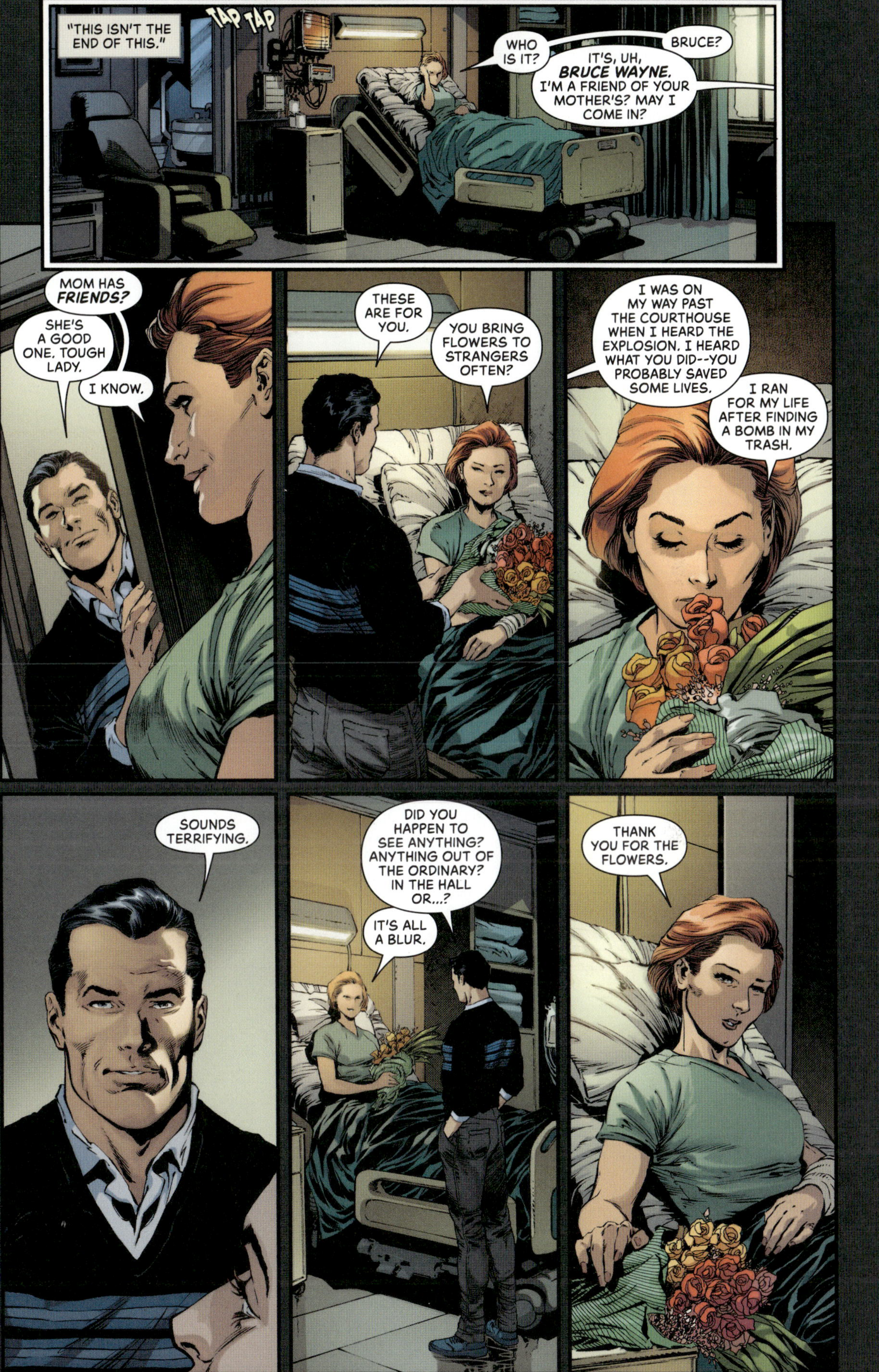
"THIS ISN'T THE END OF THIS."
TAP TAP
WHO IS IT?
BRUCE?
IT'S, UH, BRUCE WAYNE. I'M A FRIEND OF YOUR MOTHER'S? MAY I COME IN?
MOM HAS FRIENDS?
SHE'S A GOOD ONE. TOUGH LADY.
I KNOW.
THESE ARE FOR YOU.
YOU BRING FLOWERS TO STRANGERS OFTEN?
I WAS ON MY WAY PAST THE COURTHOUSE WHEN I HEARD THE EXPLOSION. I HEARD WHAT YOU DID--YOU PROBABLY SAVED SOME LIVES.
I RAN FOR MY LIFE AFTER FINDING A BOMB IN MY TRASH.
SOUNDS TERRIFYING.
DID YOU HAPPEN TO SEE ANYTHING? ANYTHING OUT OF THE ORDINARY? IN THE HALL OR...?
IT'S ALL A BLUR.
THANK YOU FOR THE FLOWERS.

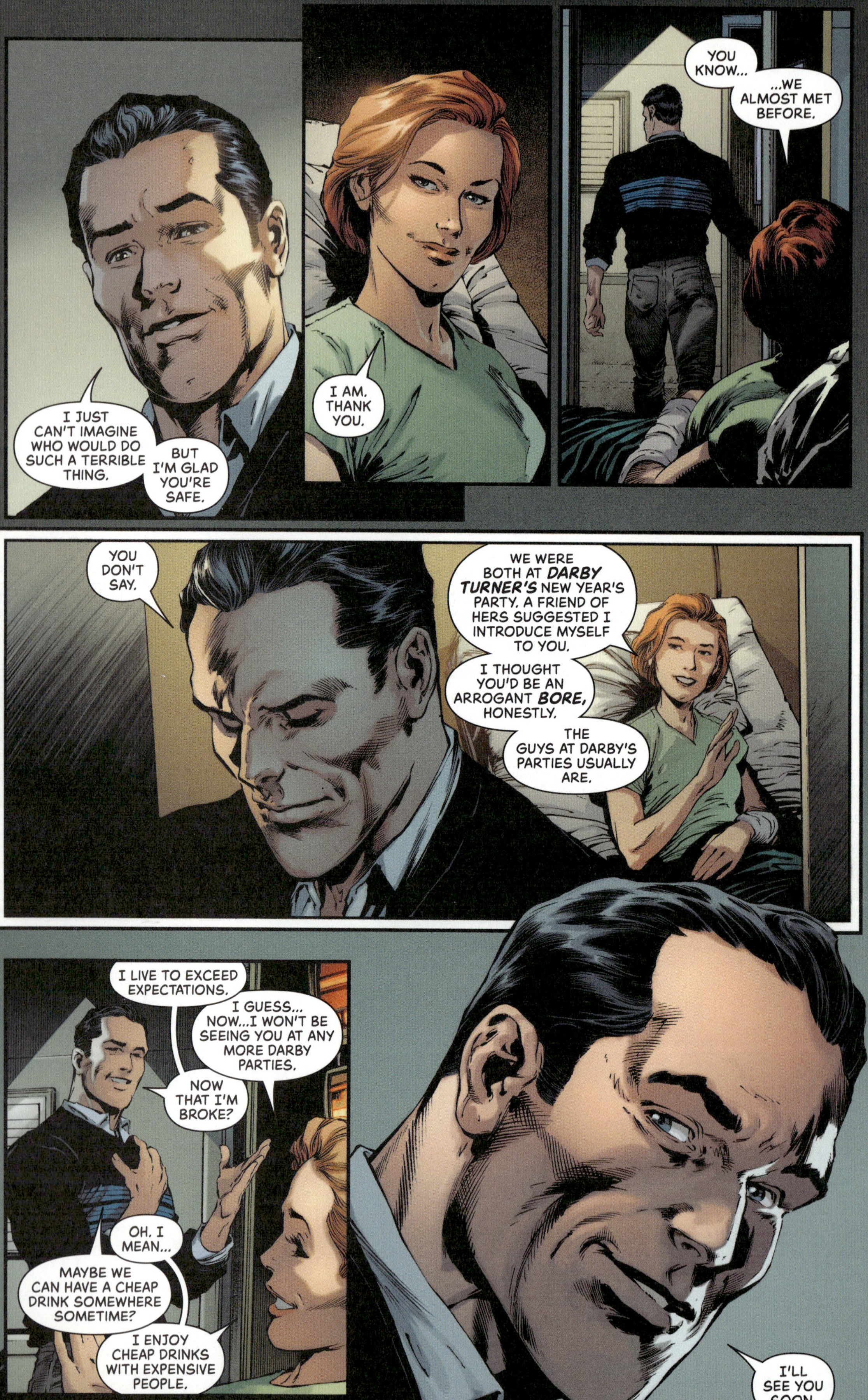
I JUST CAN'T IMAGINE WHO WOULD DO SUCH A TERRIBLE THING.
BUT I'M GLAD YOU'RE SAFE.
I AM. THANK YOU.
YOU KNOW...
...WE ALMOST MET BEFORE.
YOU DON'T SAY.
WE WERE BOTH AT DARBY TURNER'S NEW YEAR'S PARTY. A FRIEND OF HERS SUGGESTED I INTRODUCE MYSELF TO YOU.
I THOUGHT YOU'D BE AN ARROGANT BORE, HONESTLY.
THE GUYS AT DARBY'S PARTIES USUALLY ARE.
I LIVE TO EXCEED EXPECTATIONS.
I GUESS... NOW...I WON'T BE SEEING YOU AT ANY MORE DARBY PARTIES.
NOW THAT I'M BROKE?
OH, I MEAN...
MAYBE WE CAN HAVE A CHEAP DRINK SOMEWHERE SOMETIME?
I ENJOY CHEAP DRINKS WITH EXPENSIVE PEOPLE.
I'LL SEE YOU SOON.

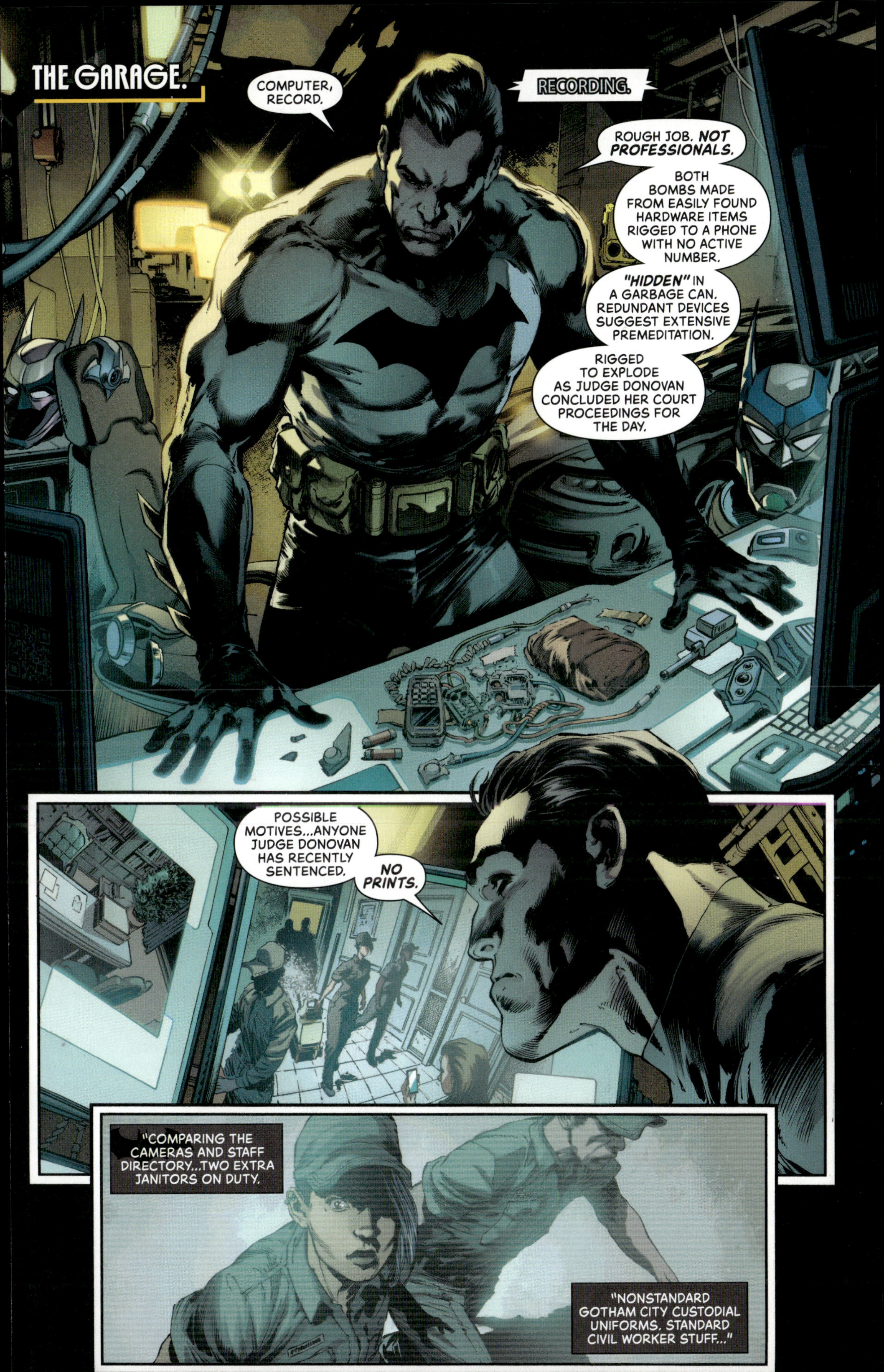

THE GARAGE.
COMPUTER, RECORD.
RECORDING.
ROUGH JOB. NOT PROFESSIONALS.
BOTH BOMBS MADE FROM EASILY FOUND HARDWARE ITEMS RIGGED TO A PHONE WITH NO ACTIVE NUMBER.
"HIDDEN" IN A GARBAGE CAN. REDUNDANT DEVICES SUGGEST EXTENSIVE PREMEDITATION.
RIGGED TO EXPLODE AS JUDGE DONOVAN CONCLUDED HER COURT PROCEEDINGS FOR THE DAY.
POSSIBLE MOTIVES...ANYONE JUDGE DONOVAN HAS RECENTLY SENTENCED.
NO PRINTS.
"COMPARING THE CAMERAS AND STAFF DIRECTORY...TWO EXTRA JANITORS ON DUTY.
"NONSTANDARD GOTHAM CITY CUSTODIAL UNIFORMS. STANDARD CIVIL WORKER STUFF..."

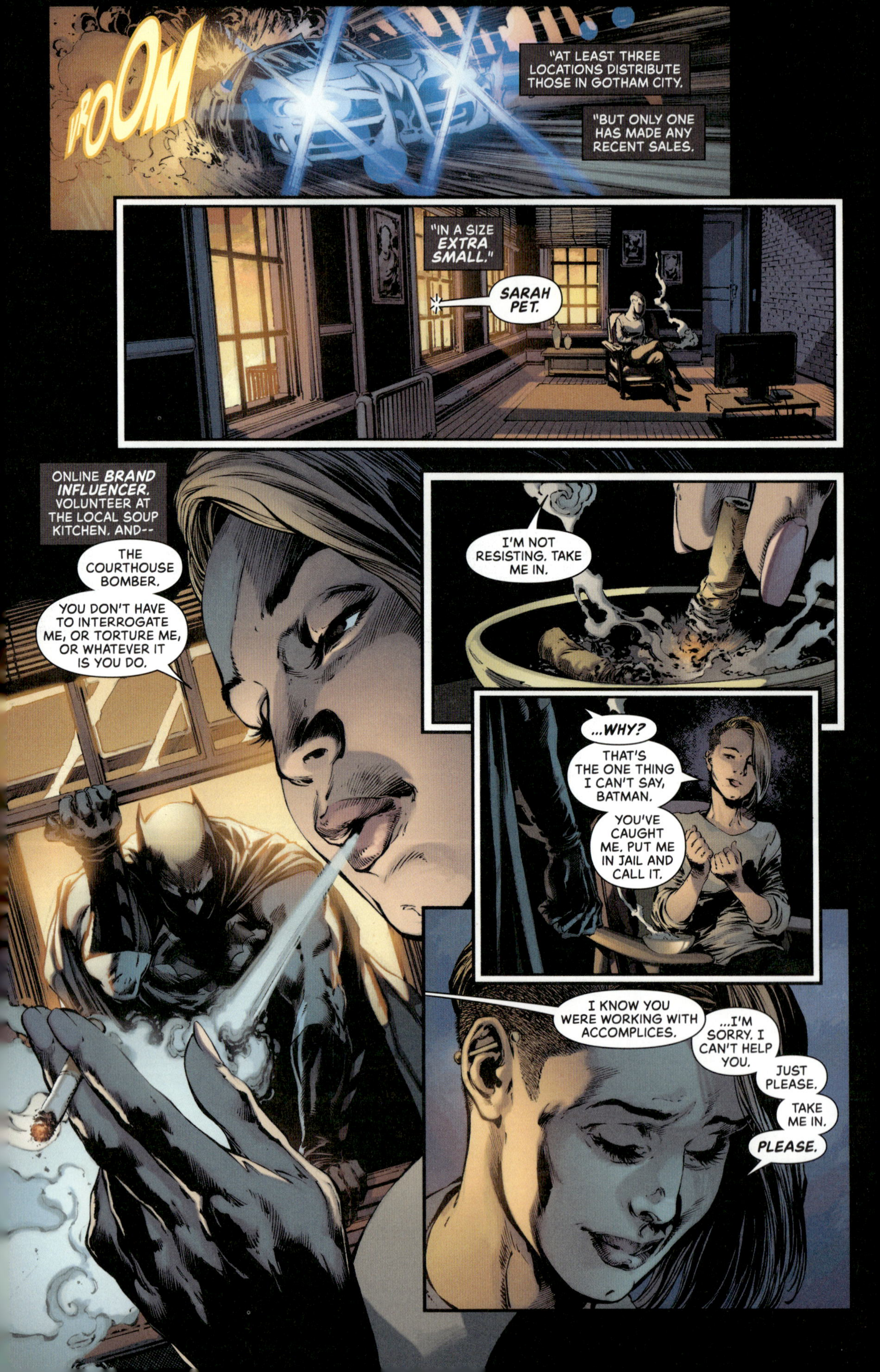
VROOM
"AT LEAST THREE LOCATIONS DISTRIBUTE THOSE IN GOTHAM CITY.
"BUT ONLY ONE HAS MADE ANY RECENT SALES.
"IN A SIZE EXTRA SMALL."
SARAH PET.
ONLINE BRAND INFLUENCER. VOLUNTEER AT THE LOCAL SOUP KITCHEN, AND--
THE COURTHOUSE BOMBER.
YOU DON'T HAVE TO INTERROGATE ME, OR TORTURE ME, OR WHATEVER IT IS YOU DO.
I'M NOT RESISTING. TAKE ME IN.
...WHY?
THAT'S THE ONE THING I CAN'T SAY, BATMAN.
YOU'VE CAUGHT ME. PUT ME IN JAIL AND CALL IT.
I KNOW YOU WERE WORKING WITH ACCOMPLICES.
...I'M SORRY. I CAN'T HELP YOU.
JUST PLEASE.
TAKE ME IN.
PLEASE.

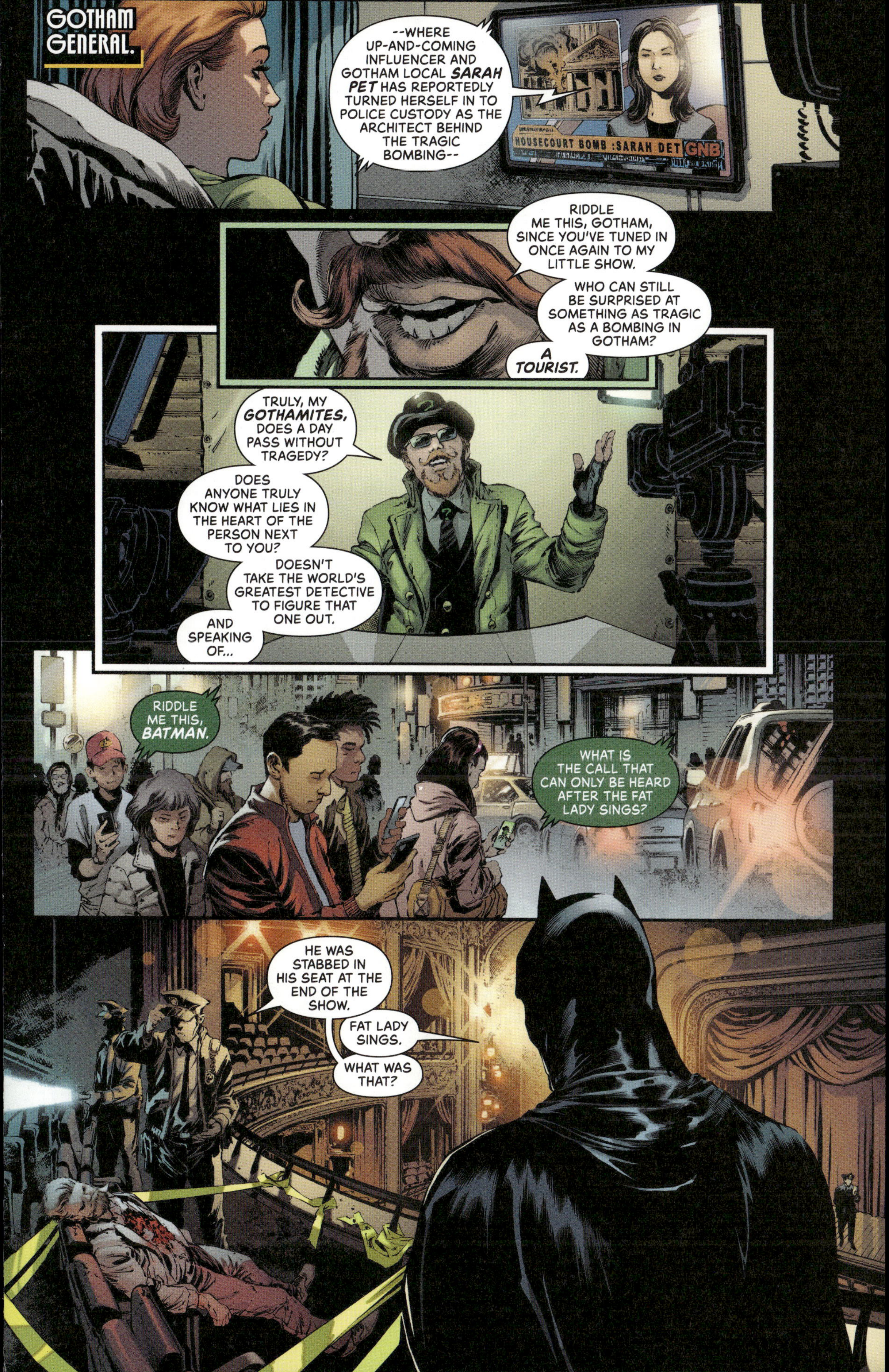
GOTHAM GENERAL.
--WHERE UP-AND-COMING INFLUENCER AND GOTHAM LOCAL SARAH PET HAS REPORTEDLY TURNED HERSELF IN TO POLICE CUSTODY AS THE ARCHITECT BEHIND THE TRAGIC BOMBING--
HOUSECOURT BOMB :SARAH DET GNB
RIDDLE ME THIS, GOTHAM, SINCE YOU'VE TUNED IN ONCE AGAIN TO MY LITTLE SHOW.
WHO CAN STILL BE SURPRISED AT SOMETHING AS TRAGIC AS A BOMBING IN GOTHAM?
A TOURIST.
TRULY, MY GOTHAMITES, DOES A DAY PASS WITHOUT TRAGEDY?
DOES ANYONE TRULY KNOW WHAT LIES IN THE HEART OF THE PERSON NEXT TO YOU?
DOESN'T TAKE THE WORLD'S GREATEST DETECTIVE TO FIGURE THAT ONE OUT.
AND SPEAKING OF...
RIDDLE ME THIS, BATMAN.
WHAT IS THE CALL THAT CAN ONLY BE HEARD AFTER THE FAT LADY SINGS?
HE WAS STABBED IN HIS SEAT AT THE END OF THE SHOW.
FAT LADY SINGS.
WHAT WAS THAT?

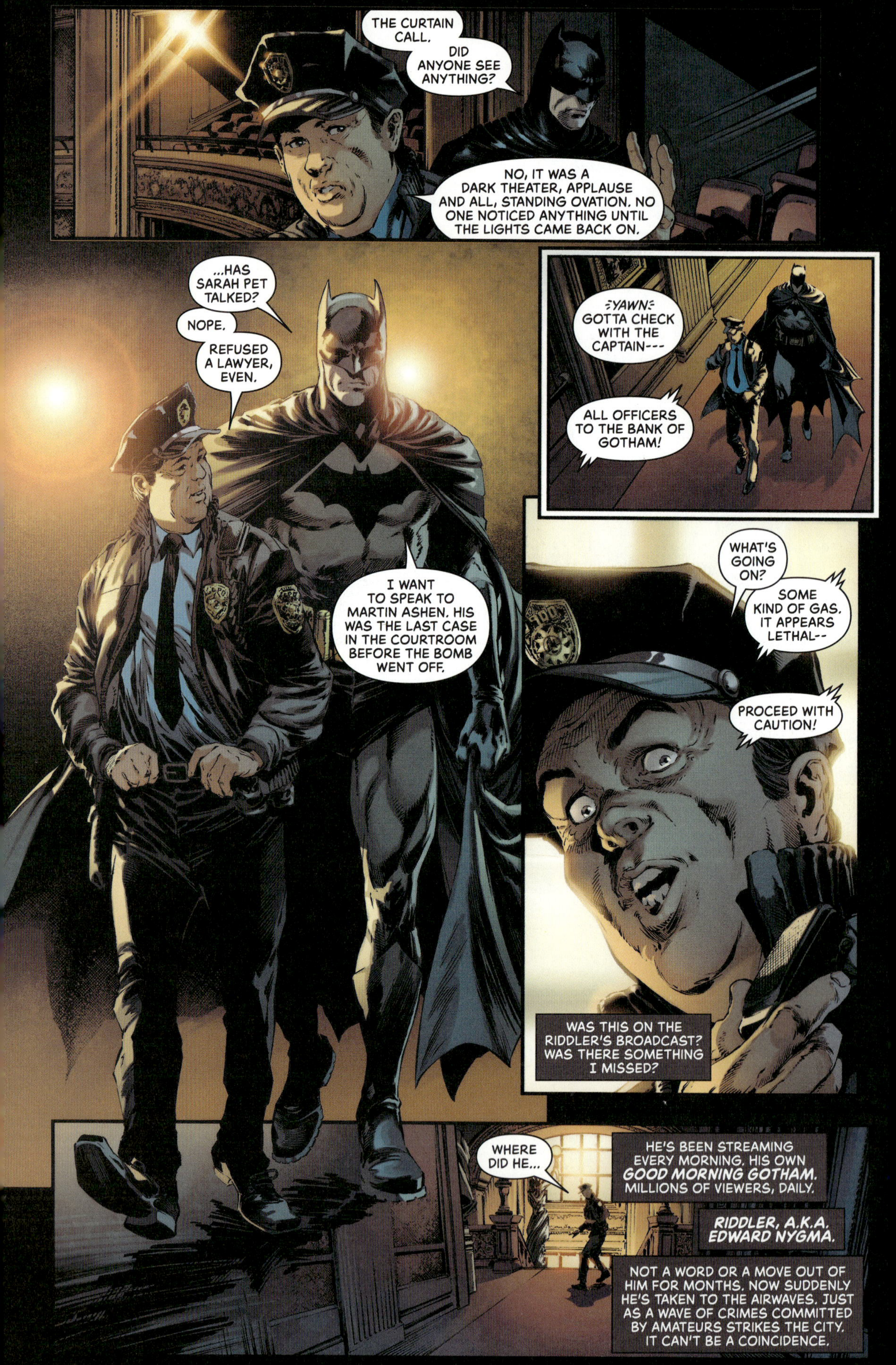
THE CURTAIN CALL.
DID ANYONE SEE ANYTHING?
NO, IT WAS A DARK THEATER, APPLAUSE AND ALL, STANDING OVATION. NO ONE NOTICED ANYTHING UNTIL THE LIGHTS CAME BACK ON.
...HAS SARAH PET TALKED?
NOPE.
REFUSED A LAWYER, EVEN.
I WANT TO SPEAK TO MARTIN ASHEN. HIS WAS THE LAST CASE IN THE COURTROOM BEFORE THE BOMB WENT OFF.
YAWN GOTTA CHECK WITH THE CAPTAIN---
ALL OFFICERS TO THE BANK OF GOTHAM!
WHAT'S GOING ON?
SOME KIND OF GAS. IT APPEARS LETHAL--
PROCEED WITH CAUTION!
WAS THIS ON THE RIDDLER'S BROADCAST? WAS THERE SOMETHING I MISSED?
WHERE DID HE...
HE'S BEEN STREAMING EVERY MORNING. HIS OWN GOOD MORNING GOTHAM. MILLIONS OF VIEWERS, DAILY.
RIDDLER, A.K.A. EDWARD NYGMA.
NOT A WORD OR A MOVE OUT OF HIM FOR MONTHS. NOW SUDDENLY HE'S TAKEN TO THE AIRWAVES. JUST AS A WAVE OF CRIMES COMMITTED BY AMATEURS STRIKES THE CITY. IT CAN'T BE A COINCIDENCE.

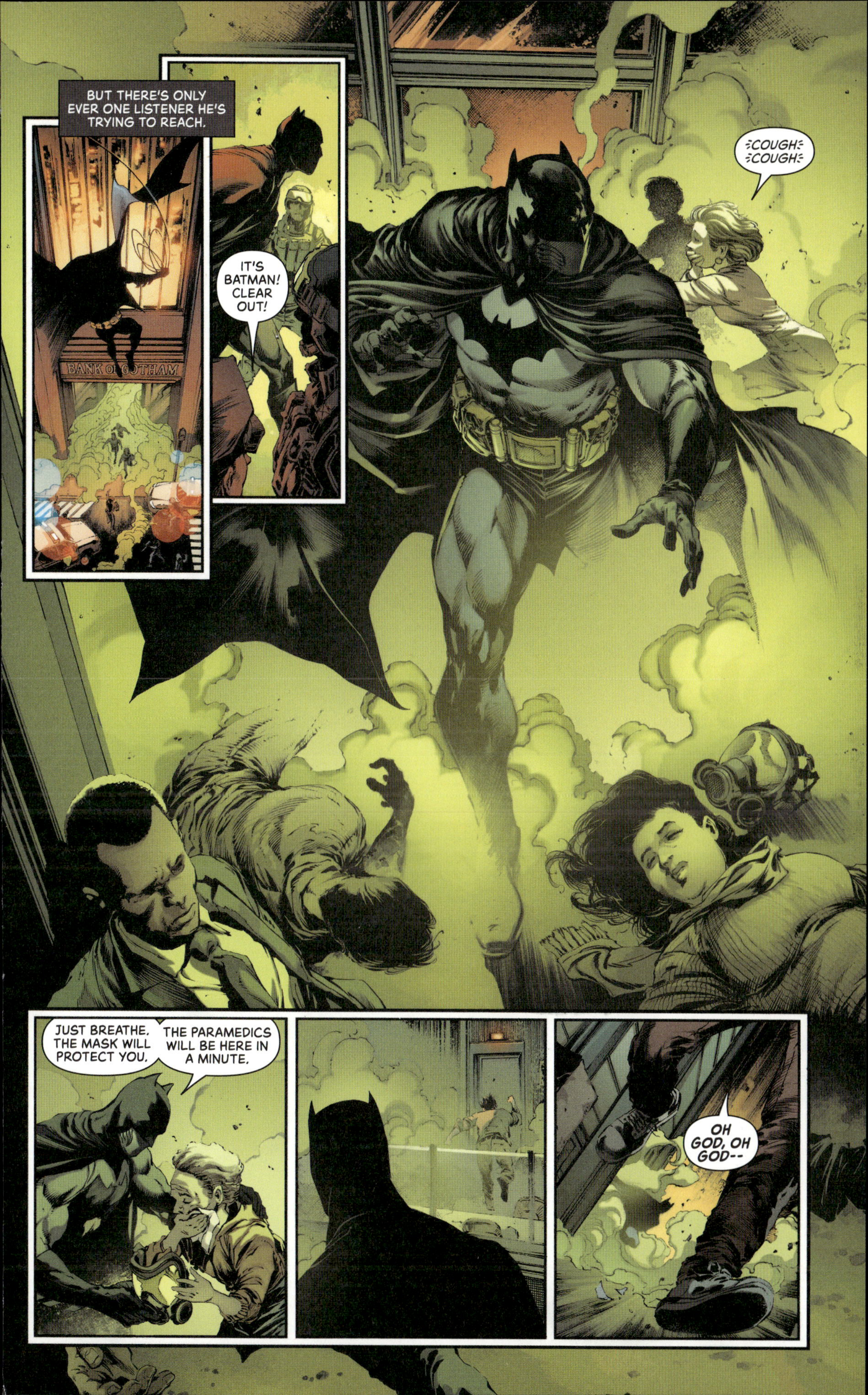
BUT THERE'S ONLY EVER ONE LISTENER HE'S TRYING TO REACH.
BANK OF GOTHAM
IT'S BATMAN! CLEAR OUT!
COUGH COUGH
JUST BREATHE. THE MASK WILL PROTECT YOU.
THE PARAMEDICS WILL BE HERE IN A MINUTE.
OH GOD, OH GOD--

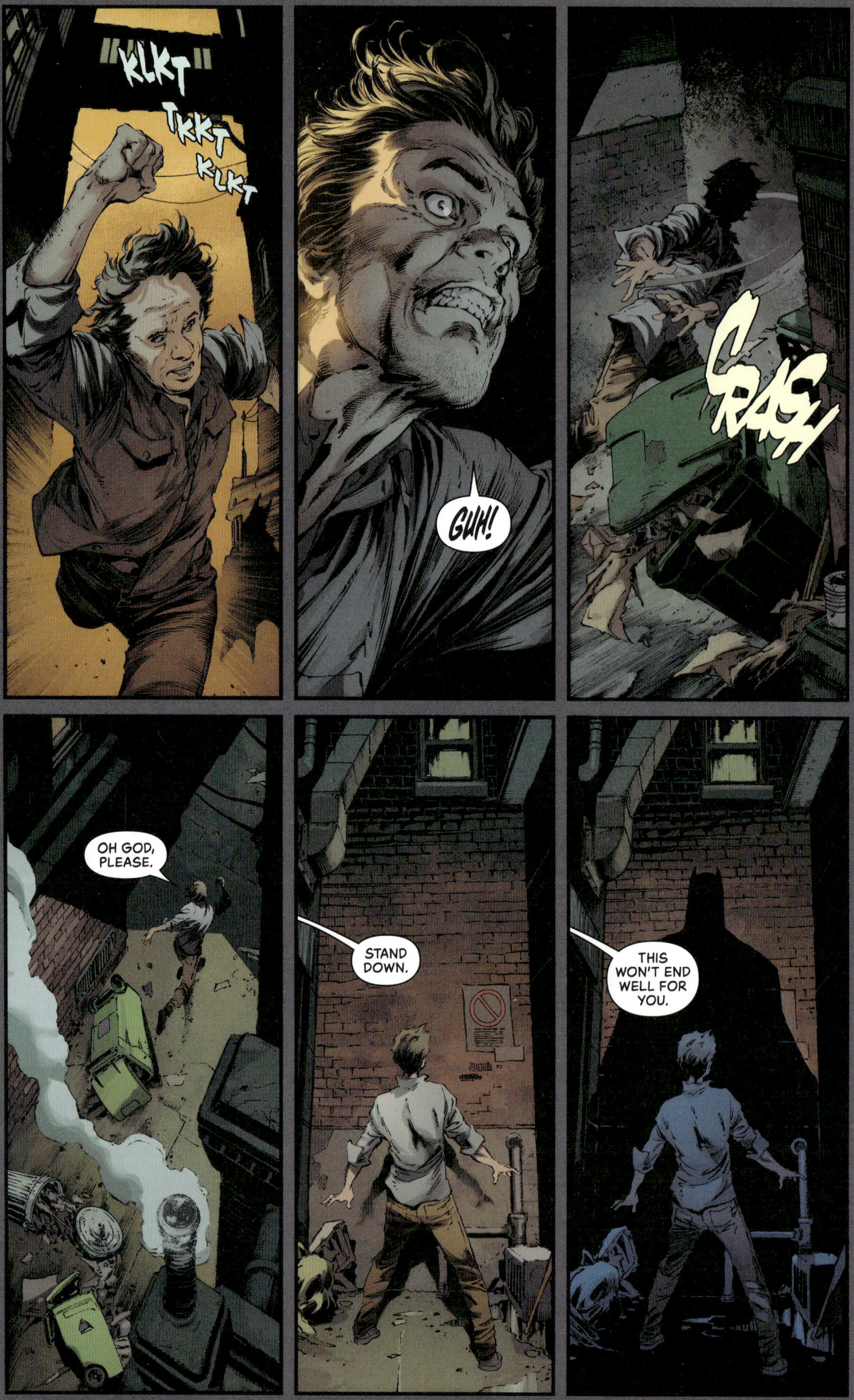

KLKT
TKKT
KLKT
GUH!
CRASH
OH GOD, PLEASE.
STAND DOWN.
THIS WON'T END WELL FOR YOU.

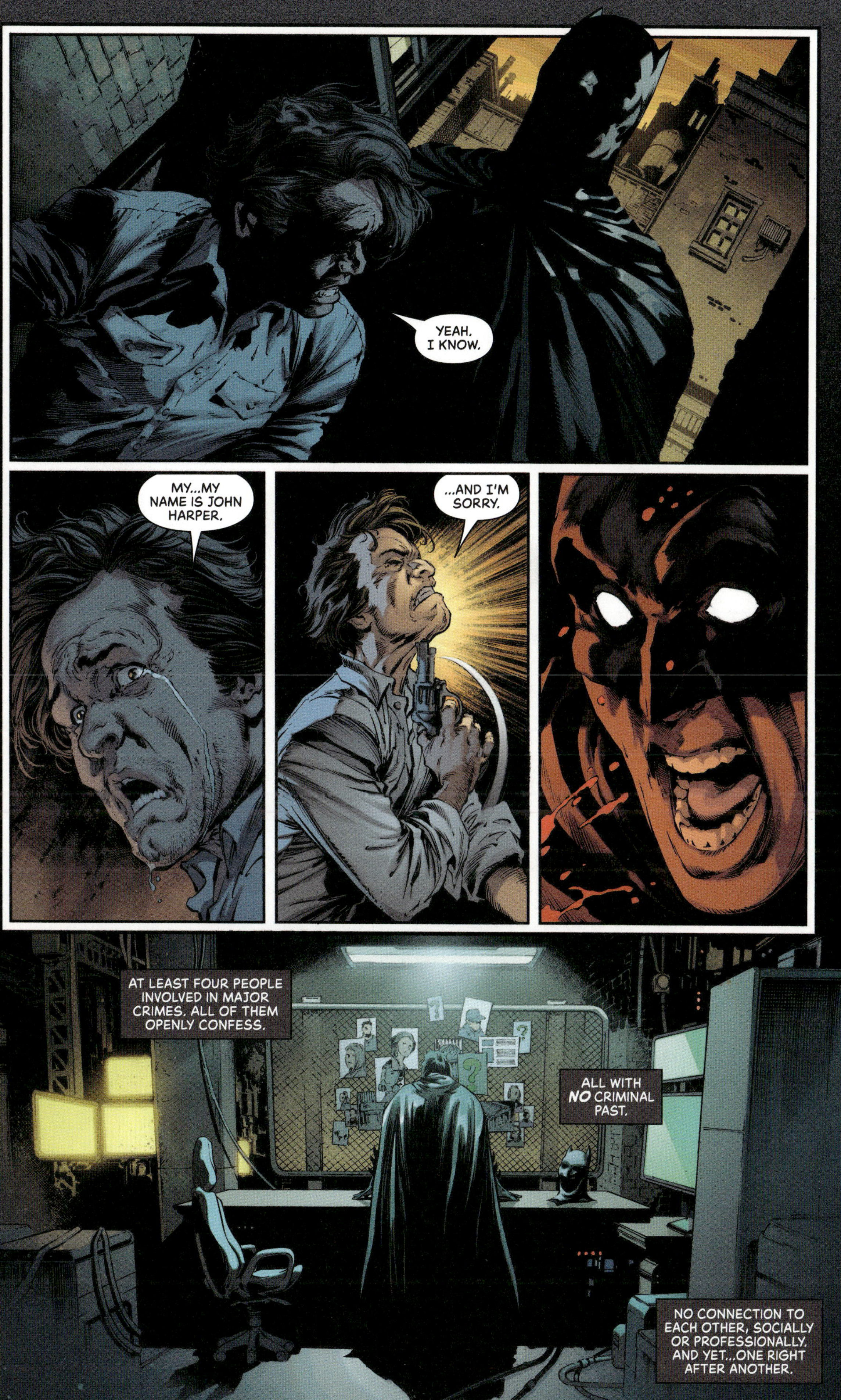
YEAH. I KNOW.
MY...MY NAME IS JOHN HARPER.
...AND I'M SORRY.
AT LEAST FOUR PEOPLE INVOLVED IN MAJOR CRIMES. ALL OF THEM OPENLY CONFESS.
ALL WITH NO CRIMINAL PAST.
NO CONNECTION TO EACH OTHER, SOCIALLY OR PROFESSIONALLY. AND YET...ONE RIGHT AFTER ANOTHER.

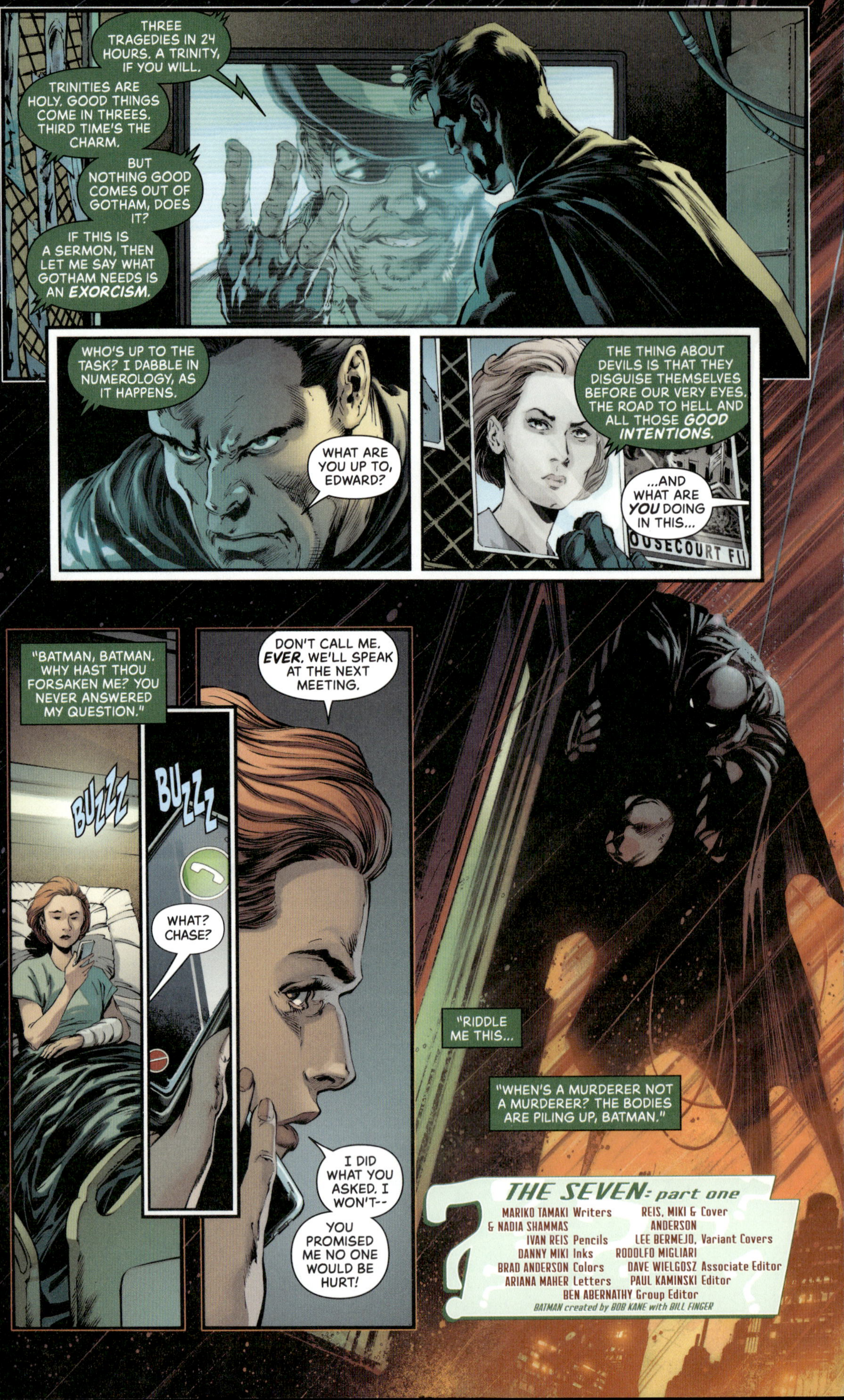
THREE TRAGEDIES IN 24 HOURS. A TRINITY, IF YOU WILL.
TRINITIES ARE HOLY. GOOD THINGS COME IN THREES. THIRD TIME'S THE CHARM.
BUT NOTHING GOOD COMES OUT OF GOTHAM, DOES IT?
IF THIS IS A SERMON, THEN LET ME SAY WHAT GOTHAM NEEDS IS AN *EXORCISM*.
WHO'S UP TO THE TASK? I DABBLE IN NUMEROLOGY, AS IT HAPPENS.
WHAT ARE YOU UP TO, EDWARD?
THE THING ABOUT DEVILS IS THAT THEY DISGUISE THEMSELVES BEFORE OUR VERY EYES. THE ROAD TO HELL AND ALL THOSE *GOOD INTENTIONS*.
...AND WHAT ARE *YOU* DOING IN THIS...
OUSECOURT FI
"BATMAN, BATMAN. WHY HAST THOU FORSAKEN ME? YOU NEVER ANSWERED MY QUESTION."
BUZZZ
BUZZZ
WHAT? CHASE?
DON'T CALL ME. *EVER*. WE'LL SPEAK AT THE NEXT MEETING.
I DID WHAT YOU ASKED. I WON'T--
YOU PROMISED ME NO ONE WOULD BE HURT!
"RIDDLE ME THIS...
"WHEN'S A MURDERER NOT A MURDERER? THE BODIES ARE PILING UP, BATMAN."
THE SEVEN: part one
MARIKO TAMAKI & NADIA SHAMMAS Writers
IVAN REIS Pencils
DANNY MIKI Inks
BRAD ANDERSON Colors
ARIANA MAHER Letters
REIS, MIKI & ANDERSON Cover
LEE BERMEJO, Variant Covers
RODOLFO MIGLIARI
DAVE WIELGOSZ Associate Editor
PAUL KAMINSKI Editor
BEN ABERNATHY Group Editor
BATMAN created by BOB KANE with BILL FINGER

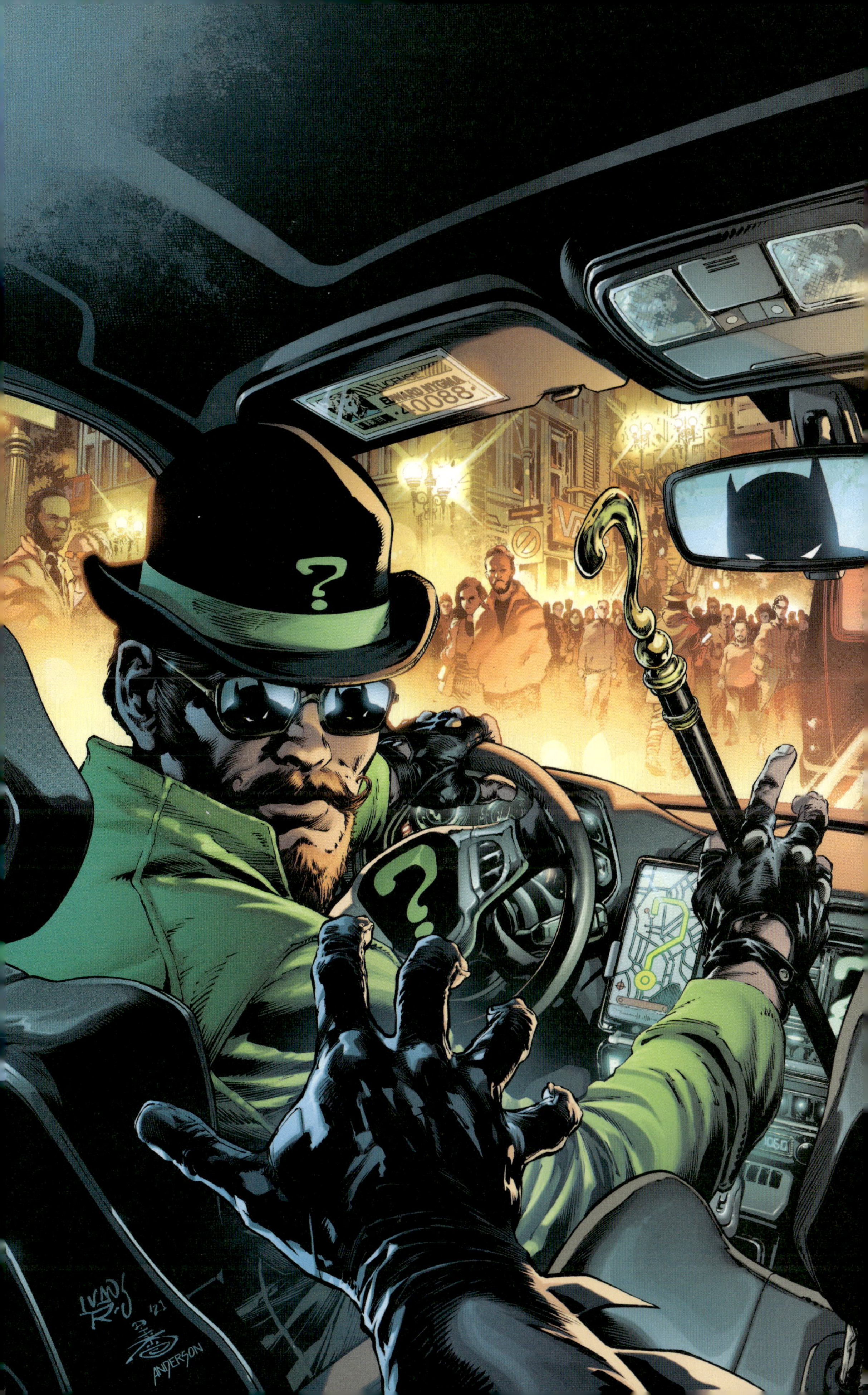
LICENSE
EDWARD NYGMA
40088
ANDERSON

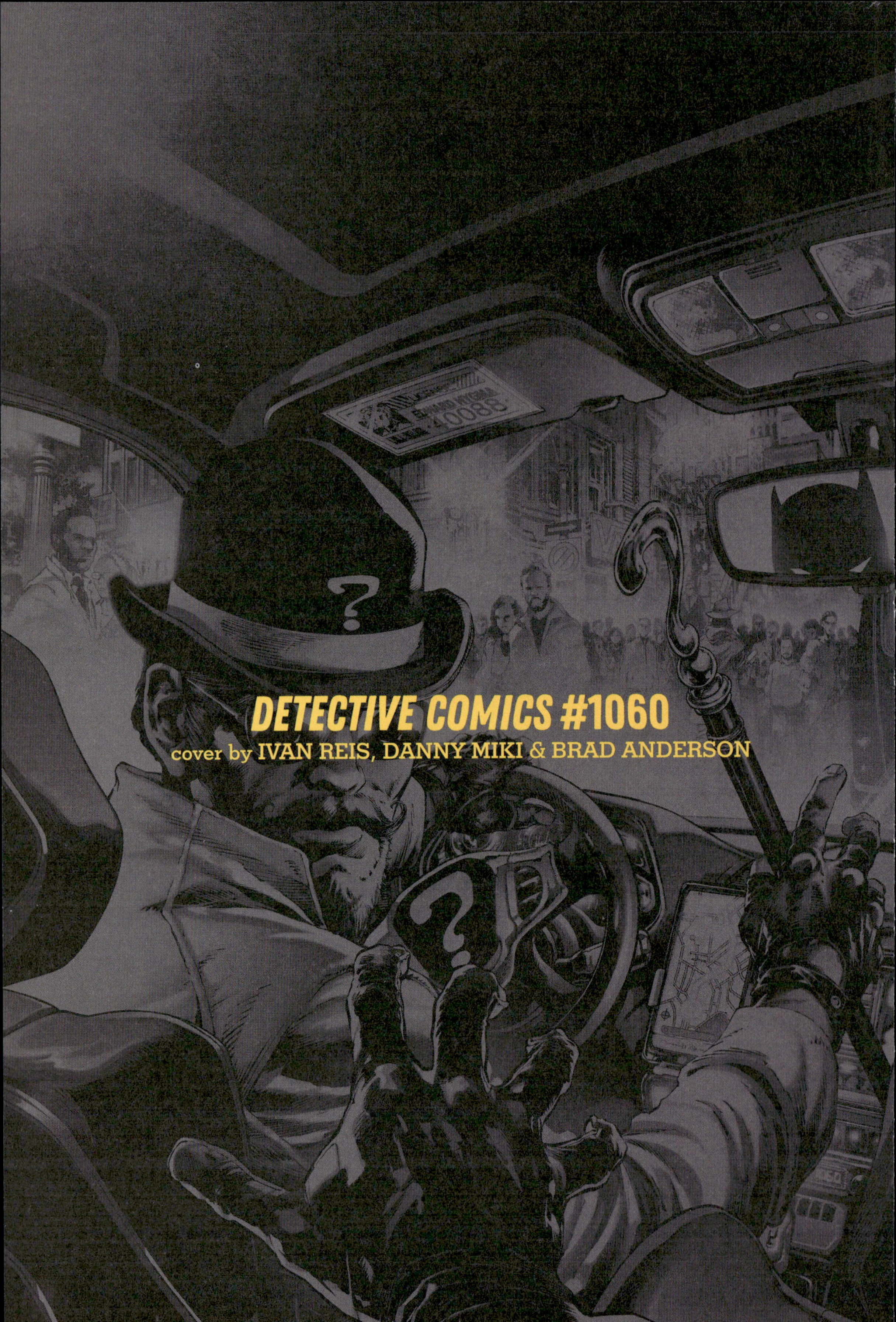

DETECTIVE COMICS #1060

cover by IVAN REIS, DANNY MIKI & BRAD ANDERSON

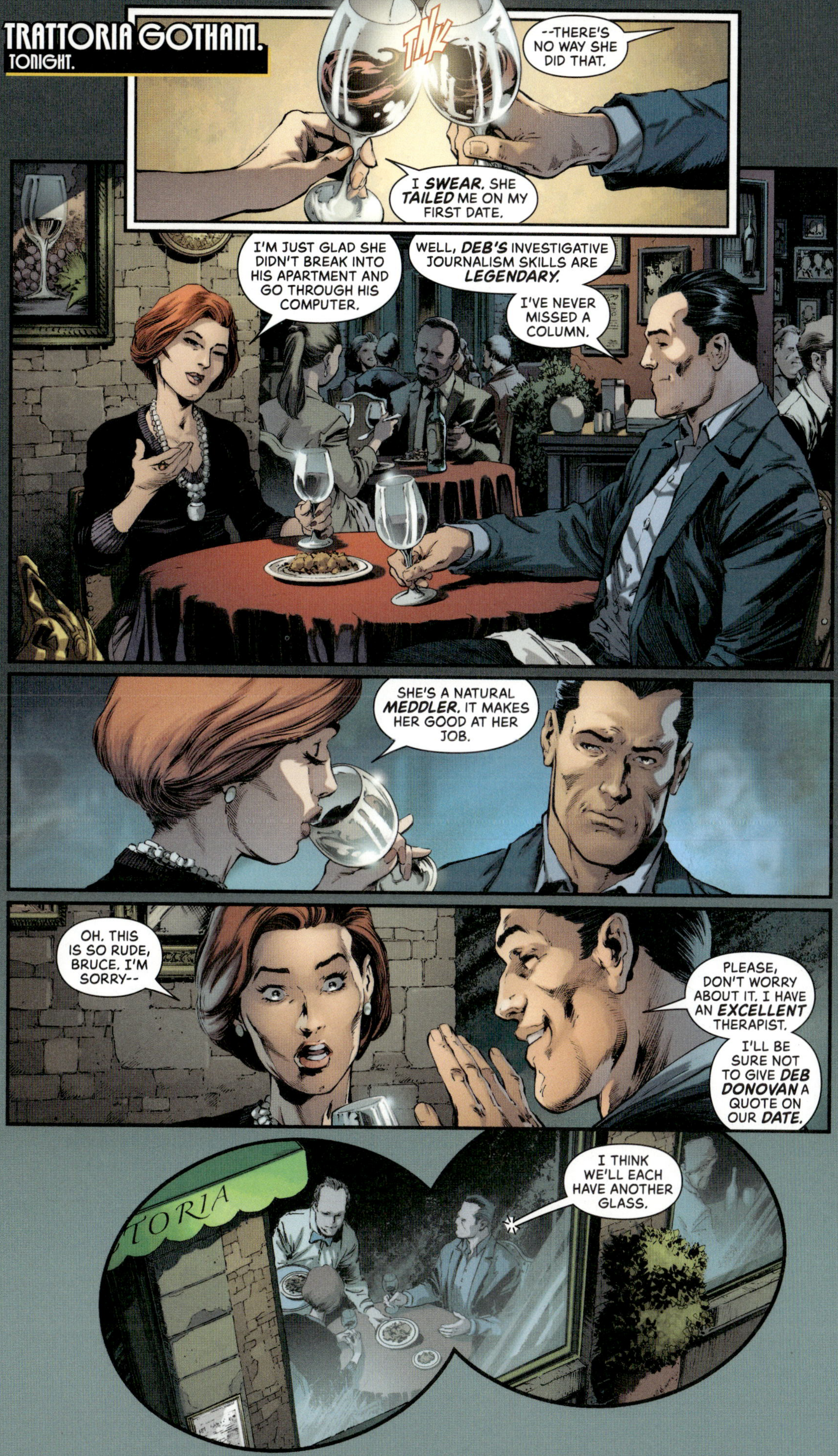
TRATTORIA GOTHAM.
TONIGHT.
TNK
--THERE'S NO WAY SHE DID THAT.
I SWEAR. SHE TAILED ME ON MY FIRST DATE.
I'M JUST GLAD SHE DIDN'T BREAK INTO HIS APARTMENT AND GO THROUGH HIS COMPUTER.
WELL, DEB'S INVESTIGATIVE JOURNALISM SKILLS ARE LEGENDARY.
I'VE NEVER MISSED A COLUMN.
SHE'S A NATURAL MEDDLER. IT MAKES HER GOOD AT HER JOB.
OH. THIS IS SO RUDE, BRUCE. I'M SORRY--
PLEASE, DON'T WORRY ABOUT IT. I HAVE AN EXCELLENT THERAPIST.
I'LL BE SURE NOT TO GIVE DEB DONOVAN A QUOTE ON OUR DATE.
TORIA
I THINK WE'LL EACH HAVE ANOTHER GLASS.

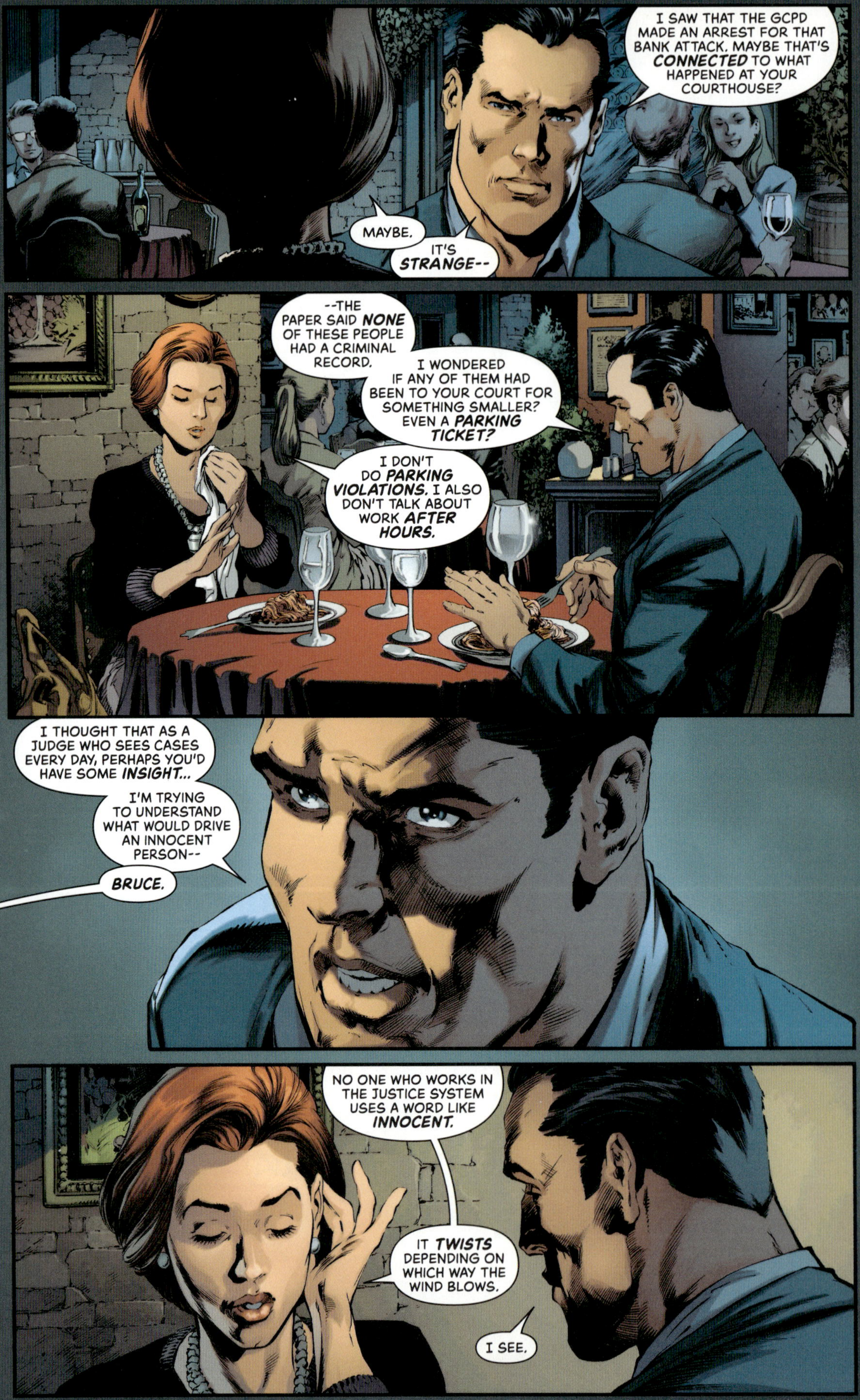
I SAW THAT THE GCPD MADE AN ARREST FOR THAT BANK ATTACK. MAYBE THAT'S CONNECTED TO WHAT HAPPENED AT YOUR COURTHOUSE?
MAYBE.
IT'S STRANGE--
--THE PAPER SAID NONE OF THESE PEOPLE HAD A CRIMINAL RECORD.
I WONDERED IF ANY OF THEM HAD BEEN TO YOUR COURT FOR SOMETHING SMALLER? EVEN A PARKING TICKET?
I DON'T DO PARKING VIOLATIONS. I ALSO DON'T TALK ABOUT WORK AFTER HOURS.
I THOUGHT THAT AS A JUDGE WHO SEES CASES EVERY DAY, PERHAPS YOU'D HAVE SOME INSIGHT...
I'M TRYING TO UNDERSTAND WHAT WOULD DRIVE AN INNOCENT PERSON--
BRUCE.
NO ONE WHO WORKS IN THE JUSTICE SYSTEM USES A WORD LIKE INNOCENT.
IT TWISTS DEPENDING ON WHICH WAY THE WIND BLOWS.
I SEE.

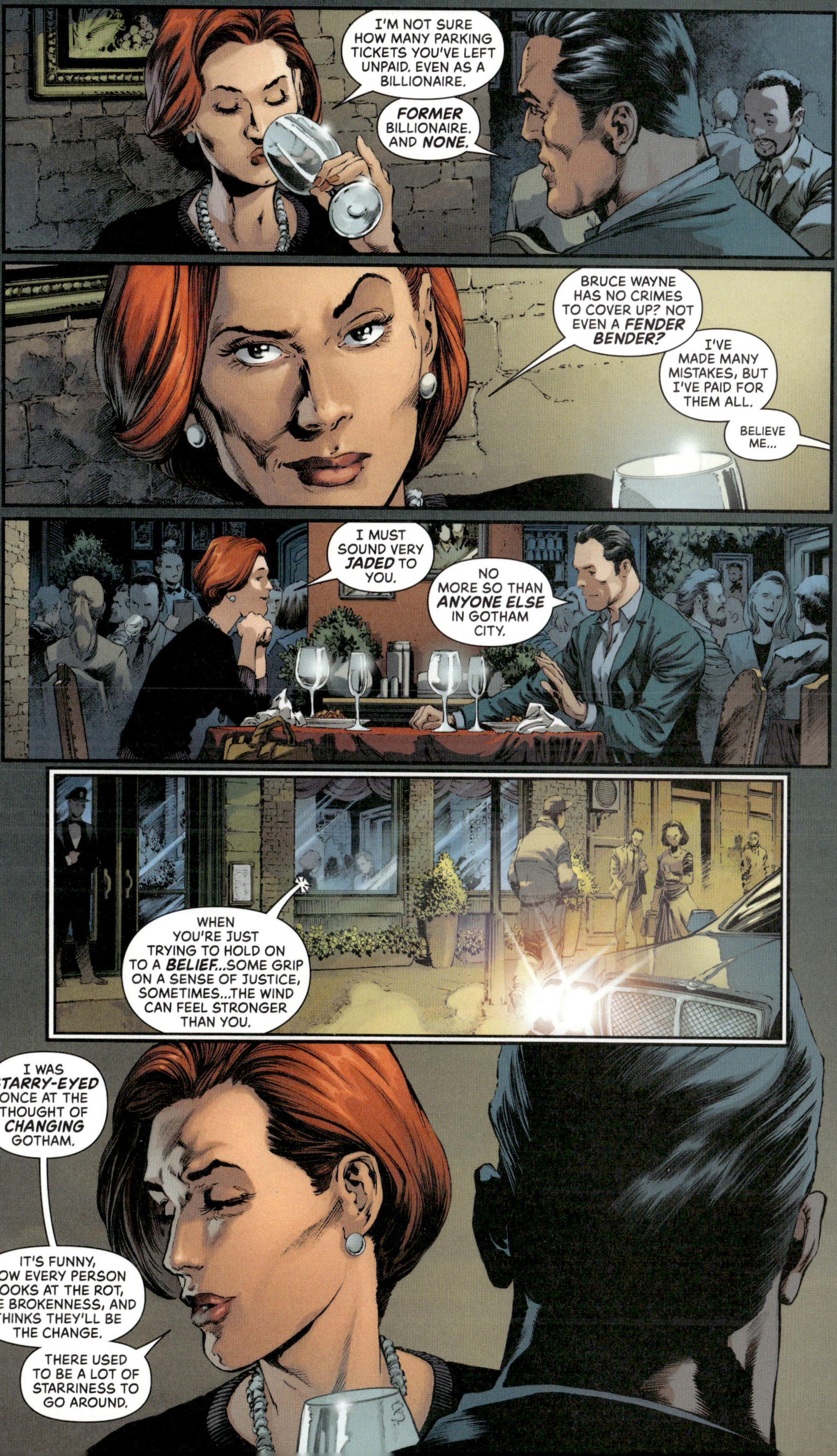
I'M NOT SURE HOW MANY PARKING TICKETS YOU'VE LEFT UNPAID, EVEN AS A BILLIONAIRE.
FORMER BILLIONAIRE, AND NONE.
BRUCE WAYNE HAS NO CRIMES TO COVER UP? NOT EVEN A FENDER BENDER?
I'VE MADE MANY MISTAKES, BUT I'VE PAID FOR THEM ALL.
BELIEVE ME...
I MUST SOUND VERY JADED TO YOU.
NO MORE SO THAN ANYONE ELSE IN GOTHAM CITY.
WHEN YOU'RE JUST TRYING TO HOLD ON TO A BELIEF...SOME GRIP ON A SENSE OF JUSTICE, SOMETIMES...THE WIND CAN FEEL STRONGER THAN YOU.
I WAS STARRY-EYED ONCE AT THE THOUGHT OF CHANGING GOTHAM.
IT'S FUNNY, HOW EVERY PERSON LOOKS AT THE ROT, THE BROKENNESS, AND THINKS THEY'LL BE THE CHANGE.
THERE USED TO BE A LOT OF STARRINESS TO GO AROUND.

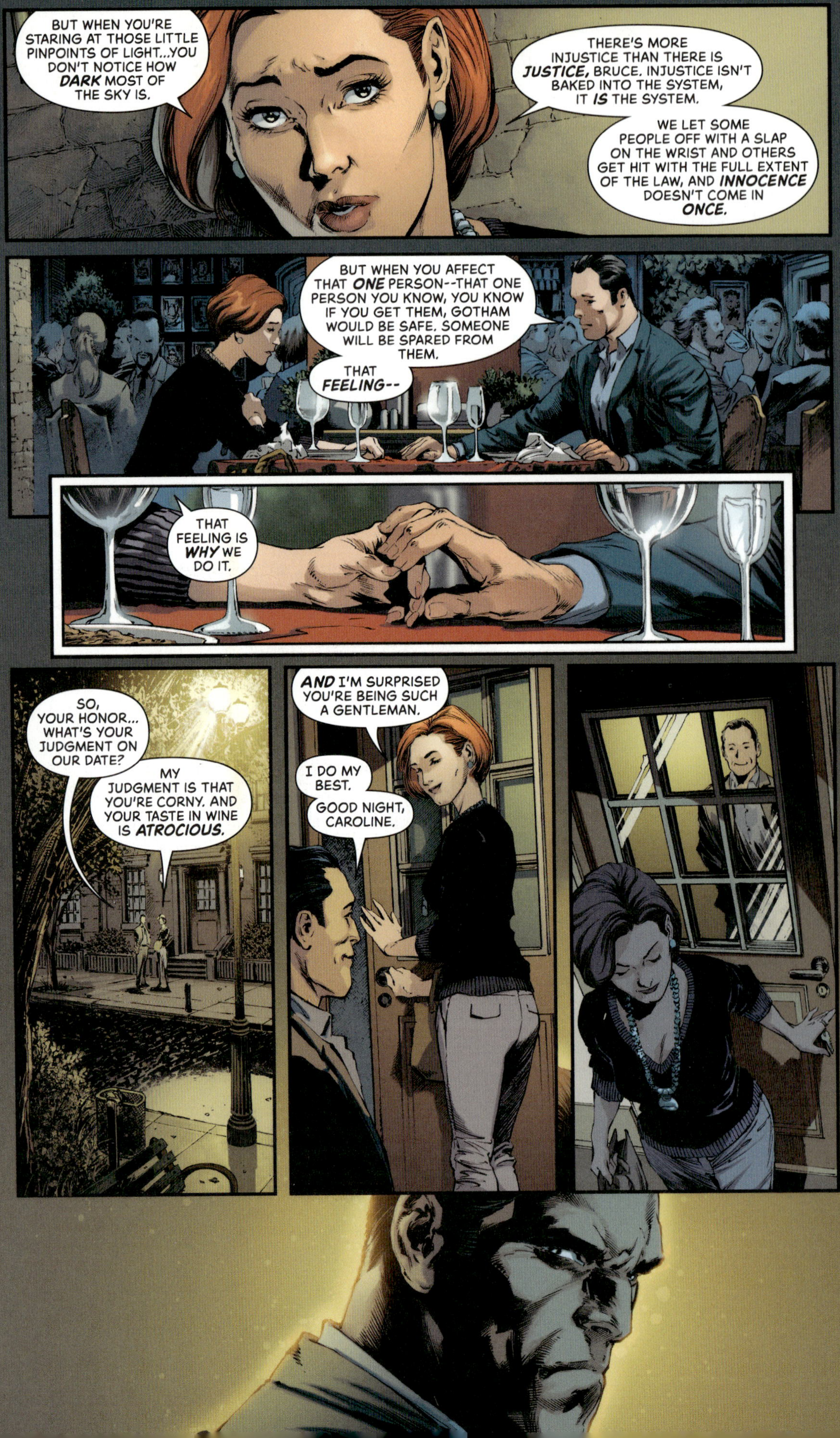
BUT WHEN YOU'RE STARING AT THOSE LITTLE PINPOINTS OF LIGHT...YOU DON'T NOTICE HOW DARK MOST OF THE SKY IS.
THERE'S MORE INJUSTICE THAN THERE IS JUSTICE, BRUCE. INJUSTICE ISN'T BAKED INTO THE SYSTEM, IT IS THE SYSTEM.
WE LET SOME PEOPLE OFF WITH A SLAP ON THE WRIST AND OTHERS GET HIT WITH THE FULL EXTENT OF THE LAW, AND INNOCENCE DOESN'T COME IN ONCE.
BUT WHEN YOU AFFECT THAT ONE PERSON--THAT ONE PERSON YOU KNOW, YOU KNOW IF YOU GET THEM, GOTHAM WOULD BE SAFE. SOMEONE WILL BE SPARED FROM THEM.
THAT FEELING--
THAT FEELING IS WHY WE DO IT.
SO, YOUR HONOR... WHAT'S YOUR JUDGMENT ON OUR DATE?
MY JUDGMENT IS THAT YOU'RE CORNY. AND YOUR TASTE IN WINE IS ATROCIOUS.
AND I'M SURPRISED YOU'RE BEING SUCH A GENTLEMAN.
I DO MY BEST.
GOOD NIGHT, CAROLINE.

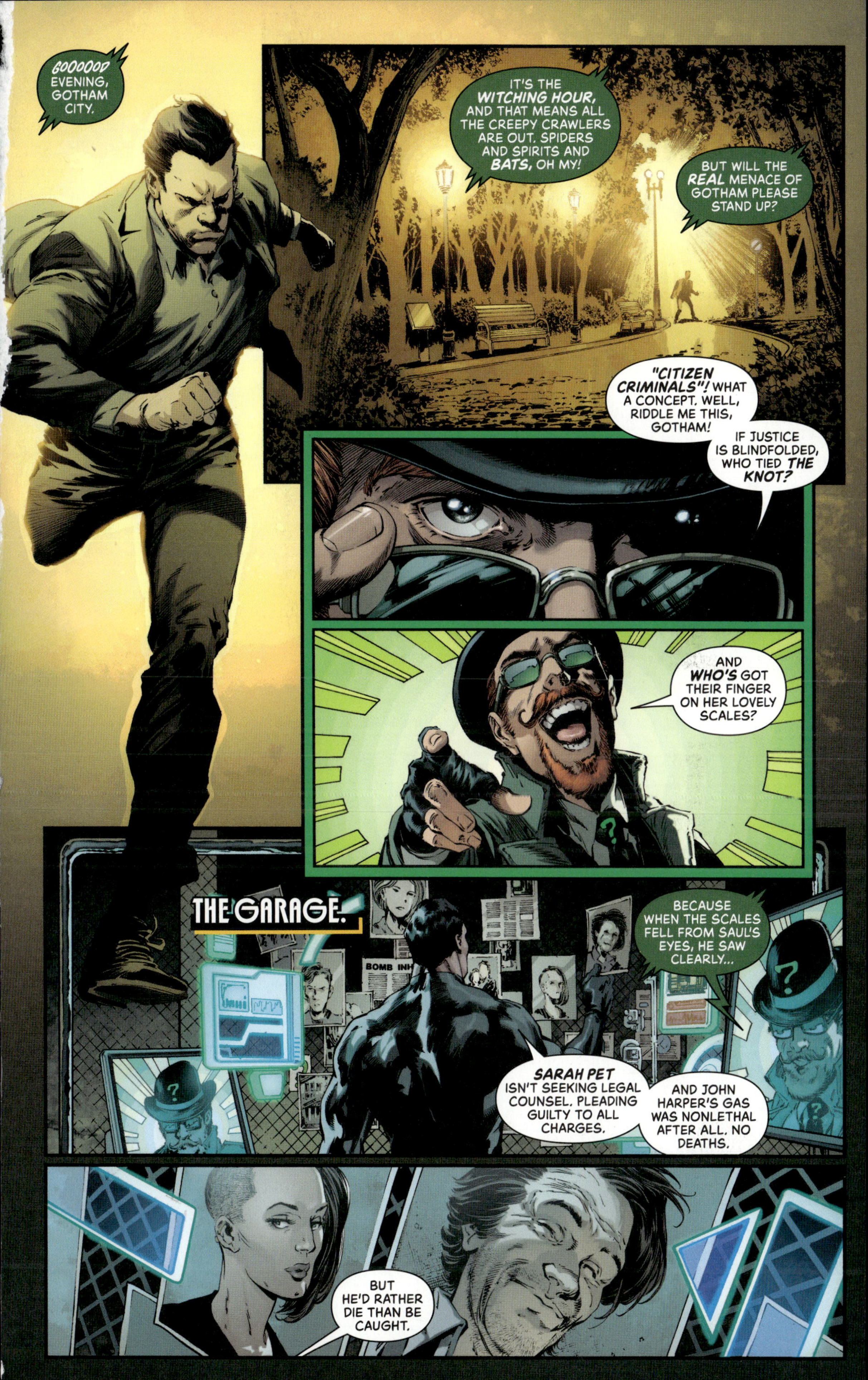

GOOOOOD EVENING, GOTHAM CITY.
IT'S THE WITCHING HOUR, AND THAT MEANS ALL THE CREEPY CRAWLERS ARE OUT. SPIDERS AND SPIRITS AND BATS, OH MY!
BUT WILL THE REAL MENACE OF GOTHAM PLEASE STAND UP?
"CITIZEN CRIMINALS"! WHAT A CONCEPT. WELL, RIDDLE ME THIS, GOTHAM!
IF JUSTICE IS BLINDFOLDED, WHO TIED THE KNOT?
AND WHO'S GOT THEIR FINGER ON HER LOVELY SCALES?
THE GARAGE.
BECAUSE WHEN THE SCALES FELL FROM SAUL'S EYES, HE SAW CLEARLY...
BOMB INH
SARAH PET ISN'T SEEKING LEGAL COUNSEL. PLEADING GUILTY TO ALL CHARGES.
AND JOHN HARPER'S GAS WAS NONLETHAL AFTER ALL. NO DEATHS.
BUT HE'D RATHER DIE THAN BE CAUGHT.

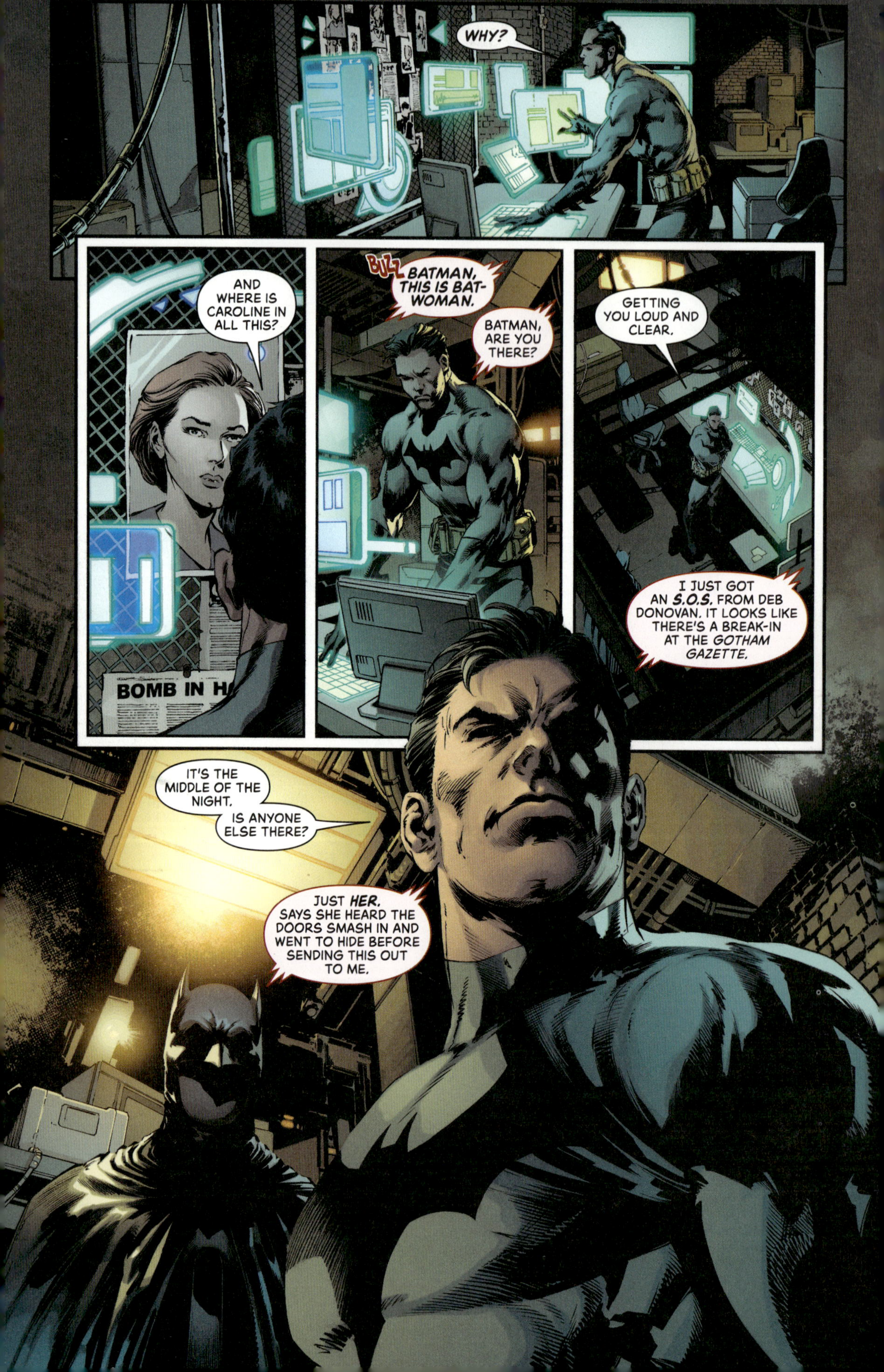
WHY?
AND WHERE IS CAROLINE IN ALL THIS?
BOMB IN H
BUZZ
BATMAN, THIS IS BAT-WOMAN.
BATMAN, ARE YOU THERE?
GETTING YOU LOUD AND CLEAR.
I JUST GOT AN S.O.S. FROM DEB DONOVAN. IT LOOKS LIKE THERE'S A BREAK-IN AT THE GOTHAM GAZETTE.
IT'S THE MIDDLE OF THE NIGHT.
IS ANYONE ELSE THERE?
JUST HER. SAYS SHE HEARD THE DOORS SMASH IN AND WENT TO HIDE BEFORE SENDING THIS OUT TO ME.

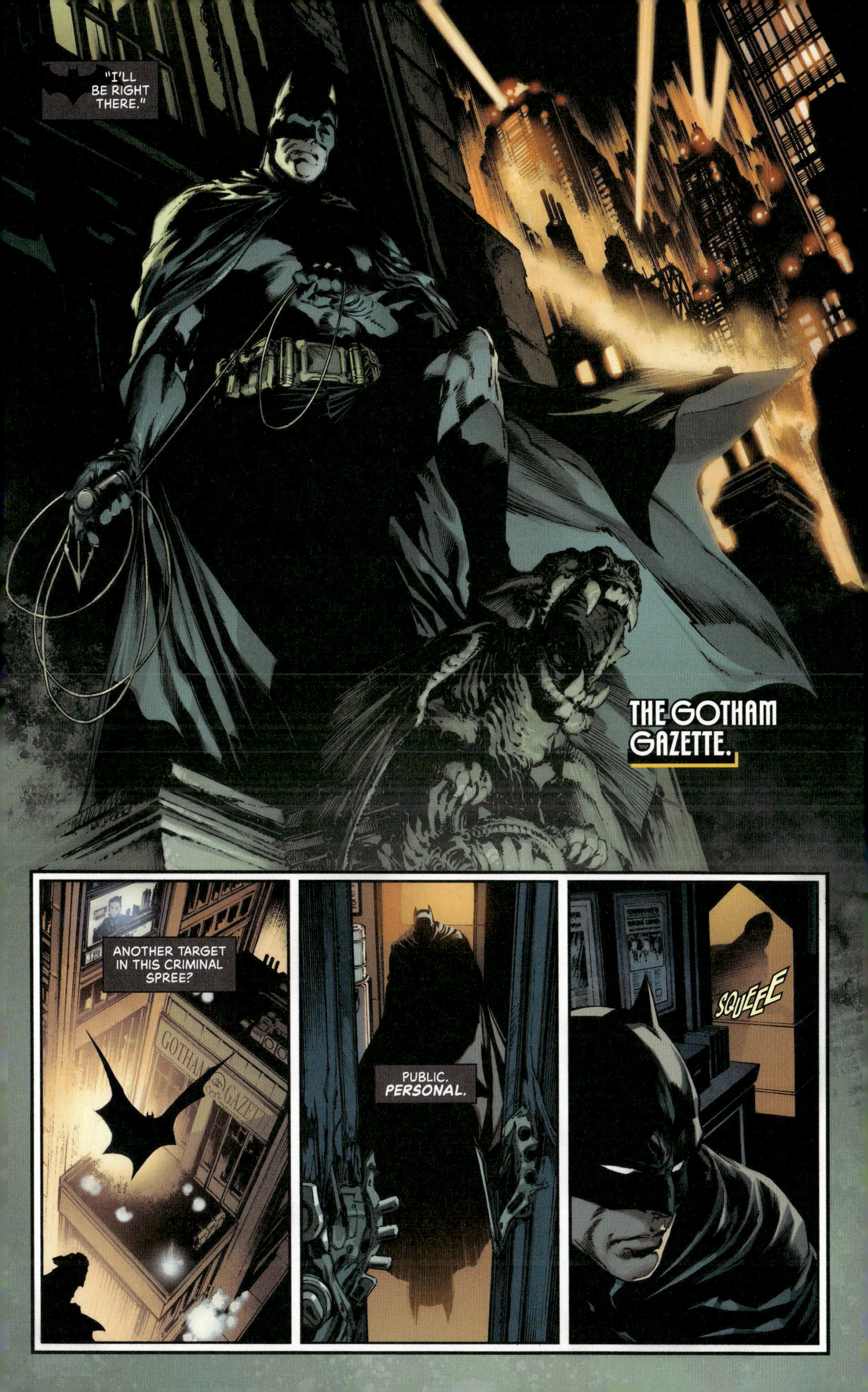
"I'LL BE RIGHT THERE."
THE GOTHAM GAZETTE.
ANOTHER TARGET IN THIS CRIMINAL SPREE?
GOTHAM GAZETTE
PUBLIC. PERSONAL.
SQUEEEE

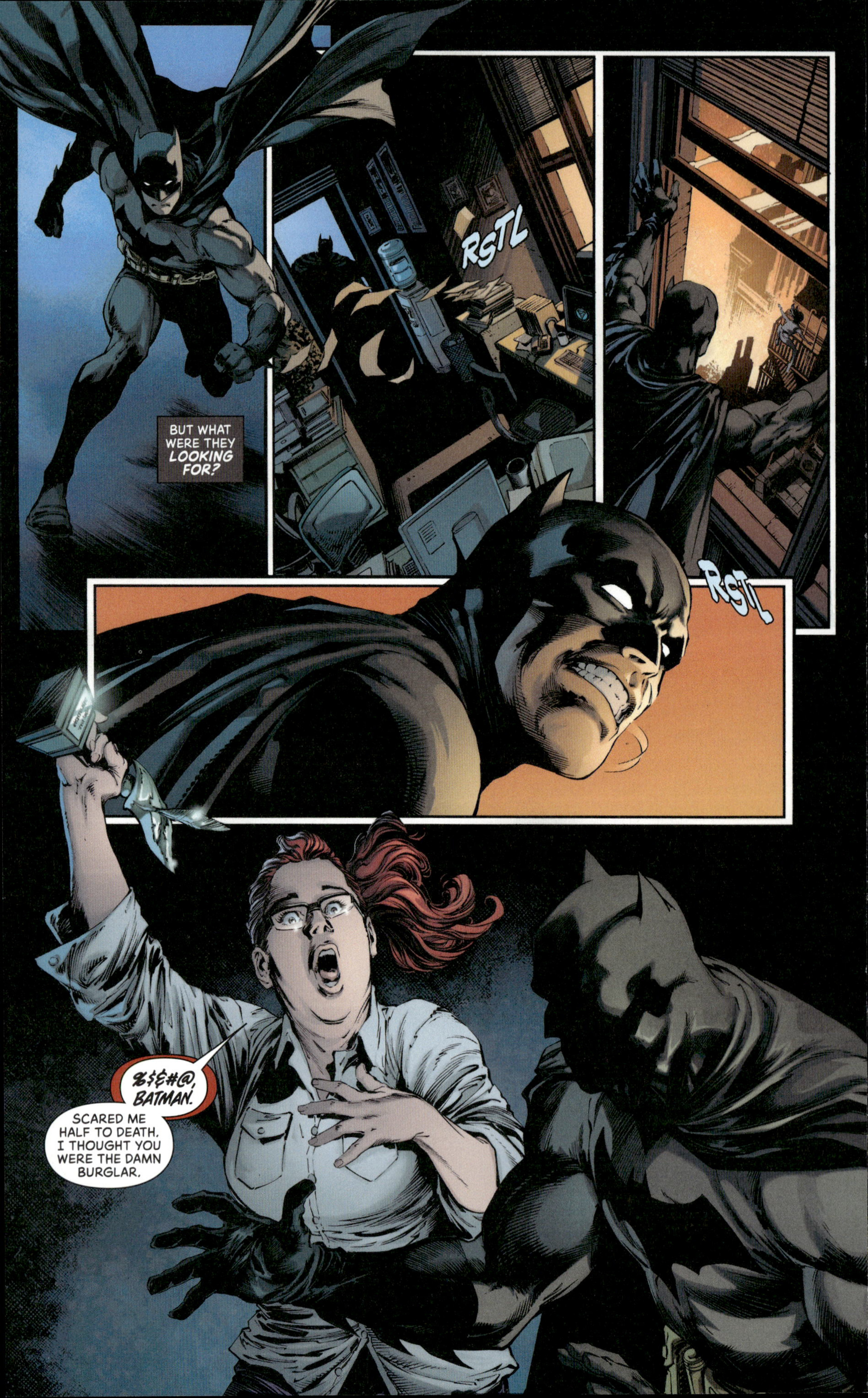
BUT WHAT WERE THEY LOOKING FOR?
RSTL
RSTL
%$&#@, BATMAN.
SCARED ME HALF TO DEATH. I THOUGHT YOU WERE THE DAMN BURGLAR.

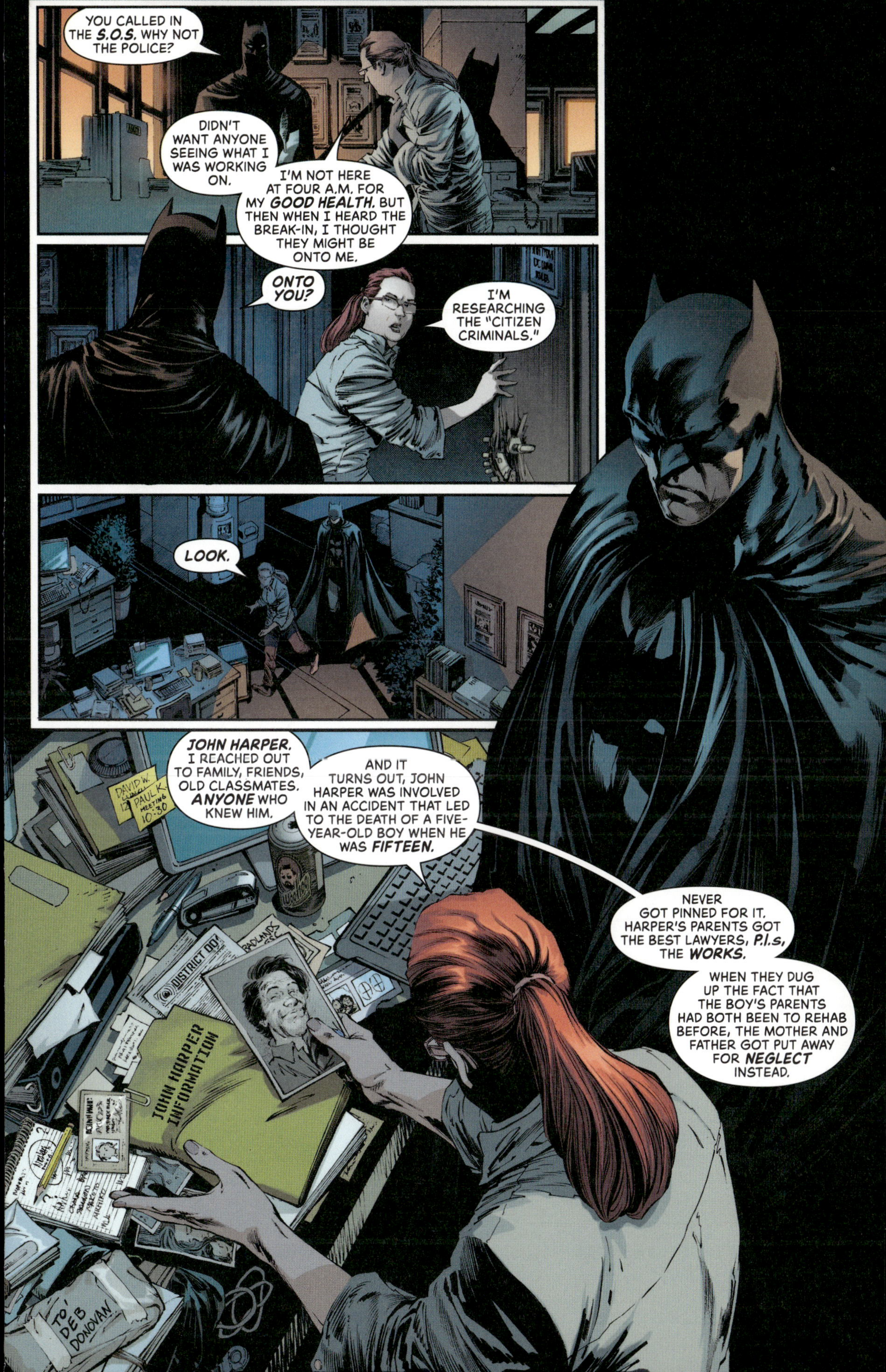
YOU CALLED IN THE S.O.S. WHY NOT THE POLICE?
DIDN'T WANT ANYONE SEEING WHAT I WAS WORKING ON.
I'M NOT HERE AT FOUR A.M. FOR MY GOOD HEALTH. BUT THEN WHEN I HEARD THE BREAK-IN, I THOUGHT THEY MIGHT BE ONTO ME.
ONTO YOU?
I'M RESEARCHING THE "CITIZEN CRIMINALS."
LOOK.
JOHN HARPER. I REACHED OUT TO FAMILY, FRIENDS, OLD CLASSMATES. ANYONE WHO KNEW HIM.
AND IT TURNS OUT, JOHN HARPER WAS INVOLVED IN AN ACCIDENT THAT LED TO THE DEATH OF A FIVE-YEAR-OLD BOY WHEN HE WAS FIFTEEN.
NEVER GOT PINNED FOR IT. HARPER'S PARENTS GOT THE BEST LAWYERS, P.I.s, THE WORKS.
WHEN THEY DUG UP THE FACT THAT THE BOY'S PARENTS HAD BOTH BEEN TO REHAB BEFORE, THE MOTHER AND FATHER GOT PUT AWAY FOR NEGLECT INSTEAD.
PAUL K. MEETING 10:30
JOHN HARPER INFORMATION
TO: DEB DONOVAN

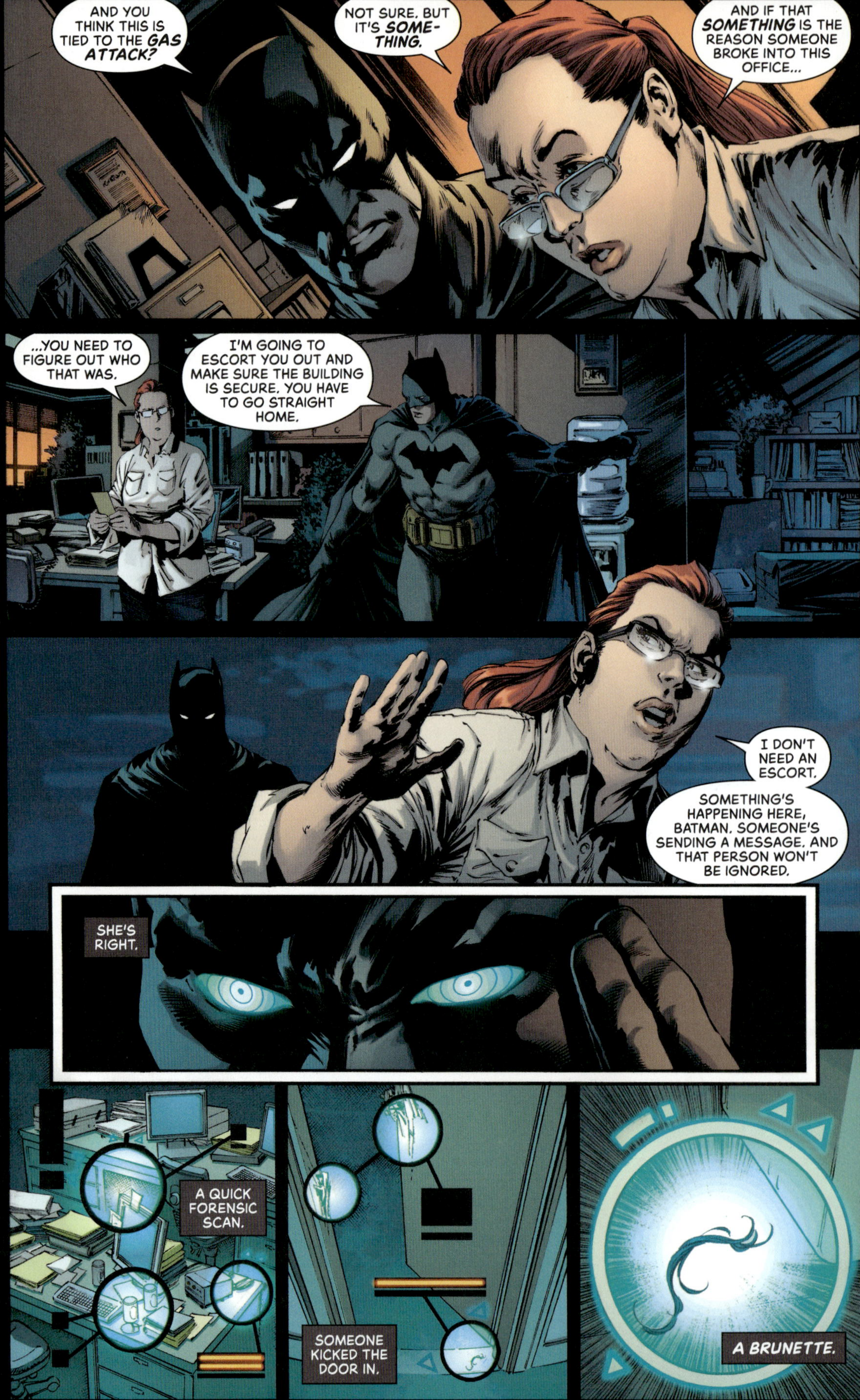
AND YOU THINK THIS IS TIED TO THE GAS ATTACK?
NOT SURE. BUT IT'S SOMETHING.
AND IF THAT SOMETHING IS THE REASON SOMEONE BROKE INTO THIS OFFICE...
...YOU NEED TO FIGURE OUT WHO THAT WAS.
I'M GOING TO ESCORT YOU OUT AND MAKE SURE THE BUILDING IS SECURE. YOU HAVE TO GO STRAIGHT HOME.
I DON'T NEED AN ESCORT.
SOMETHING'S HAPPENING HERE, BATMAN. SOMEONE'S SENDING A MESSAGE. AND THAT PERSON WON'T BE IGNORED.
SHE'S RIGHT.
A QUICK FORENSIC SCAN.
SOMEONE KICKED THE DOOR IN.
A BRUNETTE.

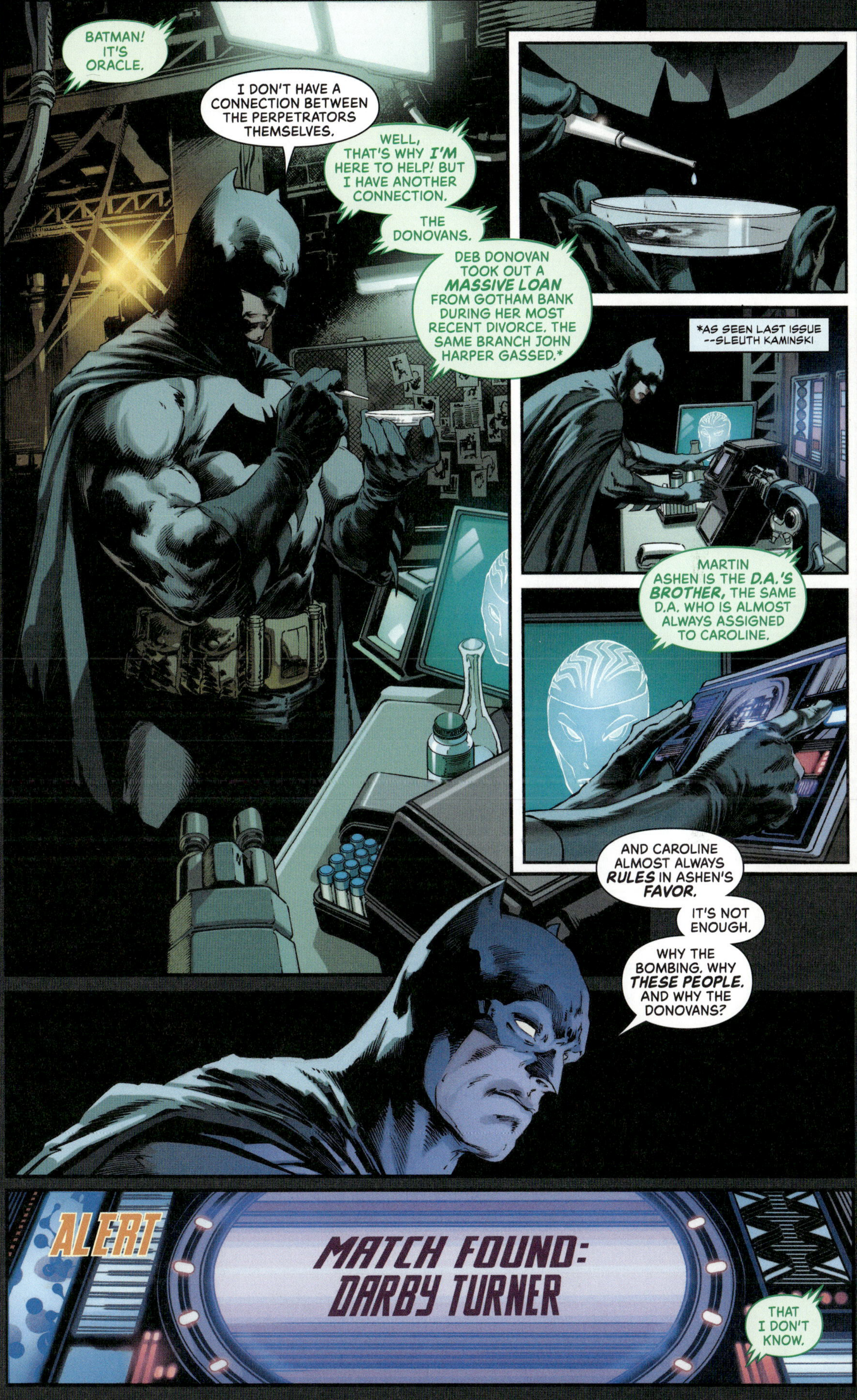
BATMAN! IT'S ORACLE.
I DON'T HAVE A CONNECTION BETWEEN THE PERPETRATORS THEMSELVES.
WELL, THAT'S WHY I'M HERE TO HELP! BUT I HAVE ANOTHER CONNECTION.
THE DONOVANS.
DEB DONOVAN TOOK OUT A MASSIVE LOAN FROM GOTHAM BANK DURING HER MOST RECENT DIVORCE. THE SAME BRANCH JOHN HARPER GASSED.*
*AS SEEN LAST ISSUE --SLEUTH KAMINSKI
MARTIN ASHEN IS THE D.A.'S BROTHER, THE SAME D.A. WHO IS ALMOST ALWAYS ASSIGNED TO CAROLINE.
AND CAROLINE ALMOST ALWAYS RULES IN ASHEN'S FAVOR.
IT'S NOT ENOUGH.
WHY THE BOMBING, WHY THESE PEOPLE, AND WHY THE DONOVANS?
ALERT
MATCH FOUND: DARBY TURNER
THAT I DON'T KNOW.

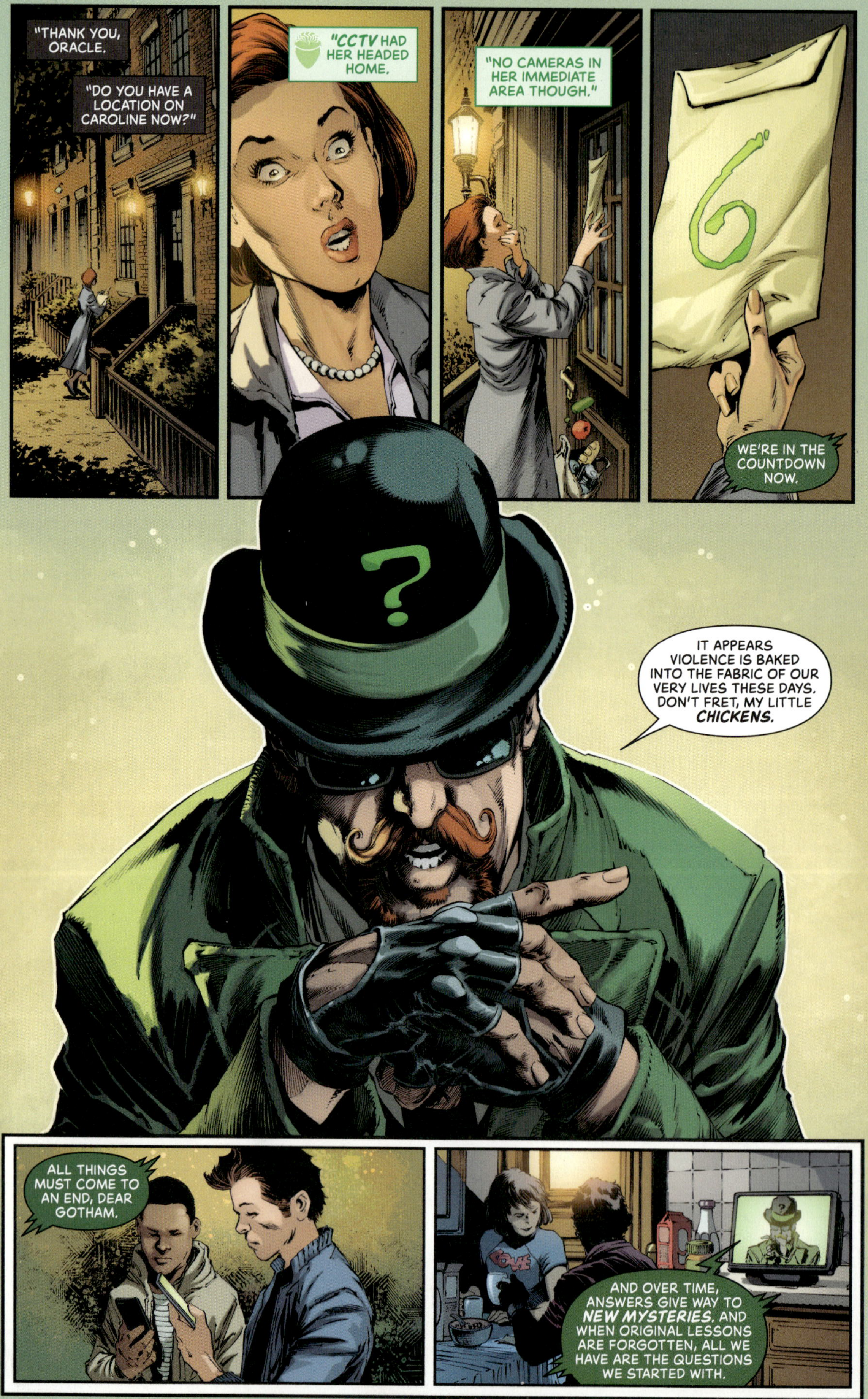
"THANK YOU, ORACLE.
"DO YOU HAVE A LOCATION ON CAROLINE NOW?"
"CCTV HAD HER HEADED HOME.
"NO CAMERAS IN HER IMMEDIATE AREA THOUGH."
6
WE'RE IN THE COUNTDOWN NOW.
IT APPEARS VIOLENCE IS BAKED INTO THE FABRIC OF OUR VERY LIVES THESE DAYS. DON'T FRET, MY LITTLE CHICKENS.
ALL THINGS MUST COME TO AN END, DEAR GOTHAM.
AND OVER TIME, ANSWERS GIVE WAY TO NEW MYSTERIES. AND WHEN ORIGINAL LESSONS ARE FORGOTTEN, ALL WE HAVE ARE THE QUESTIONS WE STARTED WITH.

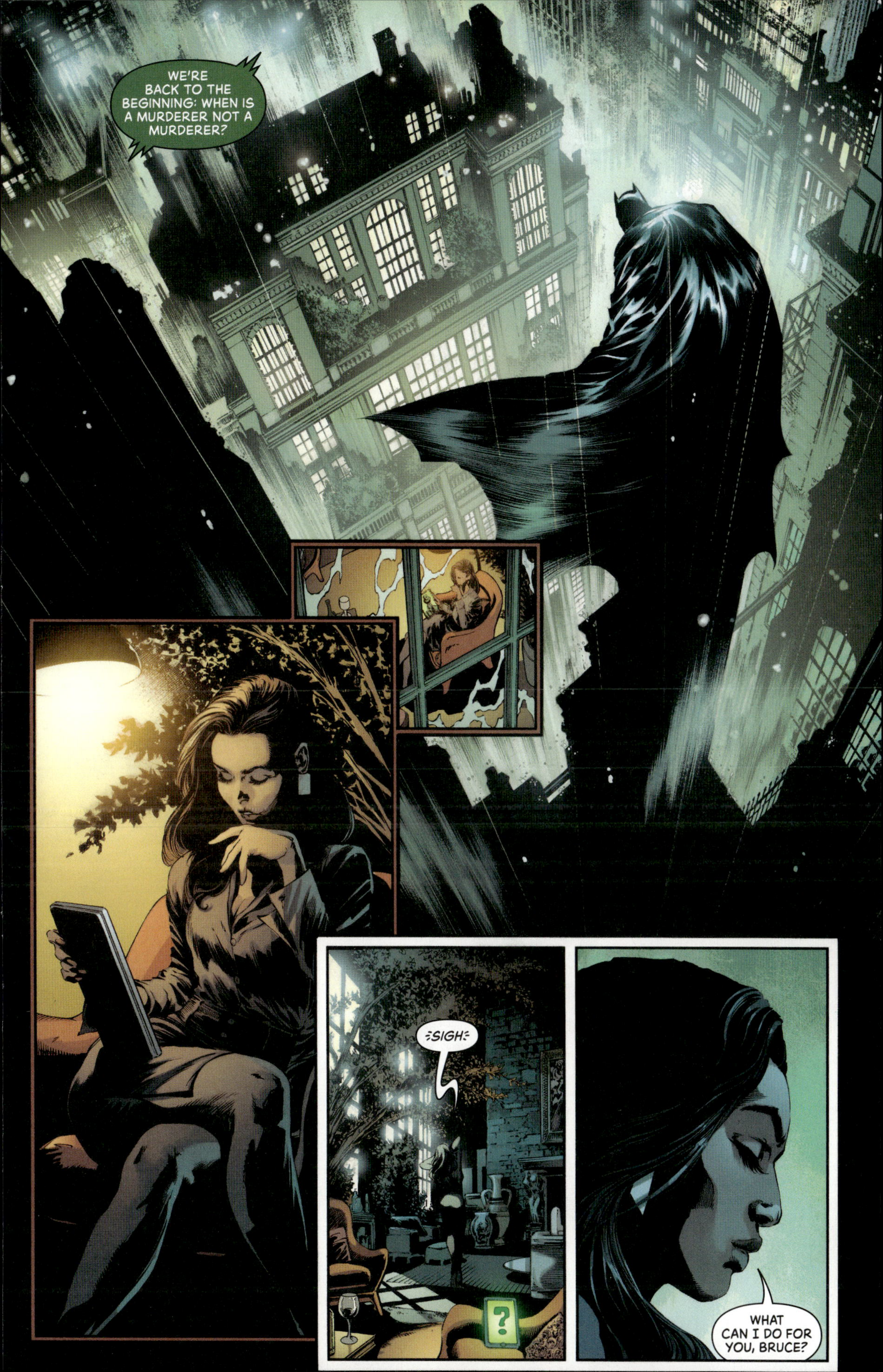
WE'RE BACK TO THE BEGINNING: WHEN IS A MURDERER NOT A MURDERER?
SIGH
WHAT CAN I DO FOR YOU, BRUCE?

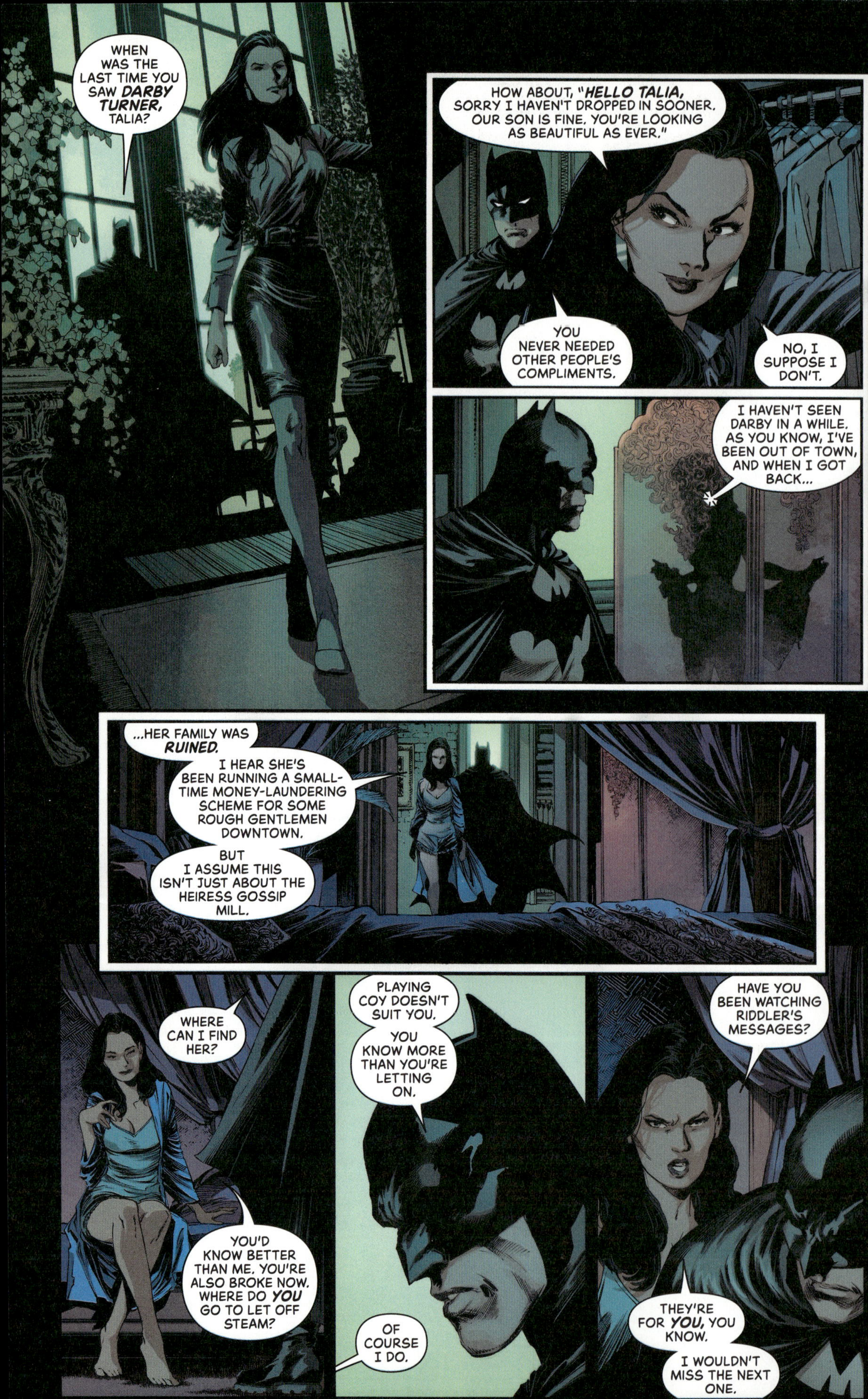

WHEN WAS THE LAST TIME YOU SAW *DARBY TURNER,* TALIA?
HOW ABOUT, "*HELLO TALIA,* SORRY I HAVEN'T DROPPED IN SOONER. OUR SON IS FINE. YOU'RE LOOKING AS BEAUTIFUL AS EVER."
YOU NEVER NEEDED OTHER PEOPLE'S COMPLIMENTS.
NO, I SUPPOSE I DON'T.
I HAVEN'T SEEN DARBY IN A WHILE. AS YOU KNOW, I'VE BEEN OUT OF TOWN, AND WHEN I GOT BACK...
...HER FAMILY WAS *RUINED.*
I HEAR SHE'S BEEN RUNNING A SMALL-TIME MONEY-LAUNDERING SCHEME FOR SOME ROUGH GENTLEMEN DOWNTOWN.
BUT I ASSUME THIS ISN'T JUST ABOUT THE HEIRESS GOSSIP MILL.
WHERE CAN I FIND HER?
YOU'D KNOW BETTER THAN ME. YOU'RE ALSO BROKE NOW. WHERE DO *YOU* GO TO LET OFF STEAM?
PLAYING COY DOESN'T SUIT YOU.
YOU KNOW MORE THAN YOU'RE LETTING ON.
OF COURSE I DO.
HAVE YOU BEEN WATCHING RIDDLER'S MESSAGES?
THEY'RE FOR *YOU,* YOU KNOW.
I WOULDN'T MISS THE NEXT ONE.

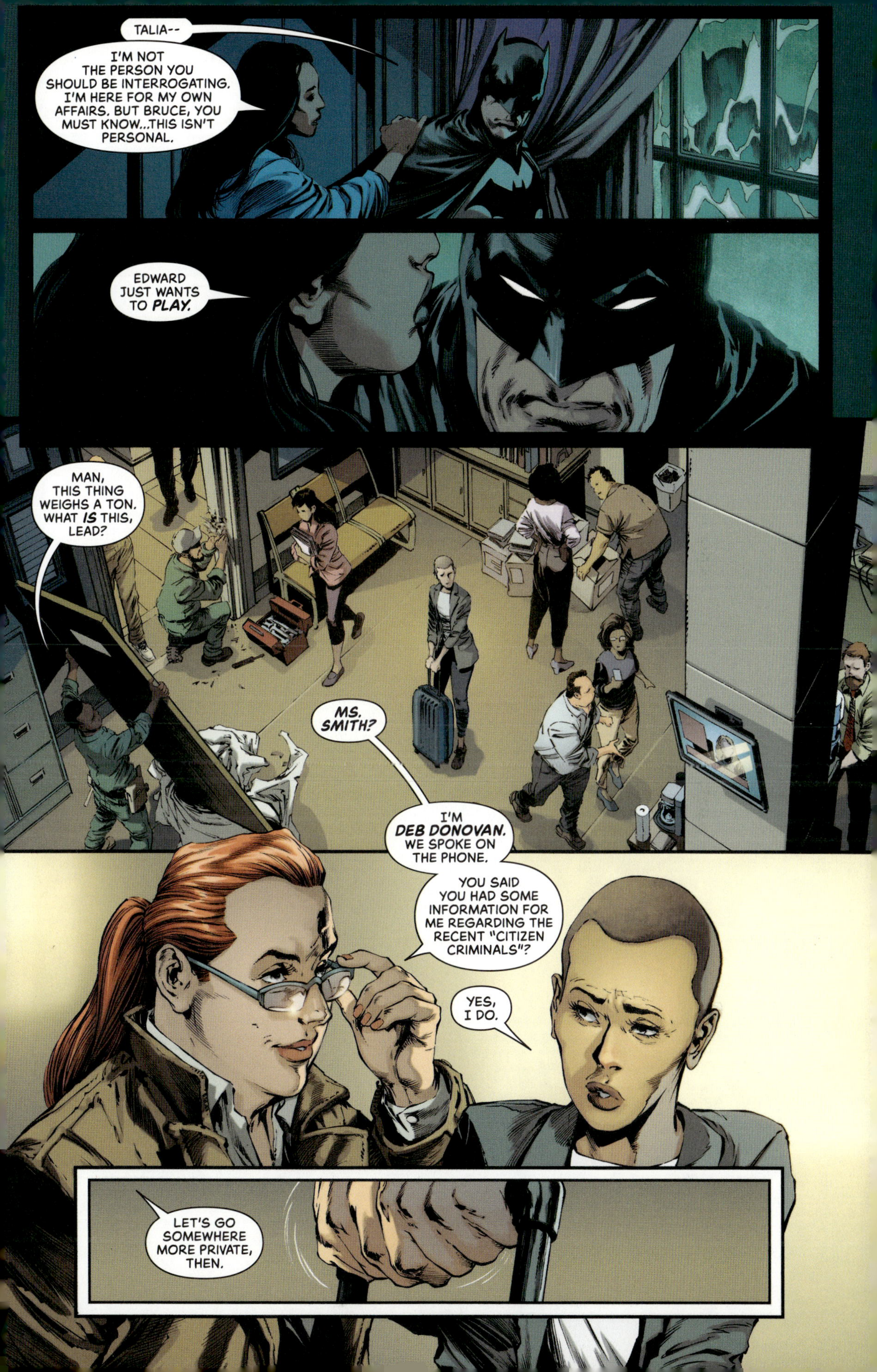
TALIA--
I'M NOT THE PERSON YOU SHOULD BE INTERROGATING. I'M HERE FOR MY OWN AFFAIRS. BUT BRUCE, YOU MUST KNOW...THIS ISN'T PERSONAL.
EDWARD JUST WANTS TO PLAY.
MAN, THIS THING WEIGHS A TON. WHAT IS THIS, LEAD?
MS. SMITH?
I'M DEB DONOVAN. WE SPOKE ON THE PHONE.
YOU SAID YOU HAD SOME INFORMATION FOR ME REGARDING THE RECENT "CITIZEN CRIMINALS"?
YES, I DO.
LET'S GO SOMEWHERE MORE PRIVATE, THEN.

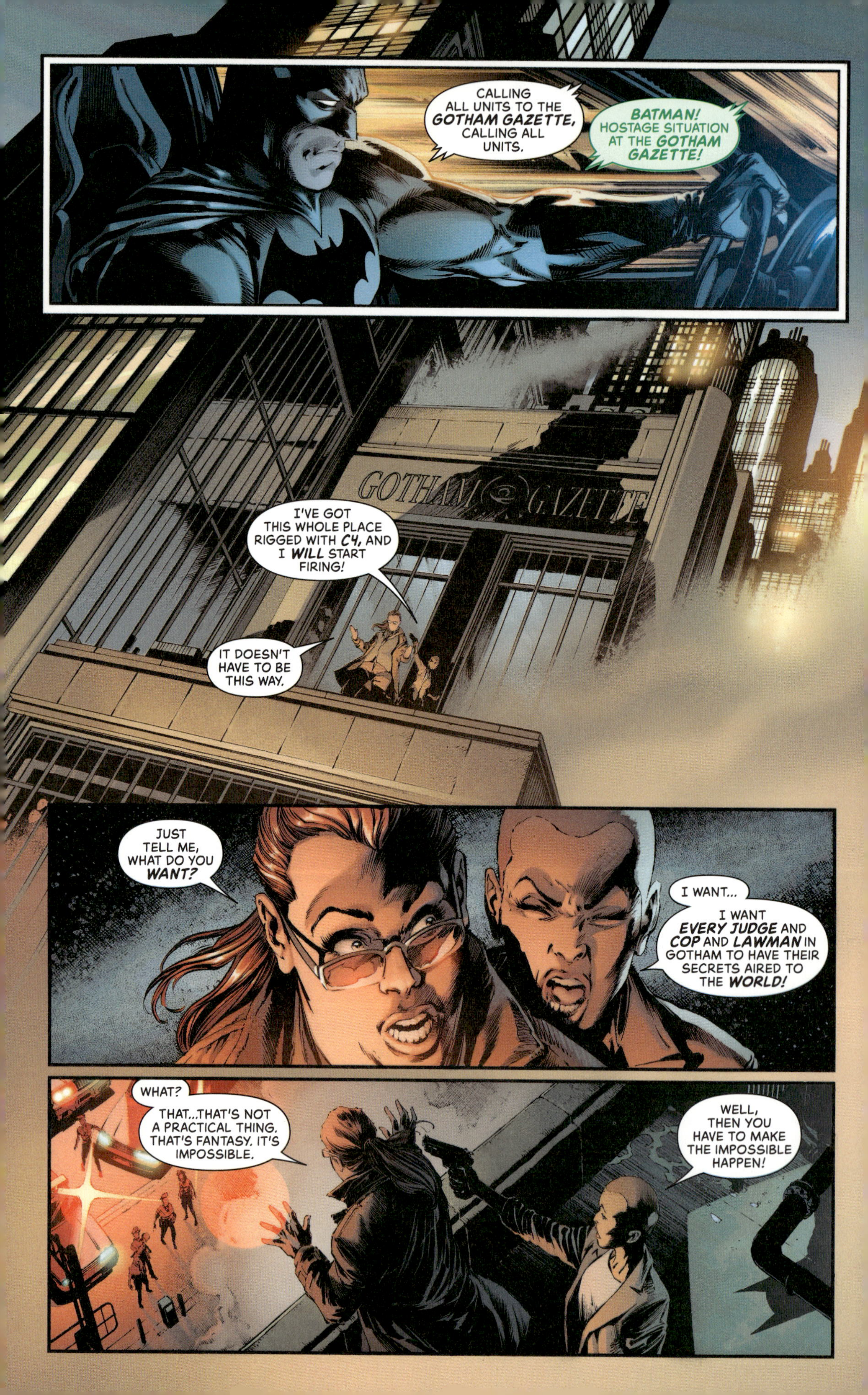
CALLING ALL UNITS TO THE GOTHAM GAZETTE, CALLING ALL UNITS.
BATMAN! HOSTAGE SITUATION AT THE GOTHAM GAZETTE!
GOTHAM GAZETTE
I'VE GOT THIS WHOLE PLACE RIGGED WITH C4, AND I WILL START FIRING!
IT DOESN'T HAVE TO BE THIS WAY.
JUST TELL ME, WHAT DO YOU WANT?
I WANT...
I WANT EVERY JUDGE AND COP AND LAWMAN IN GOTHAM TO HAVE THEIR SECRETS AIRED TO THE WORLD!
WHAT?
THAT...THAT'S NOT A PRACTICAL THING. THAT'S FANTASY. IT'S IMPOSSIBLE.
WELL, THEN YOU HAVE TO MAKE THE IMPOSSIBLE HAPPEN!

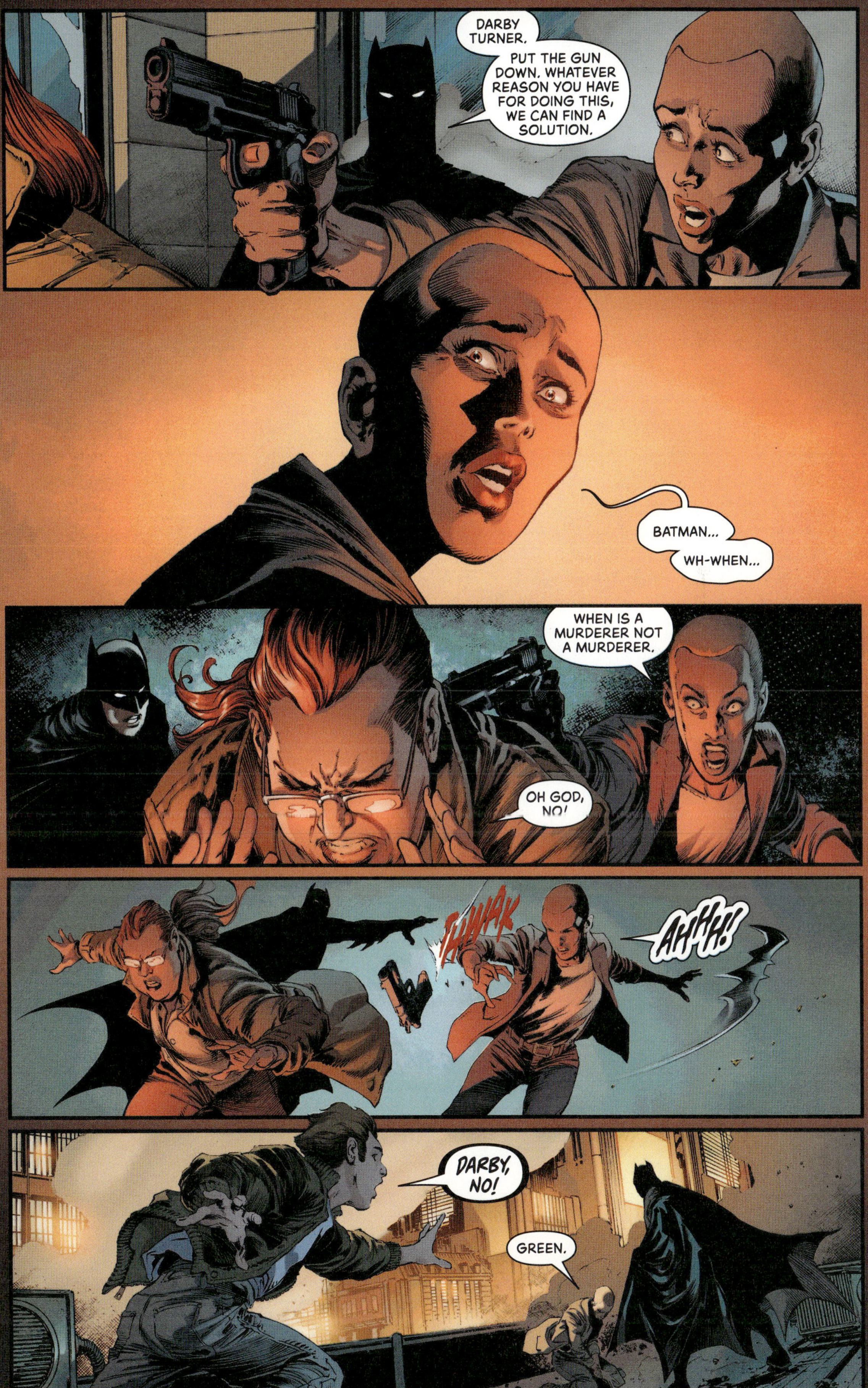
DARBY TURNER.
PUT THE GUN DOWN. WHATEVER REASON YOU HAVE FOR DOING THIS, WE CAN FIND A SOLUTION.
BATMAN...
WH-WHEN...
WHEN IS A MURDERER NOT A MURDERER.
OH GOD, NO!
THWAK
AHHH!
DARBY, NO!
GREEN.

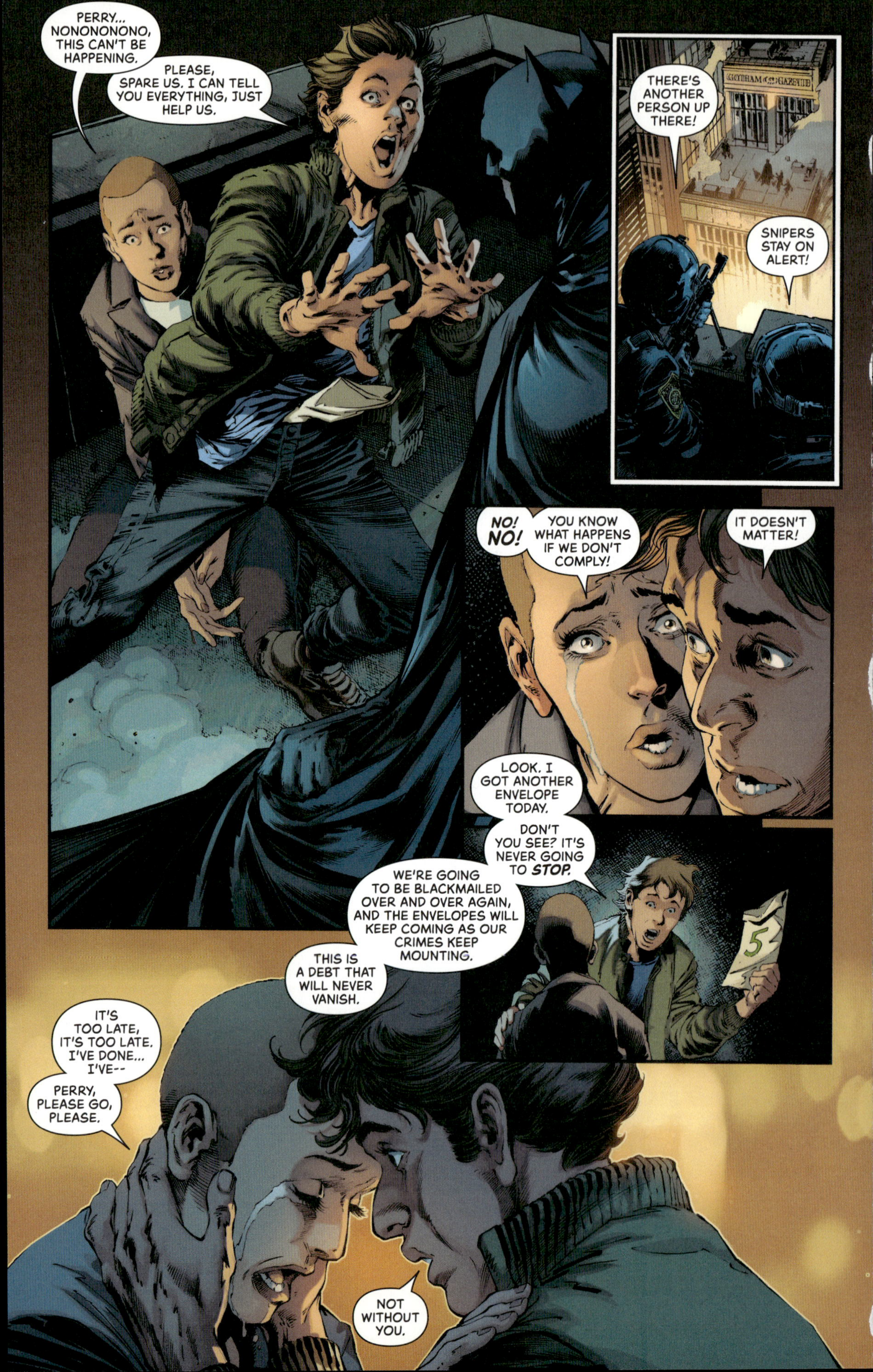
PERRY... NONONONONO, THIS CAN'T BE HAPPENING.
PLEASE, SPARE US. I CAN TELL YOU EVERYTHING, JUST HELP US.
THERE'S ANOTHER PERSON UP THERE!
SNIPERS STAY ON ALERT!
NO! NO!
YOU KNOW WHAT HAPPENS IF WE DON'T COMPLY!
IT DOESN'T MATTER!
LOOK. I GOT ANOTHER ENVELOPE TODAY.
DON'T YOU SEE? IT'S NEVER GOING TO STOP.
WE'RE GOING TO BE BLACKMAILED OVER AND OVER AGAIN, AND THE ENVELOPES WILL KEEP COMING AS OUR CRIMES KEEP MOUNTING.
THIS IS A DEBT THAT WILL NEVER VANISH.
IT'S TOO LATE, IT'S TOO LATE. I'VE DONE... I'VE--
PERRY, PLEASE GO, PLEASE.
NOT WITHOUT YOU.

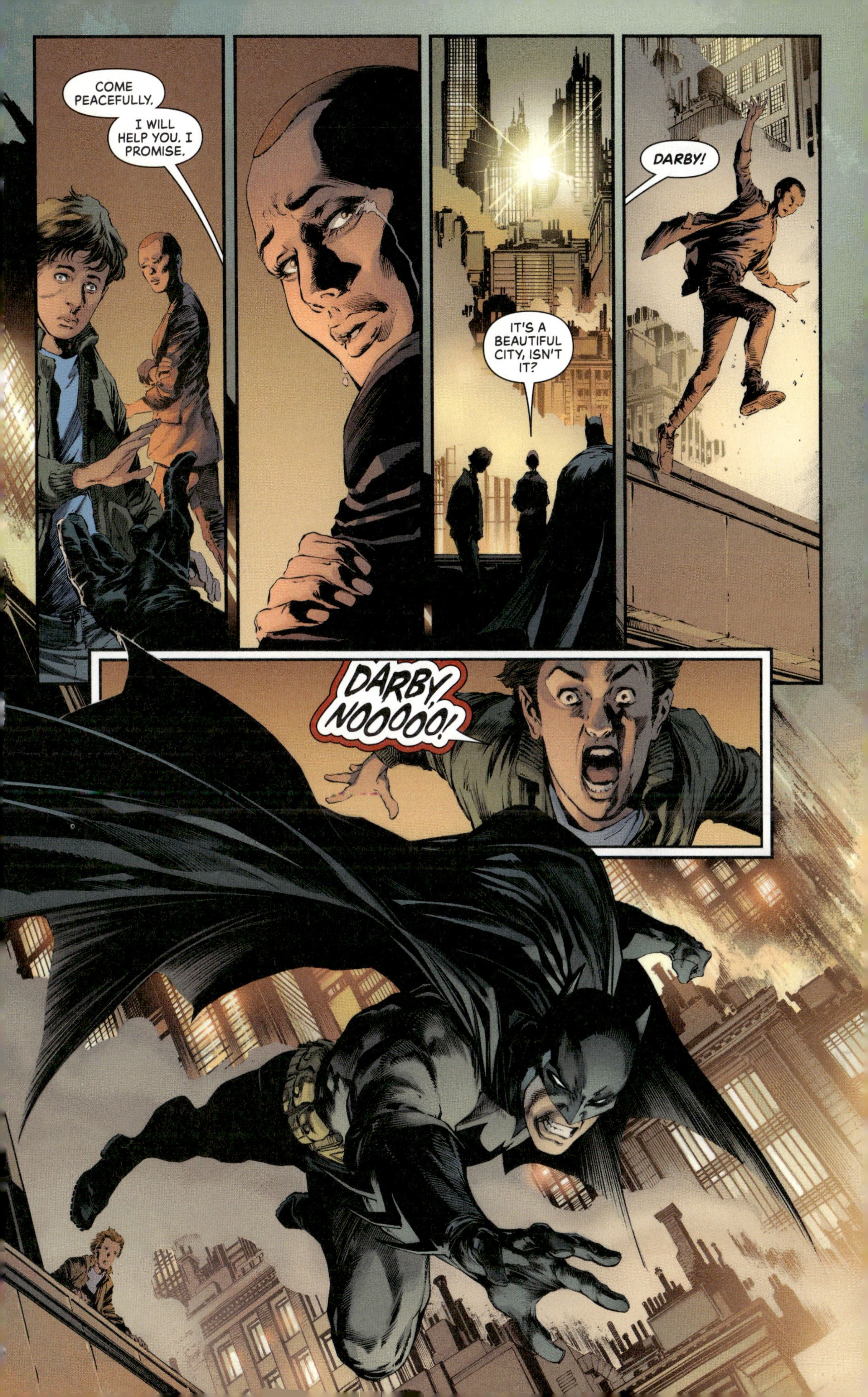
COME PEACEFULLY.
I WILL HELP YOU. I PROMISE.
IT'S A BEAUTIFUL CITY, ISN'T IT?
DARBY!
DARBY, NOOOOO!

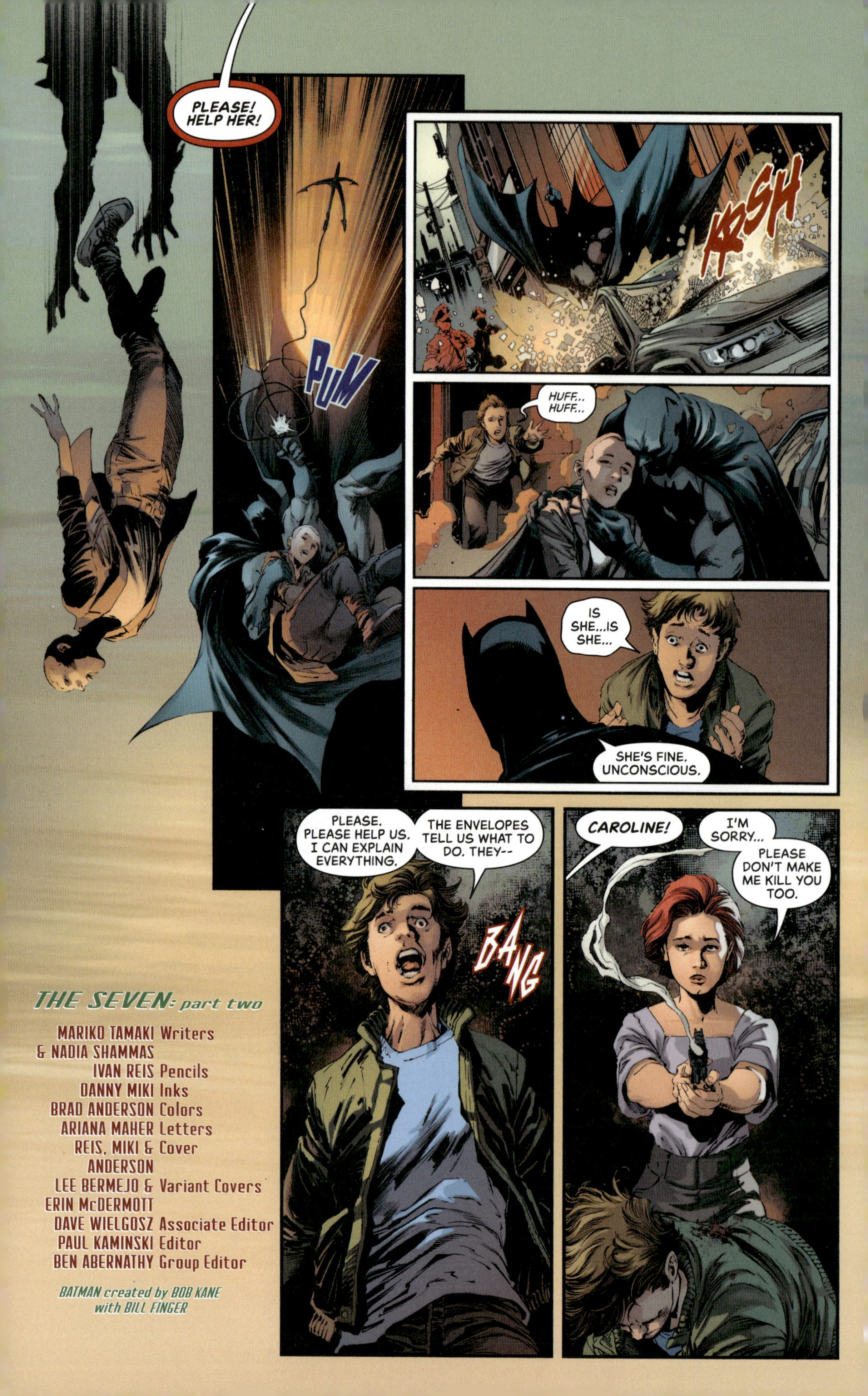

PLEASE! HELP HER!
PUM
KRSH
HUFF.. HUFF...
IS SHE...IS SHE...
SHE'S FINE. UNCONSCIOUS.
PLEASE, PLEASE HELP US. I CAN EXPLAIN EVERYTHING.
THE ENVELOPES TELL US WHAT TO DO. THEY--
BANG
CAROLINE!
I'M SORRY...
PLEASE DON'T MAKE ME KILL YOU TOO.

THE SEVEN: part two

MARIKO TAMAKI & NADIA SHAMMAS Writers
IVAN REIS Pencils
DANNY MIKI Inks
BRAD ANDERSON Colors
ARIANA MAHER Letters
REIS, MIKI & ANDERSON Cover
LEE BERMEJO & ERIN McDERMOTT Variant Covers
DAVE WIELGOSZ Associate Editor
PAUL KAMINSKI Editor
BEN ABERNATHY Group Editor

BATMAN created by BOB KANE with BILL FINGER

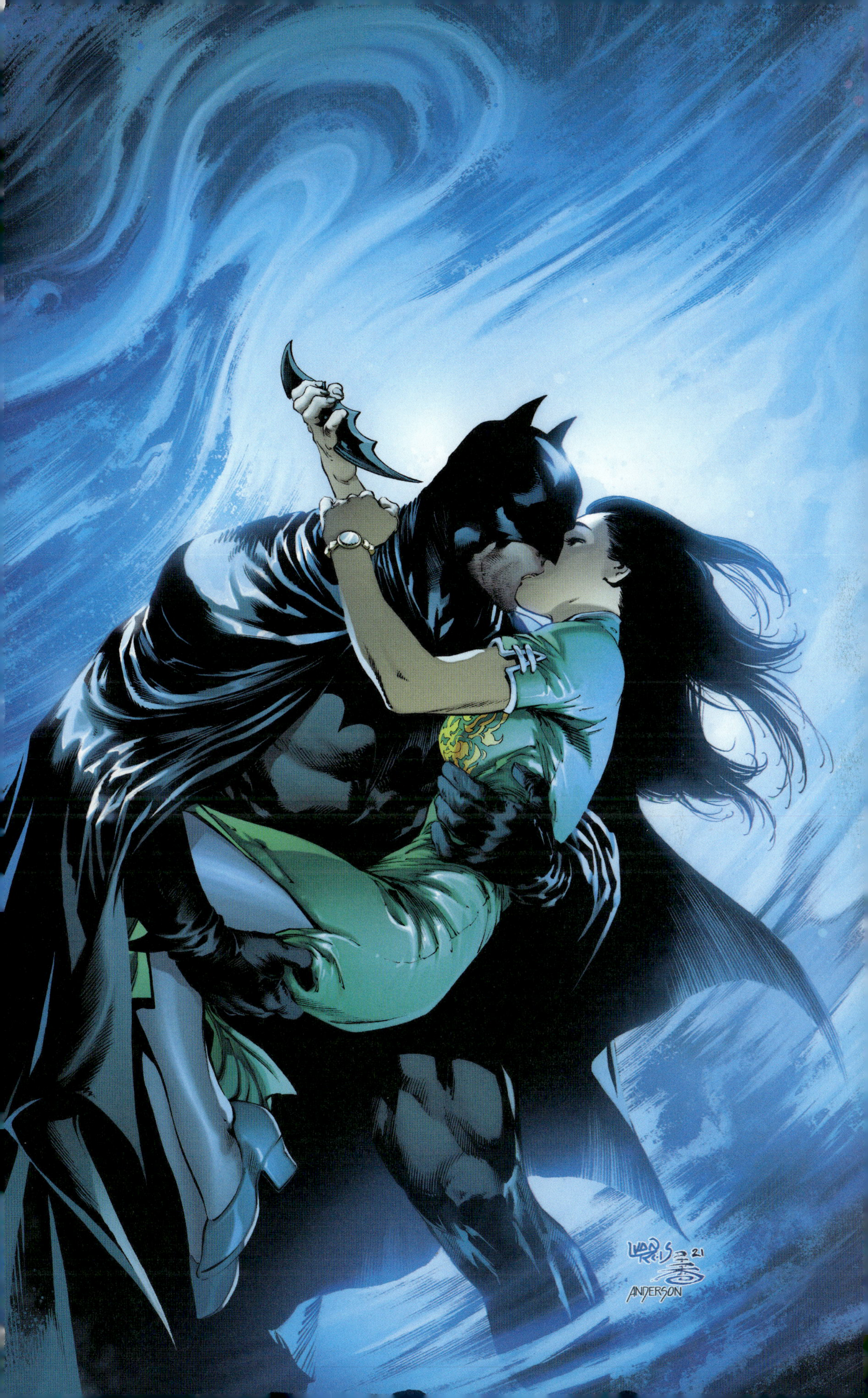
ANDERSON

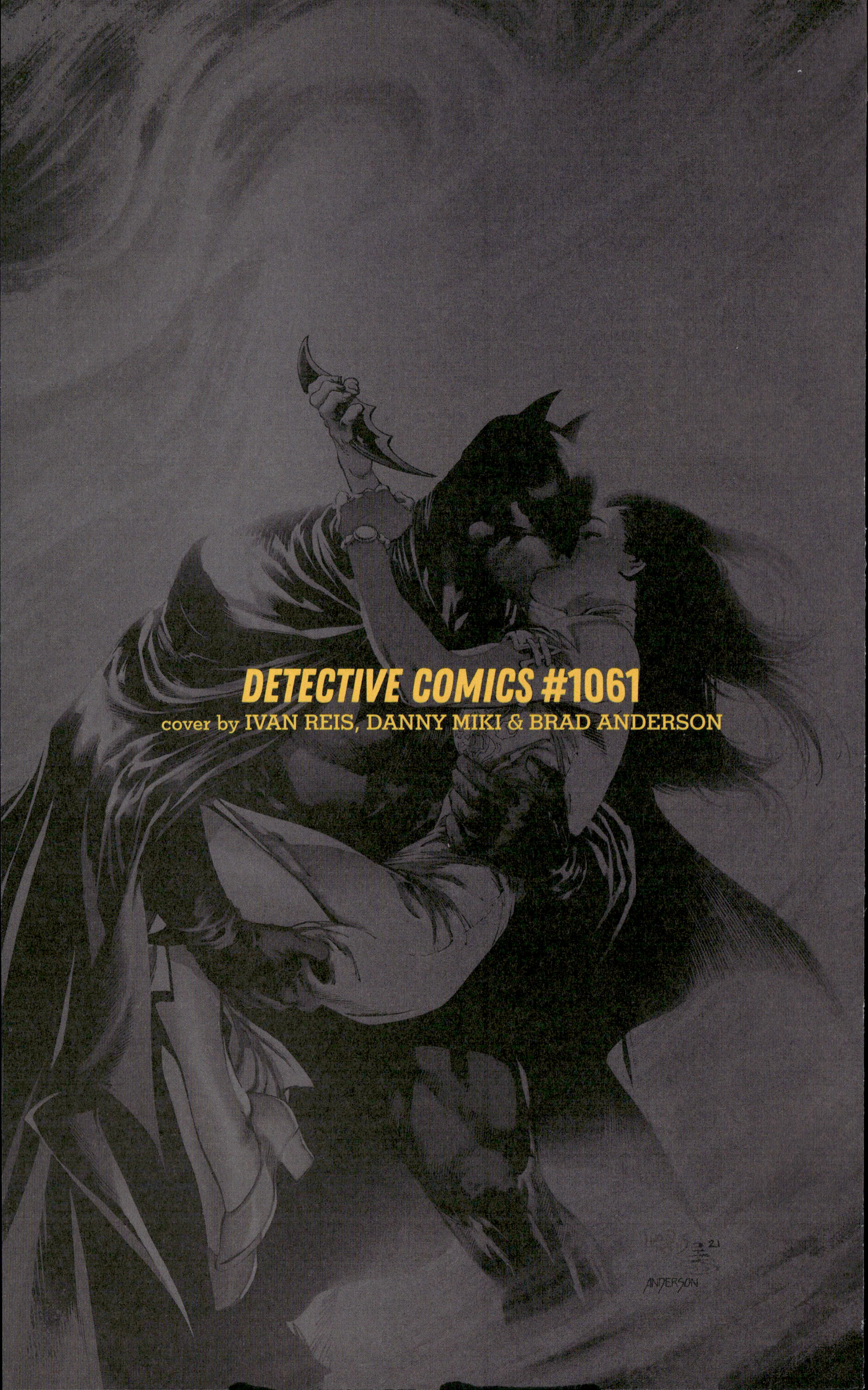
ANDERSON

DETECTIVE COMICS #1061

cover by IVAN REIS, DANNY MIKI & BRAD ANDERSON

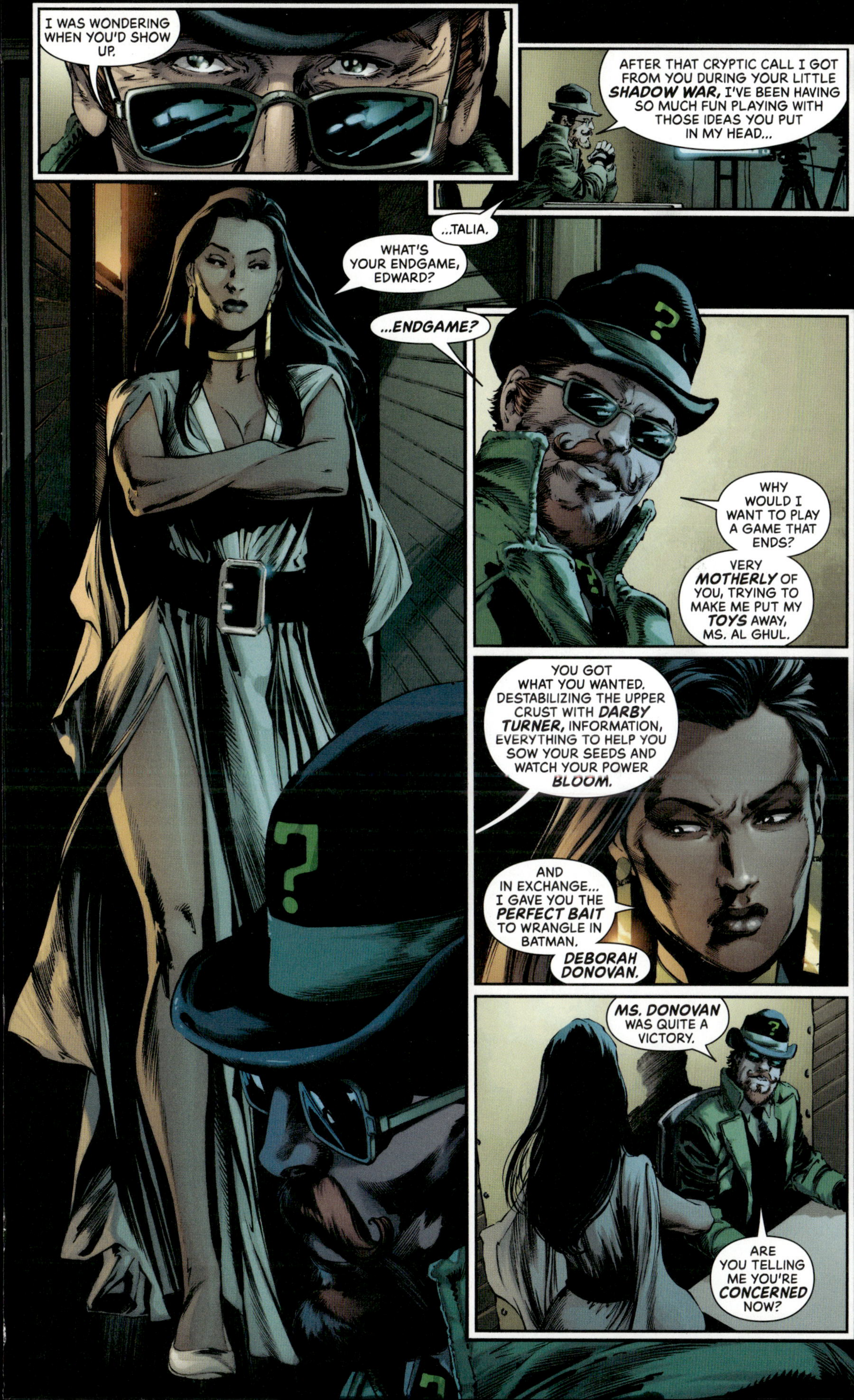
I WAS WONDERING WHEN YOU'D SHOW UP.
AFTER THAT CRYPTIC CALL I GOT FROM YOU DURING YOUR LITTLE SHADOW WAR, I'VE BEEN HAVING SO MUCH FUN PLAYING WITH THOSE IDEAS YOU PUT IN MY HEAD...
...TALIA.
WHAT'S YOUR ENDGAME, EDWARD?
...ENDGAME?
WHY WOULD I WANT TO PLAY A GAME THAT ENDS?
VERY MOTHERLY OF YOU, TRYING TO MAKE ME PUT MY TOYS AWAY, MS. AL GHUL.
YOU GOT WHAT YOU WANTED. DESTABILIZING THE UPPER CRUST WITH DARBY TURNER, INFORMATION, EVERYTHING TO HELP YOU SOW YOUR SEEDS AND WATCH YOUR POWER BLOOM.
AND IN EXCHANGE... I GAVE YOU THE PERFECT BAIT TO WRANGLE IN BATMAN.
DEBORAH DONOVAN.
MS. DONOVAN WAS QUITE A VICTORY.
ARE YOU TELLING ME YOU'RE CONCERNED NOW?

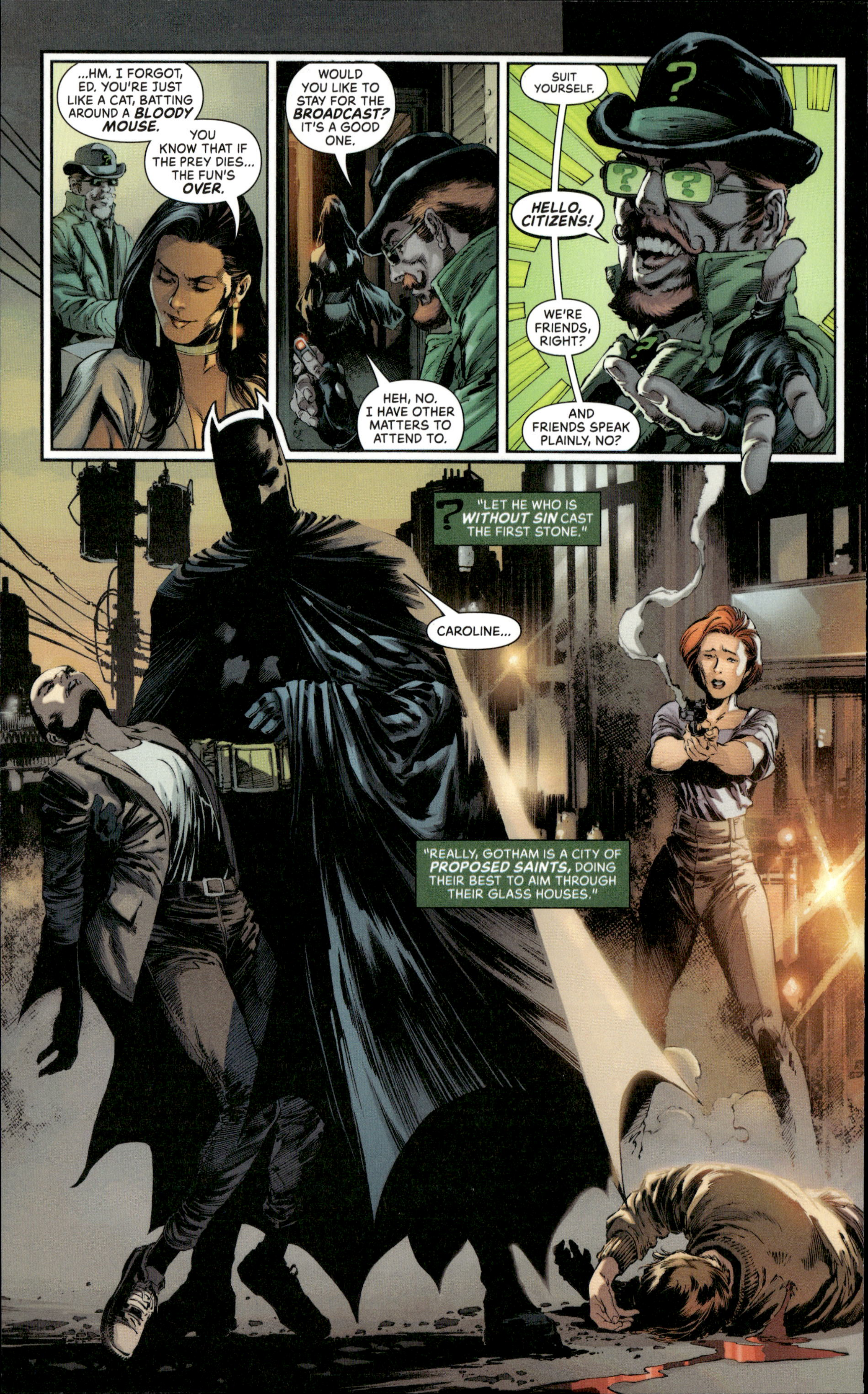
...HM. I FORGOT, ED. YOU'RE JUST LIKE A CAT, BATTING AROUND A BLOODY MOUSE.
YOU KNOW THAT IF THE PREY DIES... THE FUN'S OVER.
WOULD YOU LIKE TO STAY FOR THE BROADCAST? IT'S A GOOD ONE.
HEH, NO. I HAVE OTHER MATTERS TO ATTEND TO.
SUIT YOURSELF.
HELLO, CITIZENS!
WE'RE FRIENDS, RIGHT?
AND FRIENDS SPEAK PLAINLY, NO?
"LET HE WHO IS WITHOUT SIN CAST THE FIRST STONE."
CAROLINE...
"REALLY, GOTHAM IS A CITY OF PROPOSED SAINTS, DOING THEIR BEST TO AIM THROUGH THEIR GLASS HOUSES."

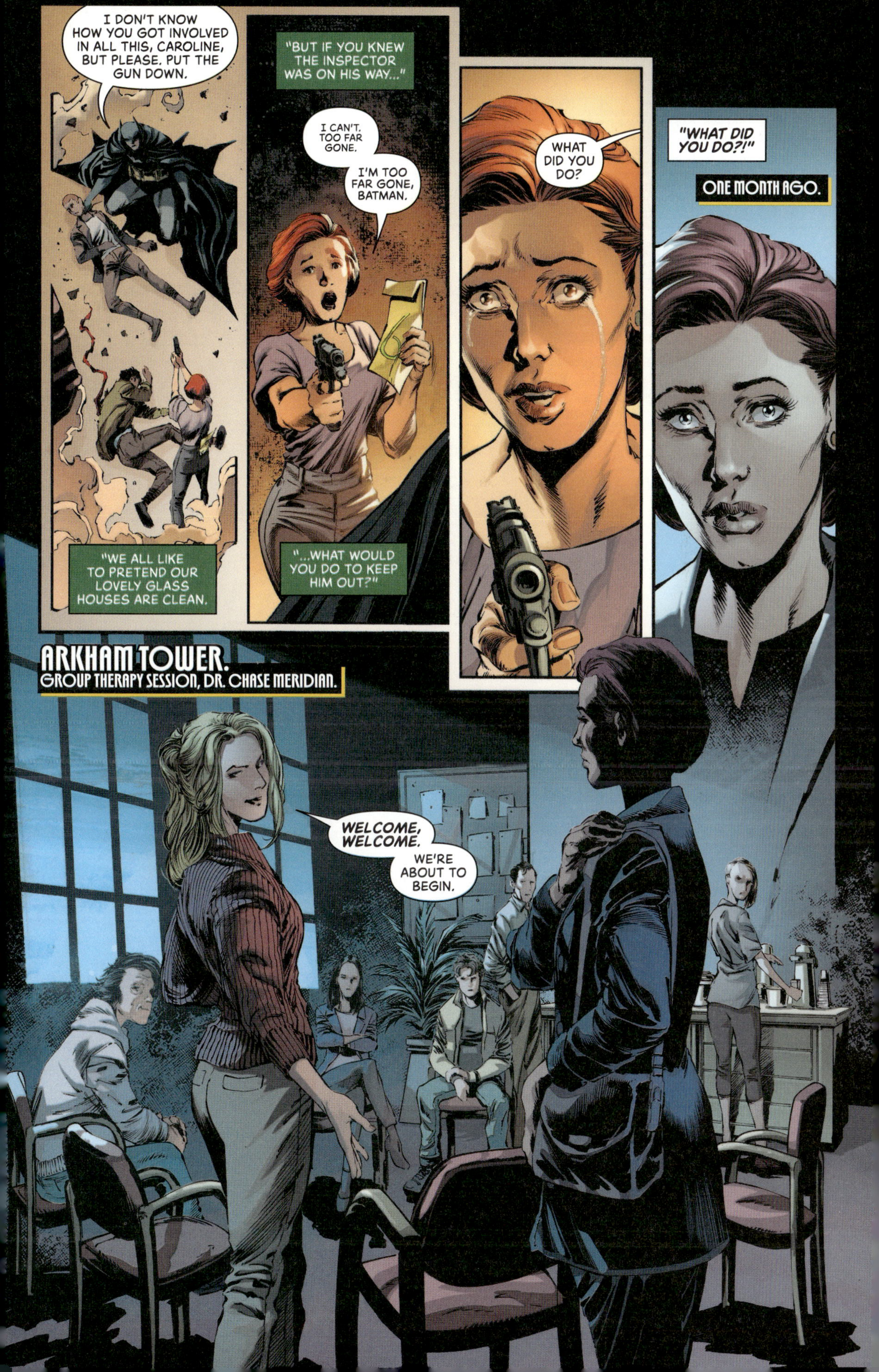

I DON'T KNOW HOW YOU GOT INVOLVED IN ALL THIS, CAROLINE, BUT PLEASE. PUT THE GUN DOWN.
"WE ALL LIKE TO PRETEND OUR LOVELY GLASS HOUSES ARE CLEAN.
"BUT IF YOU KNEW THE INSPECTOR WAS ON HIS WAY..."
I CAN'T. TOO FAR GONE.
I'M TOO FAR GONE, BATMAN.
"...WHAT WOULD YOU DO TO KEEP HIM OUT?"
WHAT DID YOU DO?
"WHAT DID YOU DO?!"
ONE MONTH AGO.
ARKHAM TOWER.
GROUP THERAPY SESSION, DR. CHASE MERIDIAN.
WELCOME, WELCOME.
WE'RE ABOUT TO BEGIN.

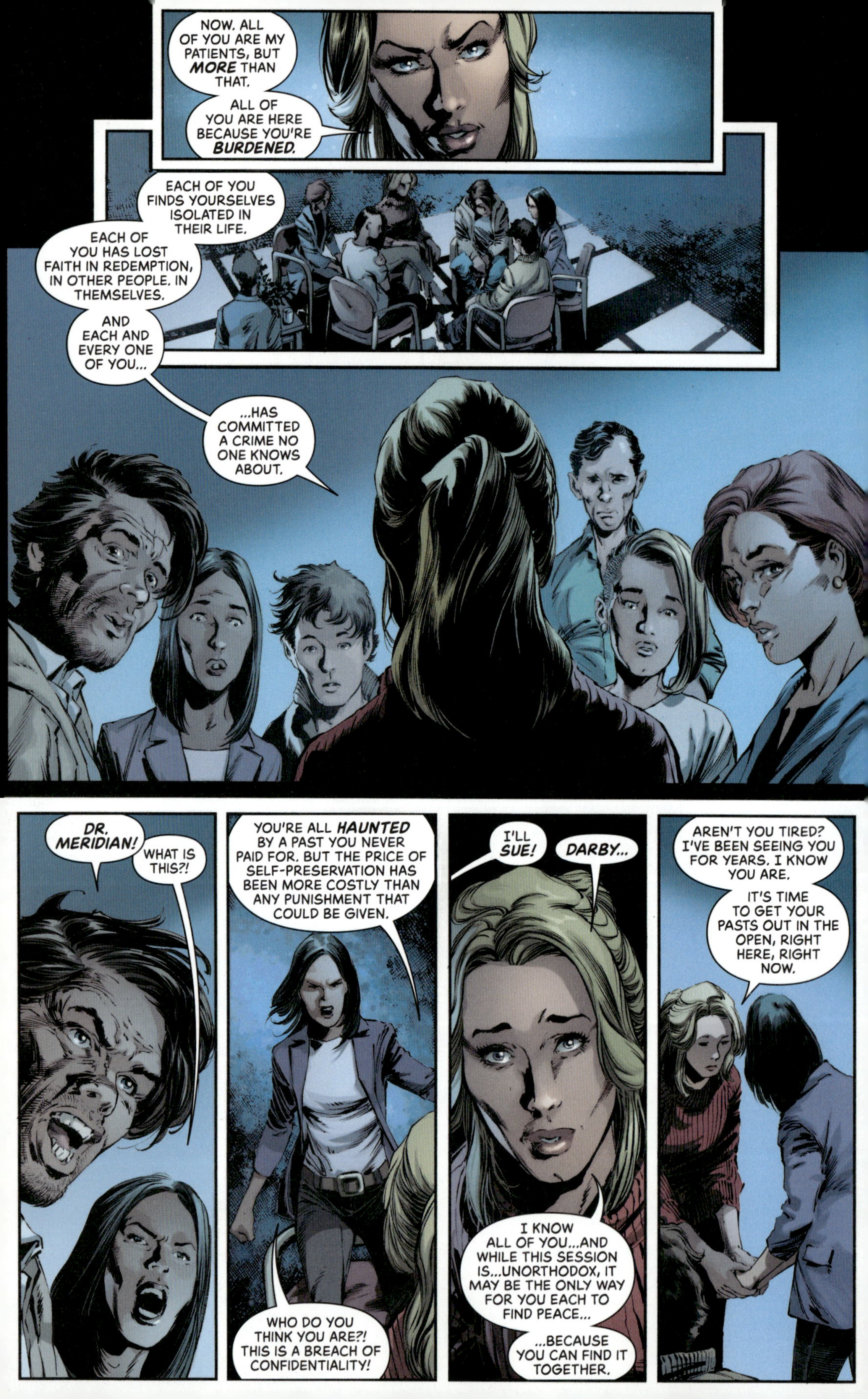
NOW. ALL OF YOU ARE MY PATIENTS, BUT *MORE* THAN THAT.
ALL OF YOU ARE HERE BECAUSE YOU'RE *BURDENED.*
EACH OF YOU FINDS YOURSELVES ISOLATED IN THEIR LIFE.
EACH OF YOU HAS LOST FAITH IN REDEMPTION, IN OTHER PEOPLE. IN THEMSELVES.
AND EACH AND EVERY ONE OF YOU...
...HAS COMMITTED A CRIME NO ONE KNOWS ABOUT.
DR. MERIDIAN!
WHAT IS THIS?!
YOU'RE ALL *HAUNTED* BY A PAST YOU NEVER PAID FOR. BUT THE PRICE OF SELF-PRESERVATION HAS BEEN MORE COSTLY THAN ANY PUNISHMENT THAT COULD BE GIVEN.
WHO DO YOU THINK YOU ARE?! THIS IS A BREACH OF CONFIDENTIALITY!
I'LL *SUE!*
DARBY...
I KNOW ALL OF YOU...AND WHILE THIS SESSION IS...UNORTHODOX, IT MAY BE THE ONLY WAY FOR YOU EACH TO FIND PEACE...
...BECAUSE YOU CAN FIND IT TOGETHER.
AREN'T YOU TIRED? I'VE BEEN SEEING YOU FOR YEARS. I KNOW YOU ARE.
IT'S TIME TO GET YOUR PASTS OUT IN THE OPEN, RIGHT HERE, RIGHT NOW.

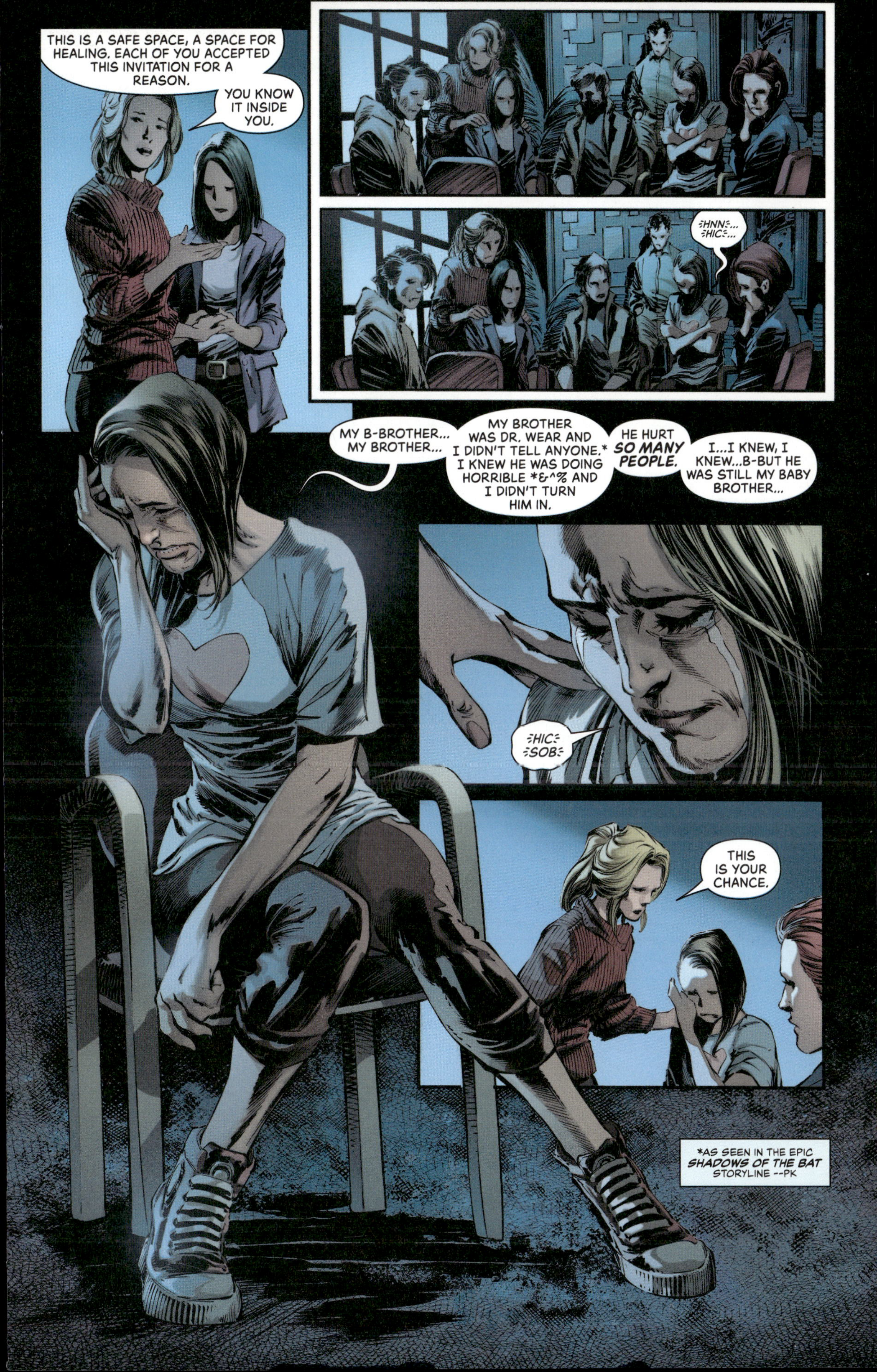
THIS IS A SAFE SPACE, A SPACE FOR HEALING. EACH OF YOU ACCEPTED THIS INVITATION FOR A REASON.
YOU KNOW IT INSIDE YOU.
HNN... HIC...
MY B-BROTHER... MY BROTHER...
MY BROTHER WAS DR. WEAR AND I DIDN'T TELL ANYONE.* I KNEW HE WAS DOING HORRIBLE *&^% AND I DIDN'T TURN HIM IN.
HE HURT SO MANY PEOPLE.
I...I KNEW, I KNEW...B-BUT HE WAS STILL MY BABY BROTHER...
HIC SOB
THIS IS YOUR CHANCE.
*AS SEEN IN THE EPIC SHADOWS OF THE BAT STORYLINE --PK

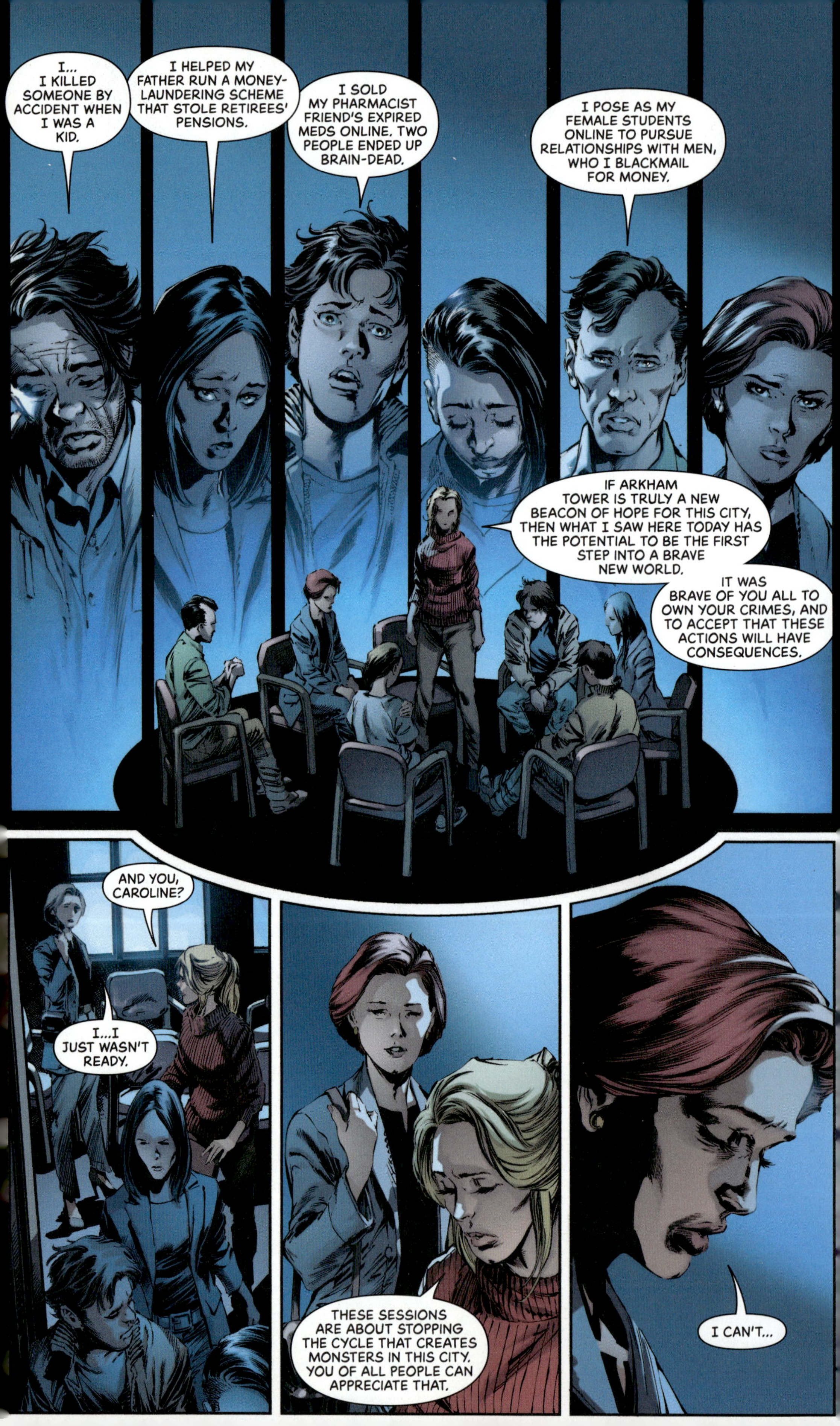
I... I KILLED SOMEONE BY ACCIDENT WHEN I WAS A KID.
I HELPED MY FATHER RUN A MONEY-LAUNDERING SCHEME THAT STOLE RETIREES' PENSIONS.
I SOLD MY PHARMACIST FRIEND'S EXPIRED MEDS ONLINE. TWO PEOPLE ENDED UP BRAIN-DEAD.
I POSE AS MY FEMALE STUDENTS ONLINE TO PURSUE RELATIONSHIPS WITH MEN, WHO I BLACKMAIL FOR MONEY.
IF ARKHAM TOWER IS TRULY A NEW BEACON OF HOPE FOR THIS CITY, THEN WHAT I SAW HERE TODAY HAS THE POTENTIAL TO BE THE FIRST STEP INTO A BRAVE NEW WORLD.
IT WAS BRAVE OF YOU ALL TO OWN YOUR CRIMES, AND TO ACCEPT THAT THESE ACTIONS WILL HAVE CONSEQUENCES.
AND YOU, CAROLINE?
I...I JUST WASN'T READY.
THESE SESSIONS ARE ABOUT STOPPING THE CYCLE THAT CREATES MONSTERS IN THIS CITY. YOU OF ALL PEOPLE CAN APPRECIATE THAT.
I CAN'T...

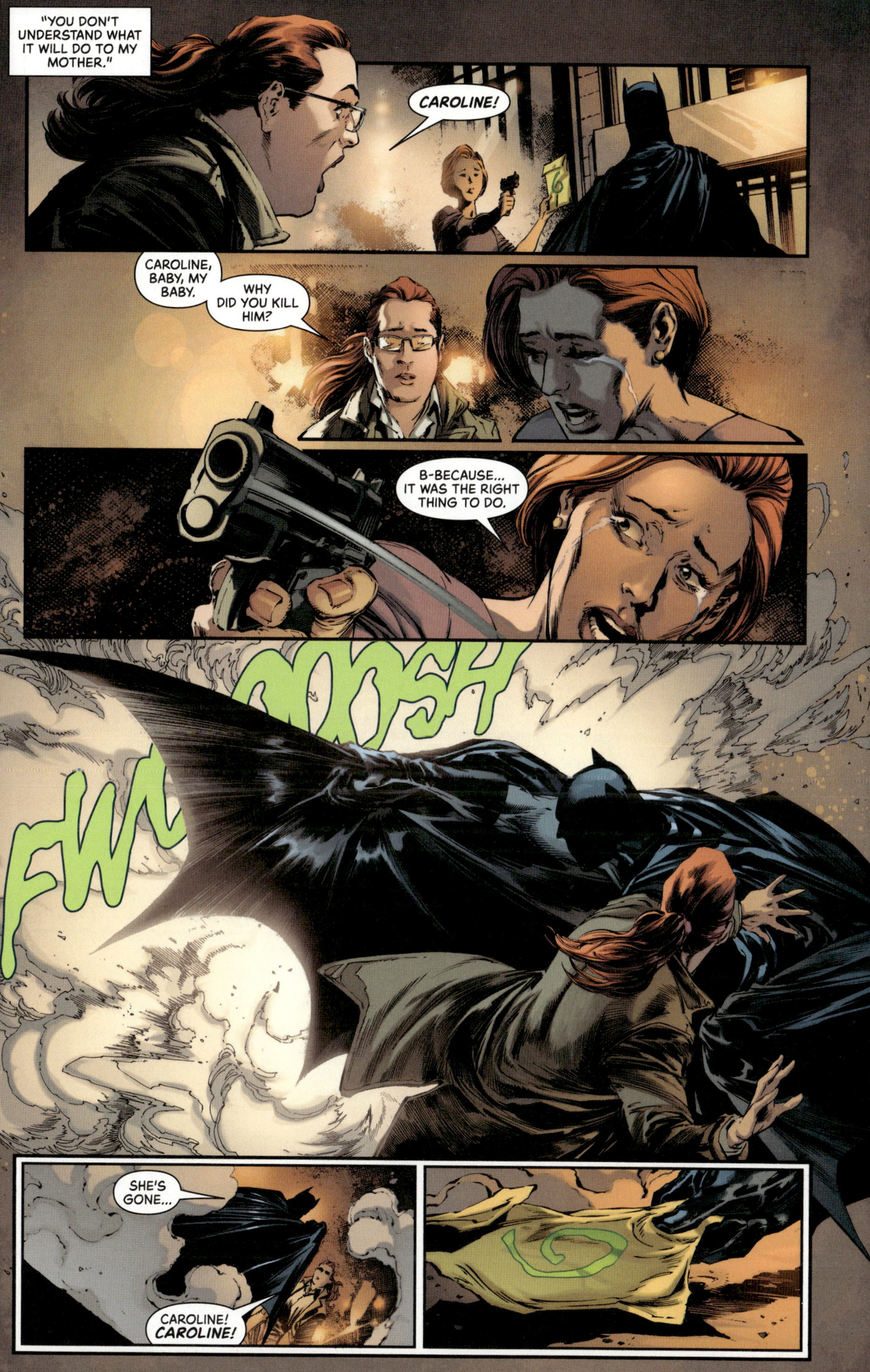

"YOU DON'T UNDERSTAND WHAT IT WILL DO TO MY MOTHER."
CAROLINE!
CAROLINE, BABY, MY BABY.
WHY DID YOU KILL HIM?
B-BECAUSE... IT WAS THE RIGHT THING TO DO.
FWOOOSH
SHE'S GONE...
CAROLINE! CAROLINE!

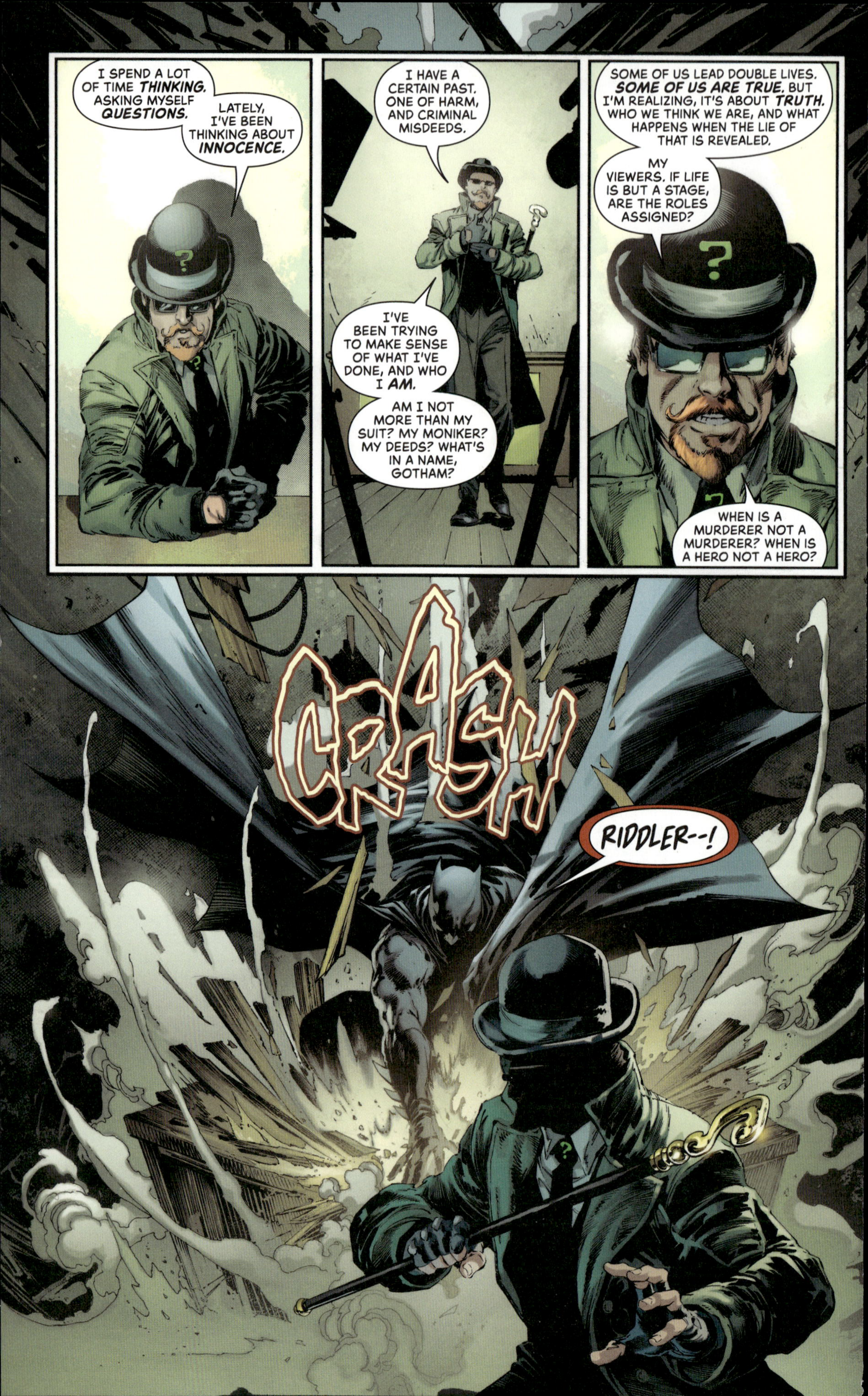
I SPEND A LOT OF TIME THINKING. ASKING MYSELF QUESTIONS.
LATELY, I'VE BEEN THINKING ABOUT INNOCENCE.
I HAVE A CERTAIN PAST. ONE OF HARM, AND CRIMINAL MISDEEDS.
I'VE BEEN TRYING TO MAKE SENSE OF WHAT I'VE DONE, AND WHO I AM.
AM I NOT MORE THAN MY SUIT? MY MONIKER? MY DEEDS? WHAT'S IN A NAME, GOTHAM?
SOME OF US LEAD DOUBLE LIVES. SOME OF US ARE TRUE. BUT I'M REALIZING, IT'S ABOUT TRUTH. WHO WE THINK WE ARE, AND WHAT HAPPENS WHEN THE LIE OF THAT IS REVEALED.
MY VIEWERS. IF LIFE IS BUT A STAGE, ARE THE ROLES ASSIGNED?
WHEN IS A MURDERER NOT A MURDERER? WHEN IS A HERO NOT A HERO?
CRASH
RIDDLER--!

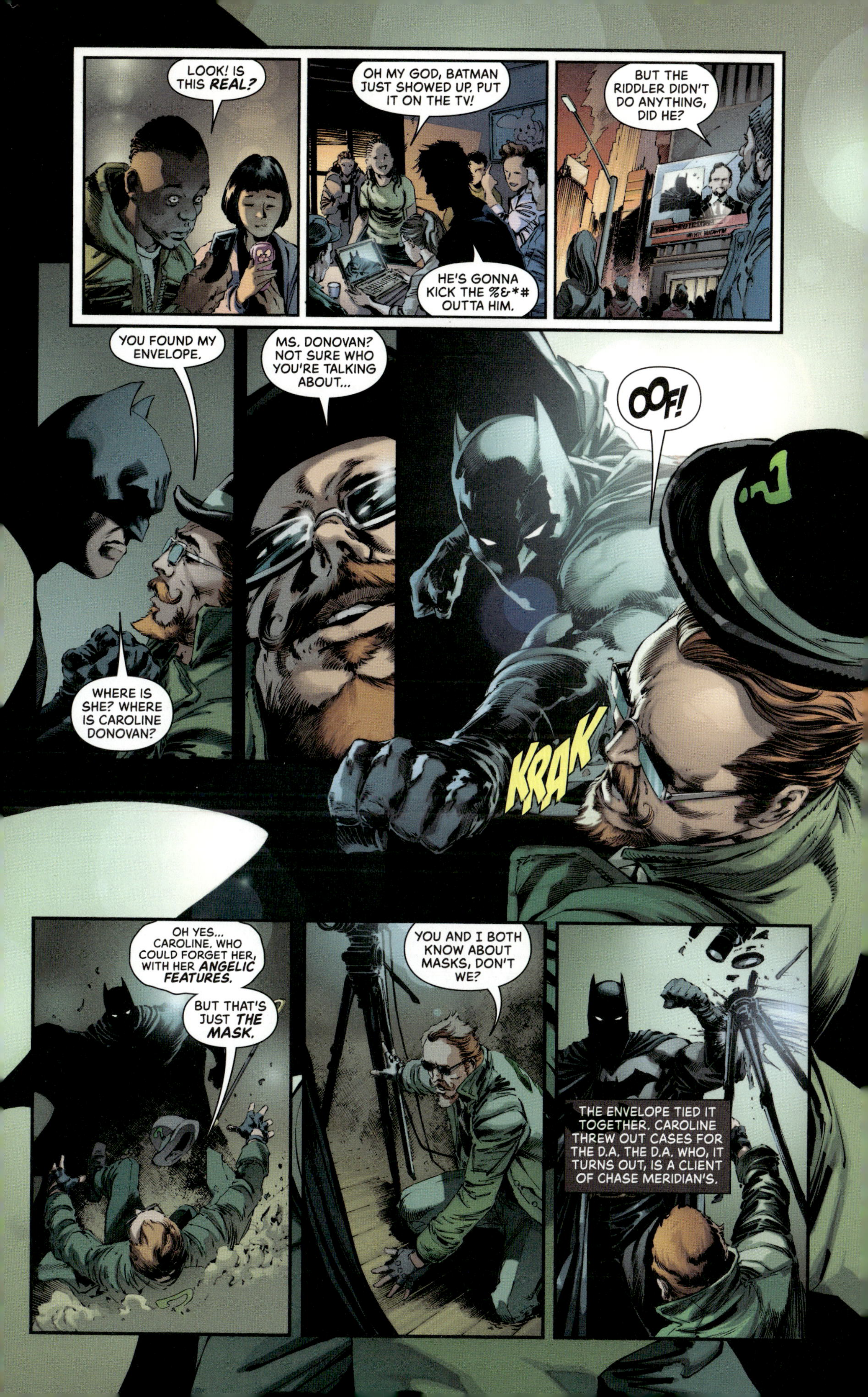

LOOK! IS THIS REAL?
OH MY GOD, BATMAN JUST SHOWED UP. PUT IT ON THE TV!
HE'S GONNA KICK THE %&*# OUTTA HIM.
BUT THE RIDDLER DIDN'T DO ANYTHING, DID HE?
YOU FOUND MY ENVELOPE.
WHERE IS SHE? WHERE IS CAROLINE DONOVAN?
MS. DONOVAN? NOT SURE WHO YOU'RE TALKING ABOUT...
OOF!
KRAK
OH YES... CAROLINE. WHO COULD FORGET HER, WITH HER ANGELIC FEATURES.
BUT THAT'S JUST THE MASK.
YOU AND I BOTH KNOW ABOUT MASKS, DON'T WE?
THE ENVELOPE TIED IT TOGETHER. CAROLINE THREW OUT CASES FOR THE D.A. THE D.A. WHO, IT TURNS OUT, IS A CLIENT OF CHASE MERIDIAN'S.

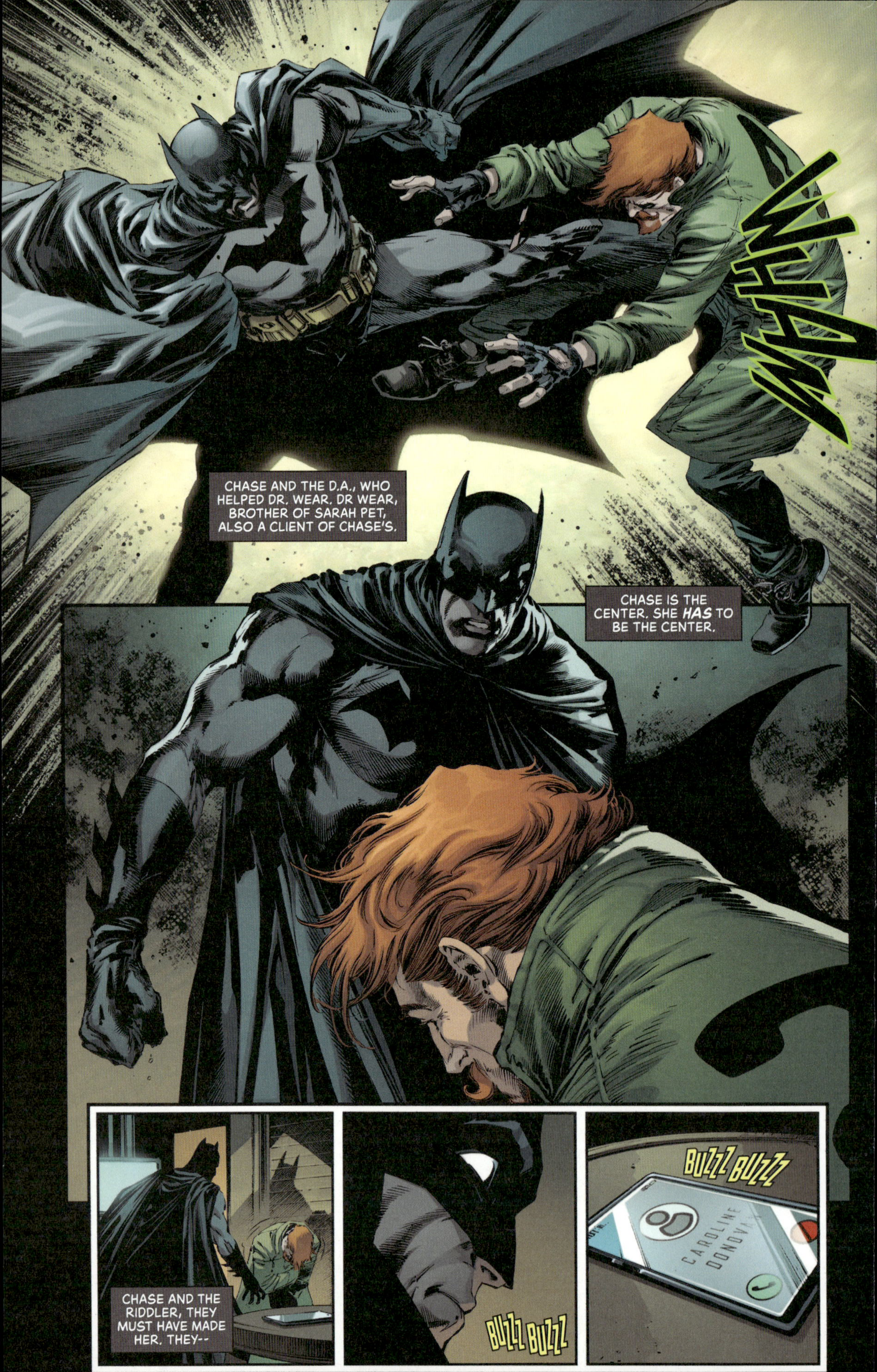
WHAM
CHASE AND THE D.A., WHO HELPED DR. WEAR. DR WEAR, BROTHER OF SARAH PET, ALSO A CLIENT OF CHASE'S.
CHASE IS THE CENTER. SHE *HAS* TO BE THE CENTER.
CHASE AND THE RIDDLER, THEY MUST HAVE MADE HER. THEY--
BUZZZ BUZZZ
BUZZZ BUZZZ
CAROLINE

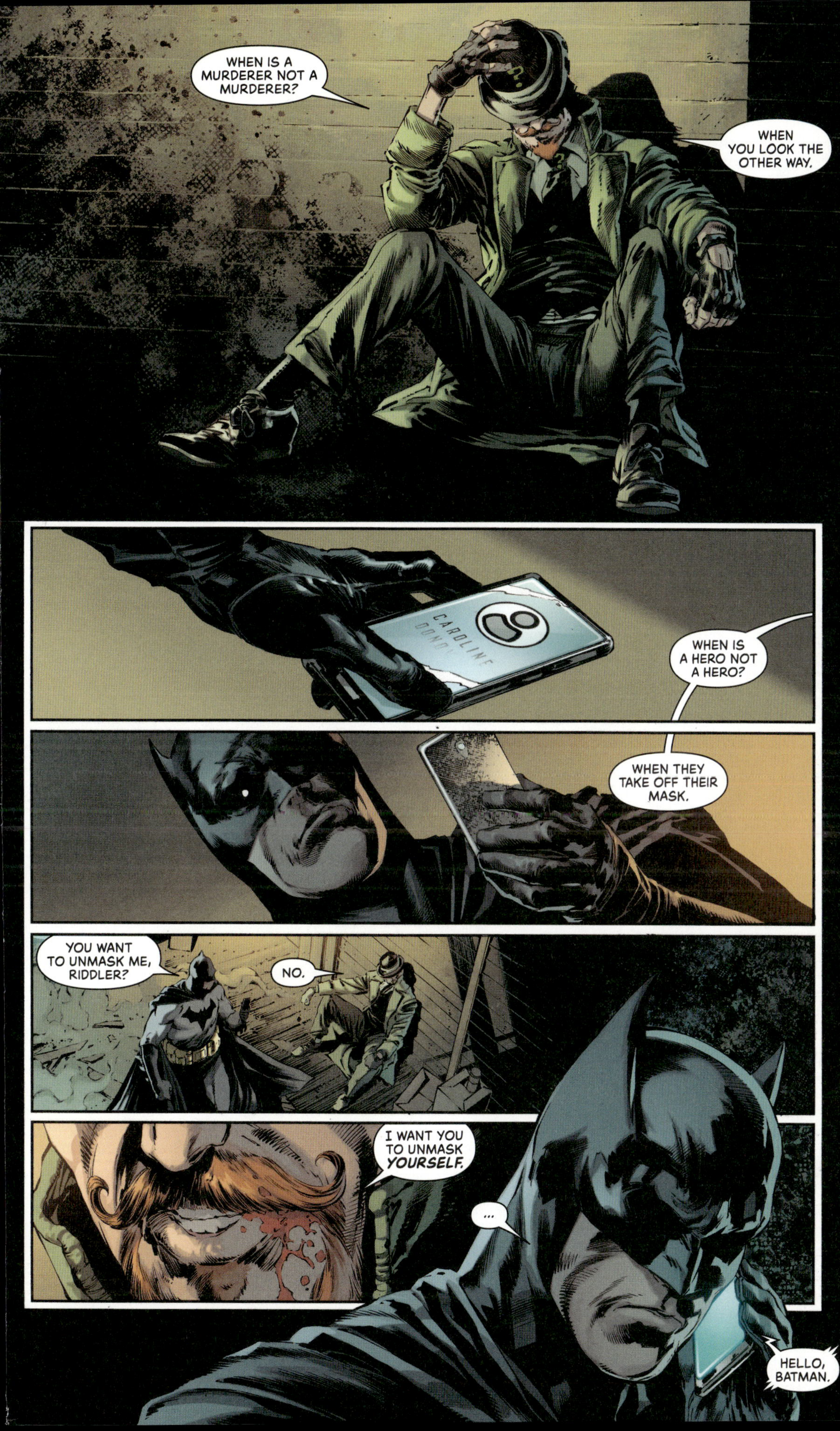
WHEN IS A MURDERER NOT A MURDERER?
WHEN YOU LOOK THE OTHER WAY.
CAROLINE DONDI
WHEN IS A HERO NOT A HERO?
WHEN THEY TAKE OFF THEIR MASK.
YOU WANT TO UNMASK ME, RIDDLER?
NO.
I WANT YOU TO UNMASK *YOURSELF*.
...
HELLO, BATMAN.

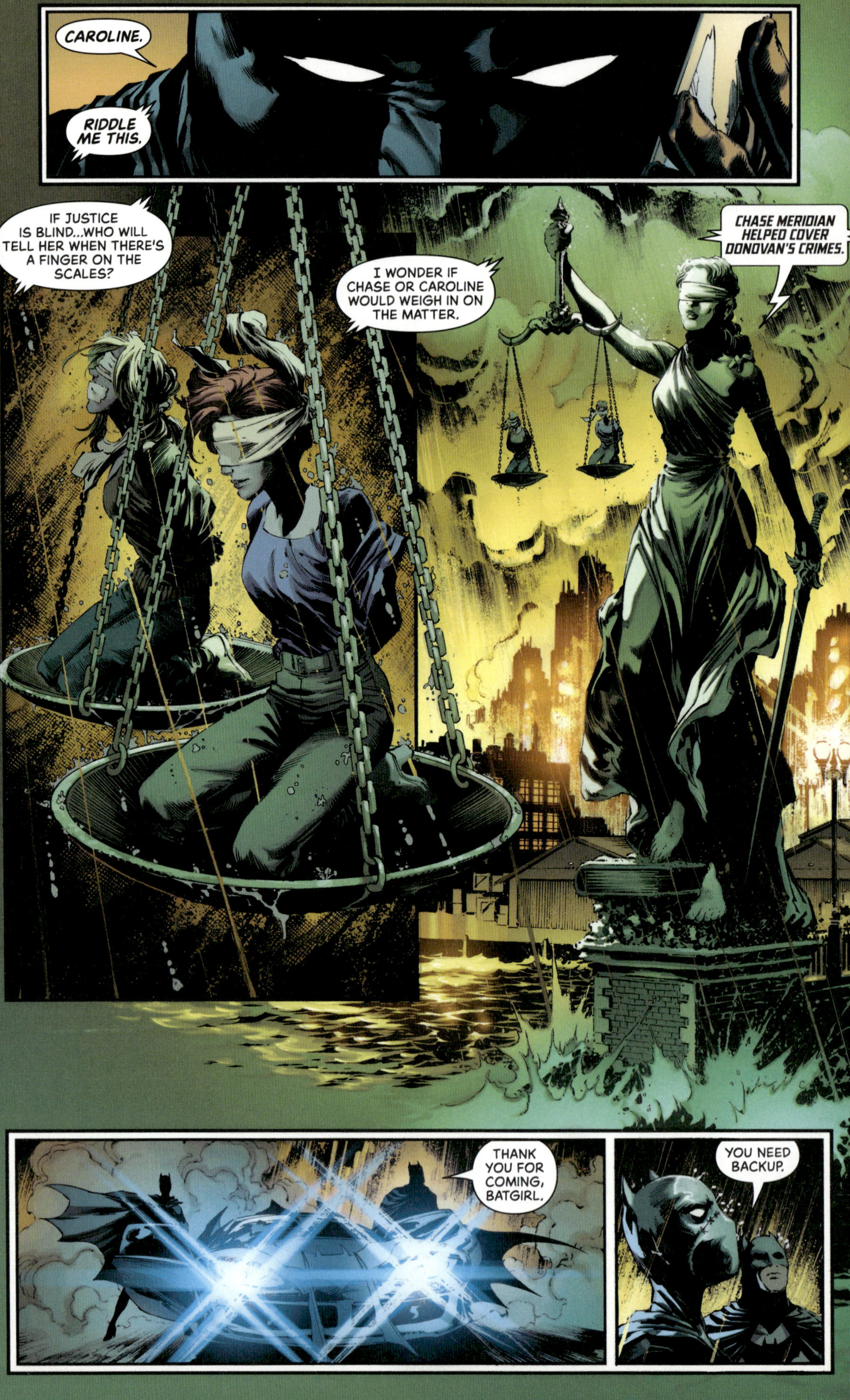
CAROLINE.
RIDDLE ME THIS.
IF JUSTICE IS BLIND...WHO WILL TELL HER WHEN THERE'S A FINGER ON THE SCALES?
I WONDER IF CHASE OR CAROLINE WOULD WEIGH IN ON THE MATTER.
CHASE MERIDIAN HELPED COVER DONOVAN'S CRIMES.
THANK YOU FOR COMING, BATGIRL.
YOU NEED BACKUP.

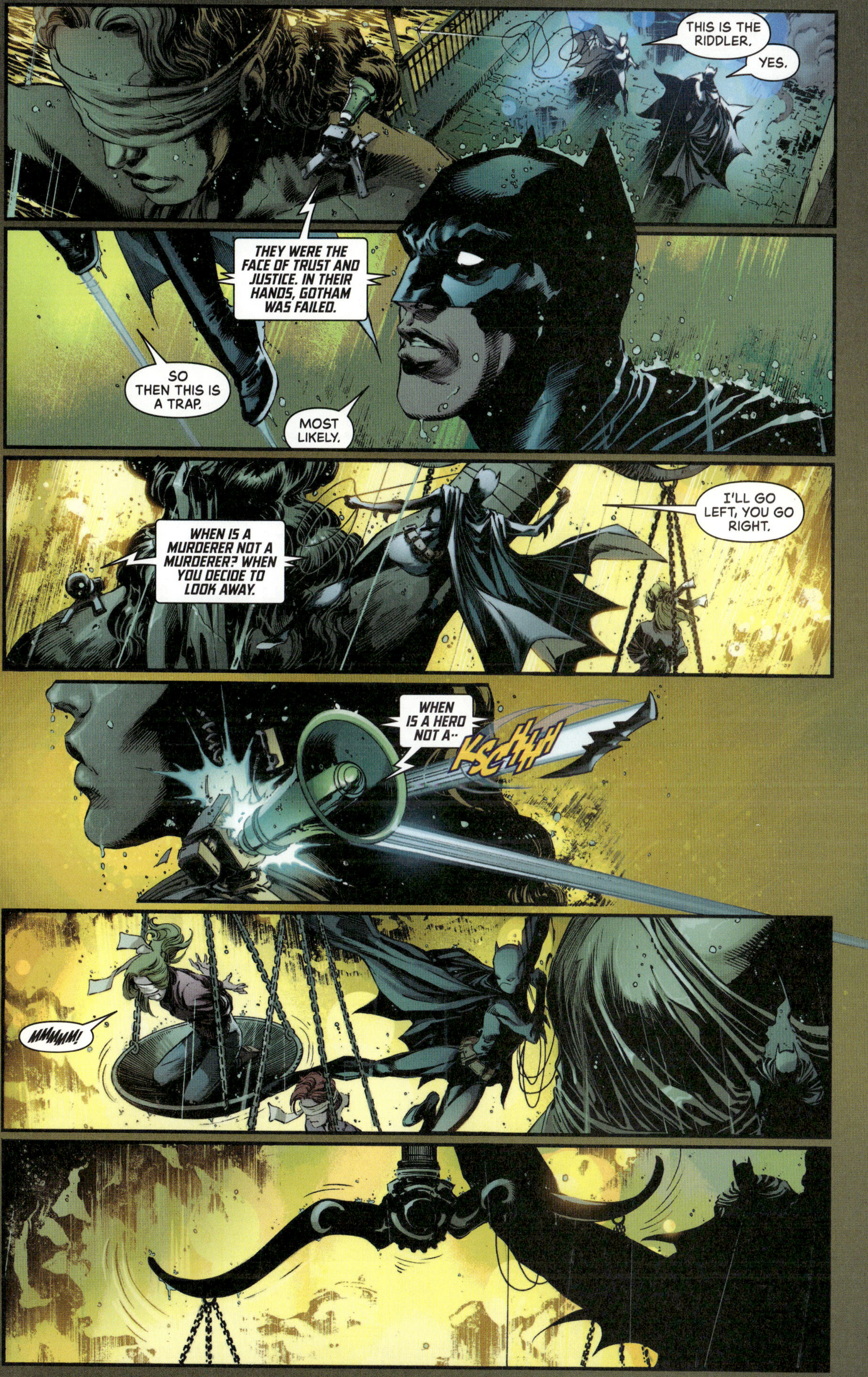
THIS IS THE RIDDLER.
YES.
THEY WERE THE FACE OF TRUST AND JUSTICE. IN THEIR HANDS, GOTHAM WAS FAILED.
SO THEN THIS IS A TRAP.
MOST LIKELY.
WHEN IS A MURDERER NOT A MURDERER? WHEN YOU DECIDE TO LOOK AWAY.
I'LL GO LEFT, YOU GO RIGHT.
WHEN IS A HERO NOT A--
KSCHHH
MMMMM!

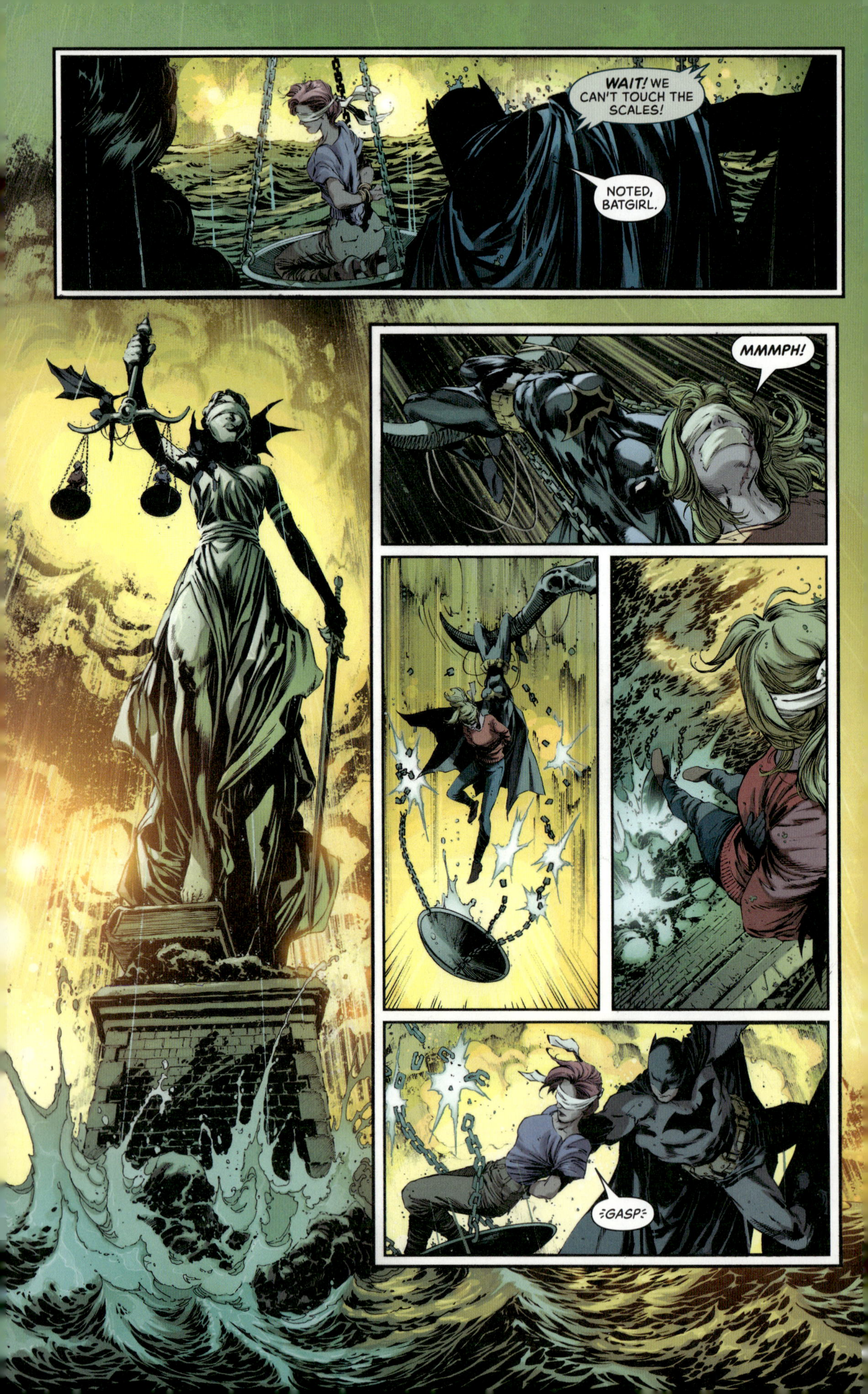
WAIT! WE CAN'T TOUCH THE SCALES!
NOTED, BATGIRL.
MMMPH!
GASP

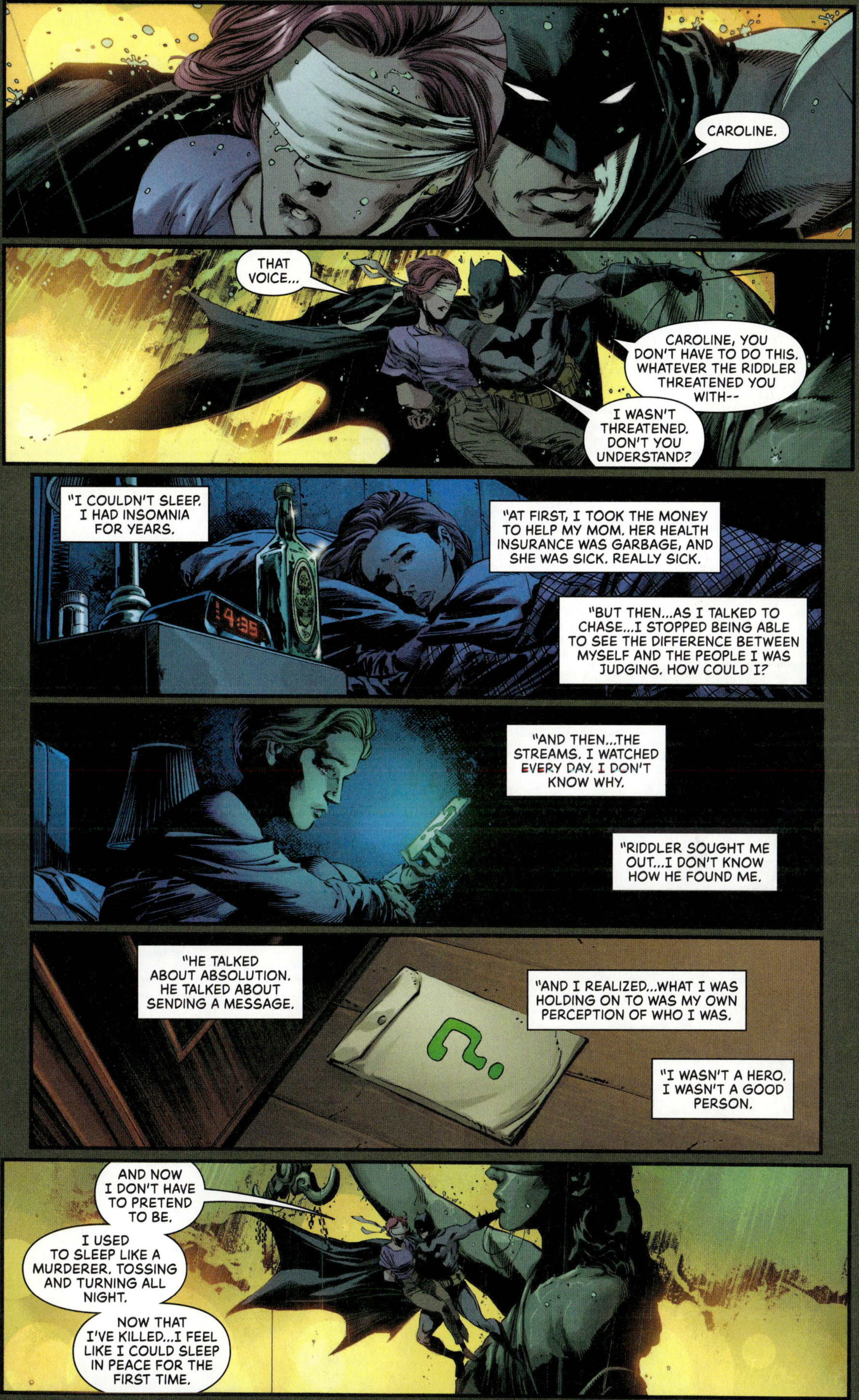
CAROLINE.
THAT VOICE...
CAROLINE, YOU DON'T HAVE TO DO THIS. WHATEVER THE RIDDLER THREATENED YOU WITH--
I WASN'T THREATENED. DON'T YOU UNDERSTAND?
"I COULDN'T SLEEP. I HAD INSOMNIA FOR YEARS.
"AT FIRST, I TOOK THE MONEY TO HELP MY MOM. HER HEALTH INSURANCE WAS GARBAGE, AND SHE WAS SICK. REALLY SICK.
4:35
"BUT THEN...AS I TALKED TO CHASE...I STOPPED BEING ABLE TO SEE THE DIFFERENCE BETWEEN MYSELF AND THE PEOPLE I WAS JUDGING. HOW COULD I?
"AND THEN...THE STREAMS. I WATCHED EVERY DAY. I DON'T KNOW WHY.
"RIDDLER SOUGHT ME OUT...I DON'T KNOW HOW HE FOUND ME.
"HE TALKED ABOUT ABSOLUTION. HE TALKED ABOUT SENDING A MESSAGE.
"AND I REALIZED...WHAT I WAS HOLDING ON TO WAS MY OWN PERCEPTION OF WHO I WAS.
"I WASN'T A HERO. I WASN'T A GOOD PERSON.
AND NOW I DON'T HAVE TO PRETEND TO BE.
I USED TO SLEEP LIKE A MURDERER, TOSSING AND TURNING ALL NIGHT.
NOW THAT I'VE KILLED...I FEEL LIKE I COULD SLEEP IN PEACE FOR THE FIRST TIME.

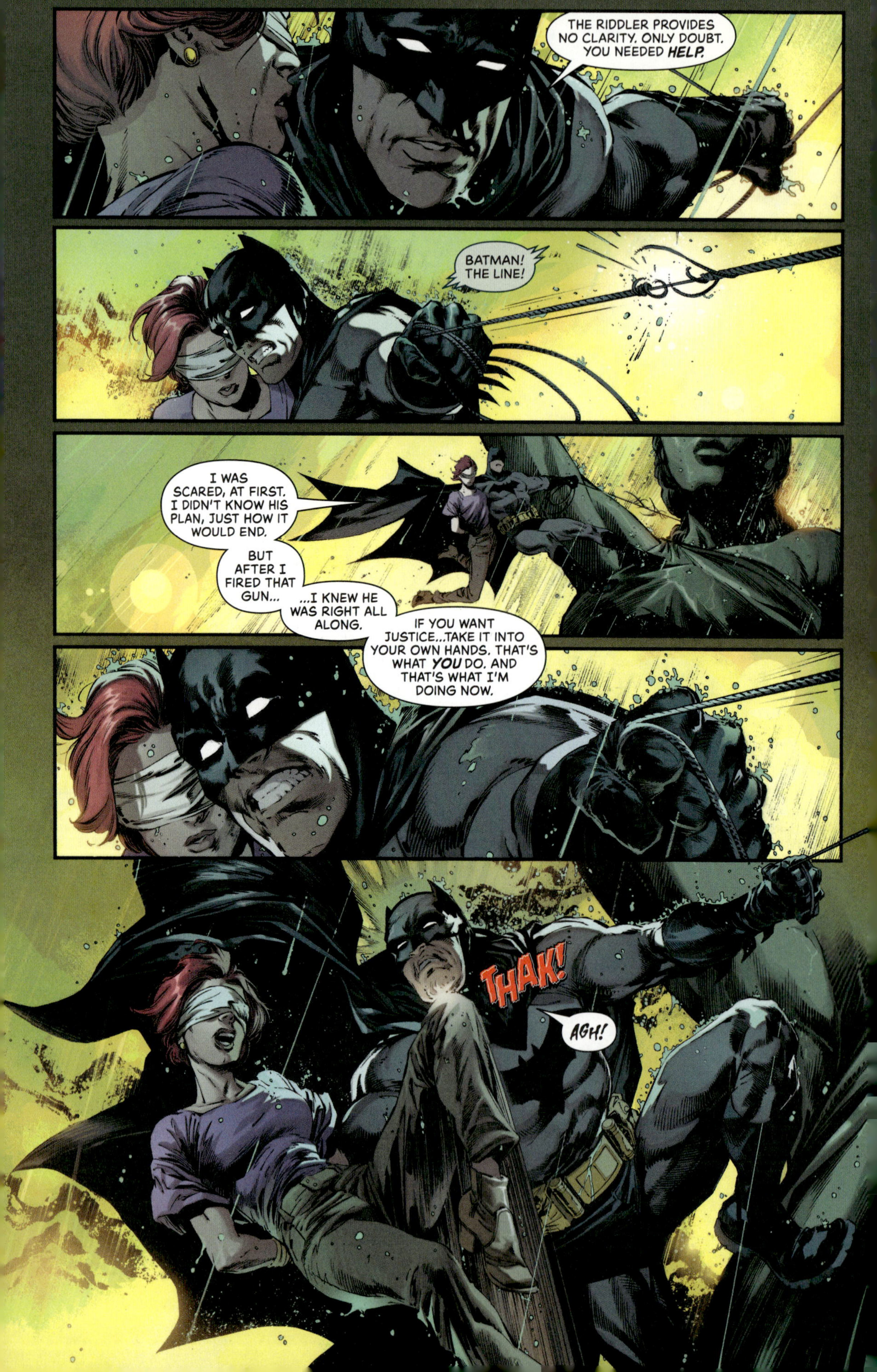
THE RIDDLER PROVIDES NO CLARITY. ONLY DOUBT. YOU NEEDED HELP.
BATMAN! THE LINE!
I WAS SCARED, AT FIRST. I DIDN'T KNOW HIS PLAN, JUST HOW IT WOULD END.
BUT AFTER I FIRED THAT GUN...
...I KNEW HE WAS RIGHT ALL ALONG.
IF YOU WANT JUSTICE...TAKE IT INTO YOUR OWN HANDS. THAT'S WHAT YOU DO. AND THAT'S WHAT I'M DOING NOW.
THAK!
AGH!

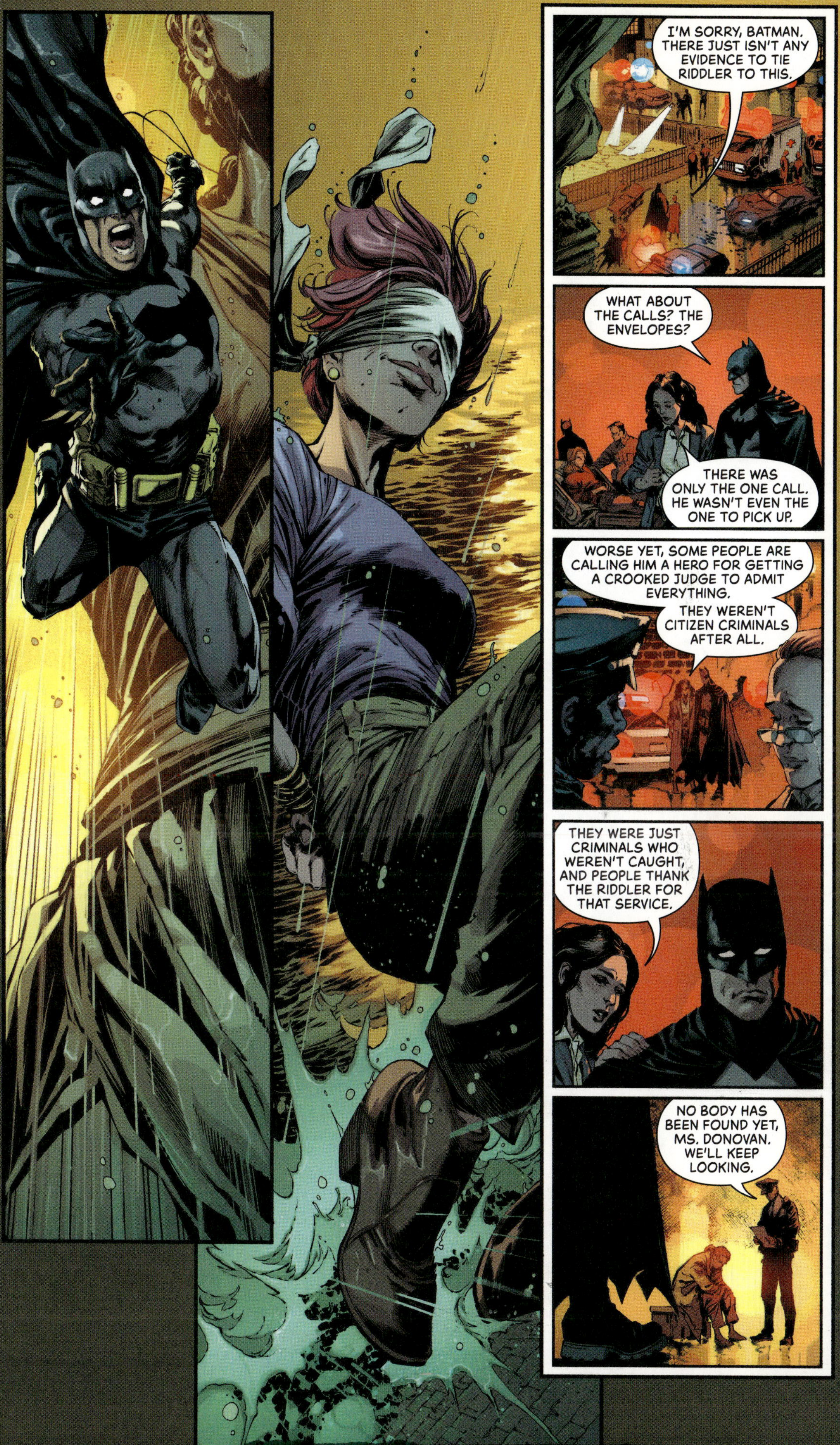
I'M SORRY, BATMAN. THERE JUST ISN'T ANY EVIDENCE TO TIE RIDDLER TO THIS.
WHAT ABOUT THE CALLS? THE ENVELOPES?
THERE WAS ONLY THE ONE CALL. HE WASN'T EVEN THE ONE TO PICK UP.
WORSE YET, SOME PEOPLE ARE CALLING HIM A HERO FOR GETTING A CROOKED JUDGE TO ADMIT EVERYTHING.
THEY WEREN'T CITIZEN CRIMINALS AFTER ALL.
THEY WERE JUST CRIMINALS WHO WEREN'T CAUGHT, AND PEOPLE THANK THE RIDDLER FOR THAT SERVICE.
NO BODY HAS BEEN FOUND YET, MS. DONOVAN. WE'LL KEEP LOOKING.

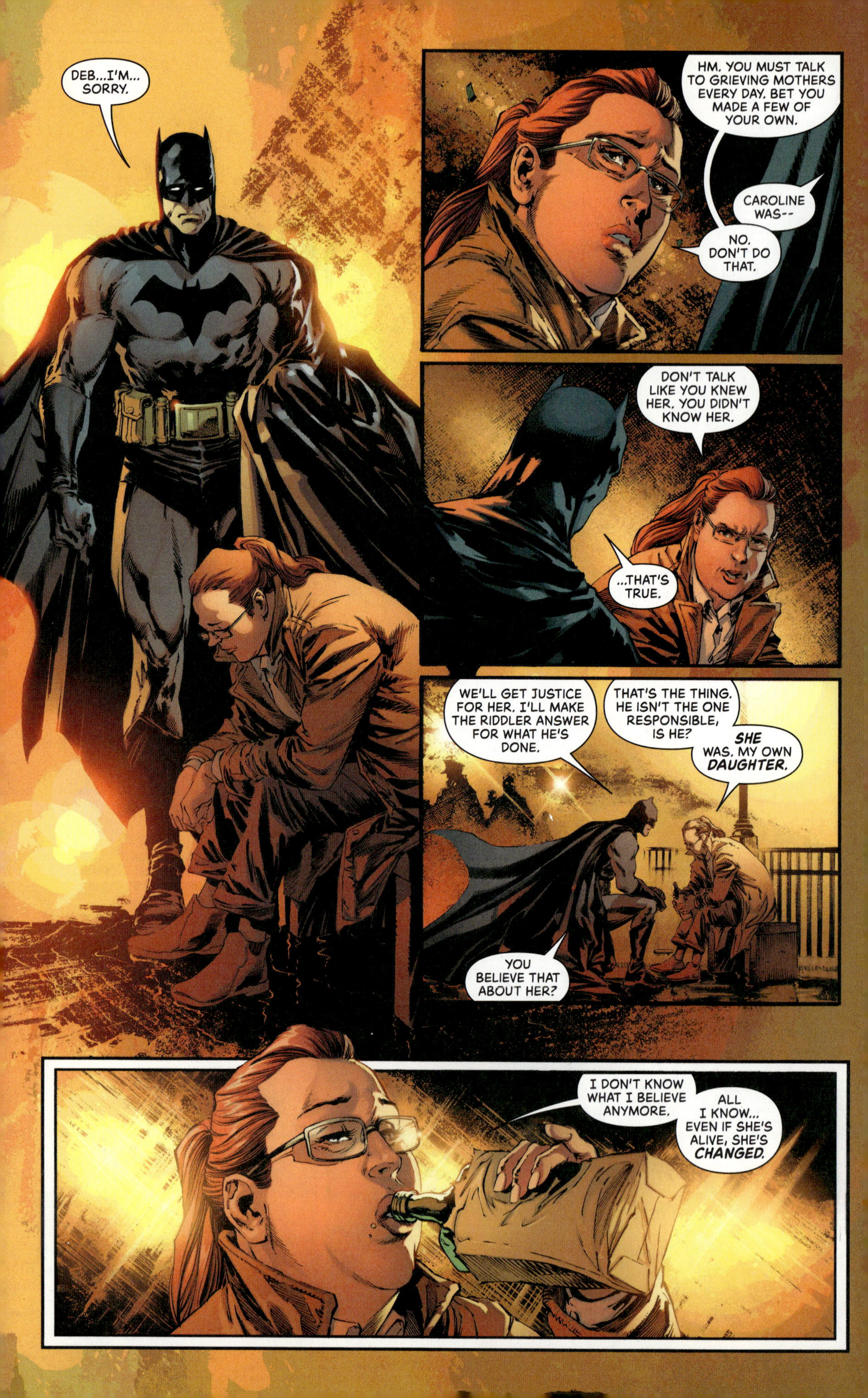
DEB...I'M... SORRY.
HM. YOU MUST TALK TO GRIEVING MOTHERS EVERY DAY. BET YOU MADE A FEW OF YOUR OWN.
CAROLINE WAS--
NO. DON'T DO THAT.
DON'T TALK LIKE YOU KNEW HER. YOU DIDN'T KNOW HER.
...THAT'S TRUE.
WE'LL GET JUSTICE FOR HER. I'LL MAKE THE RIDDLER ANSWER FOR WHAT HE'S DONE.
THAT'S THE THING. HE ISN'T THE ONE RESPONSIBLE, IS HE?
SHE WAS. MY OWN DAUGHTER.
YOU BELIEVE THAT ABOUT HER?
I DON'T KNOW WHAT I BELIEVE ANYMORE.
ALL I KNOW... EVEN IF SHE'S ALIVE, SHE'S CHANGED.

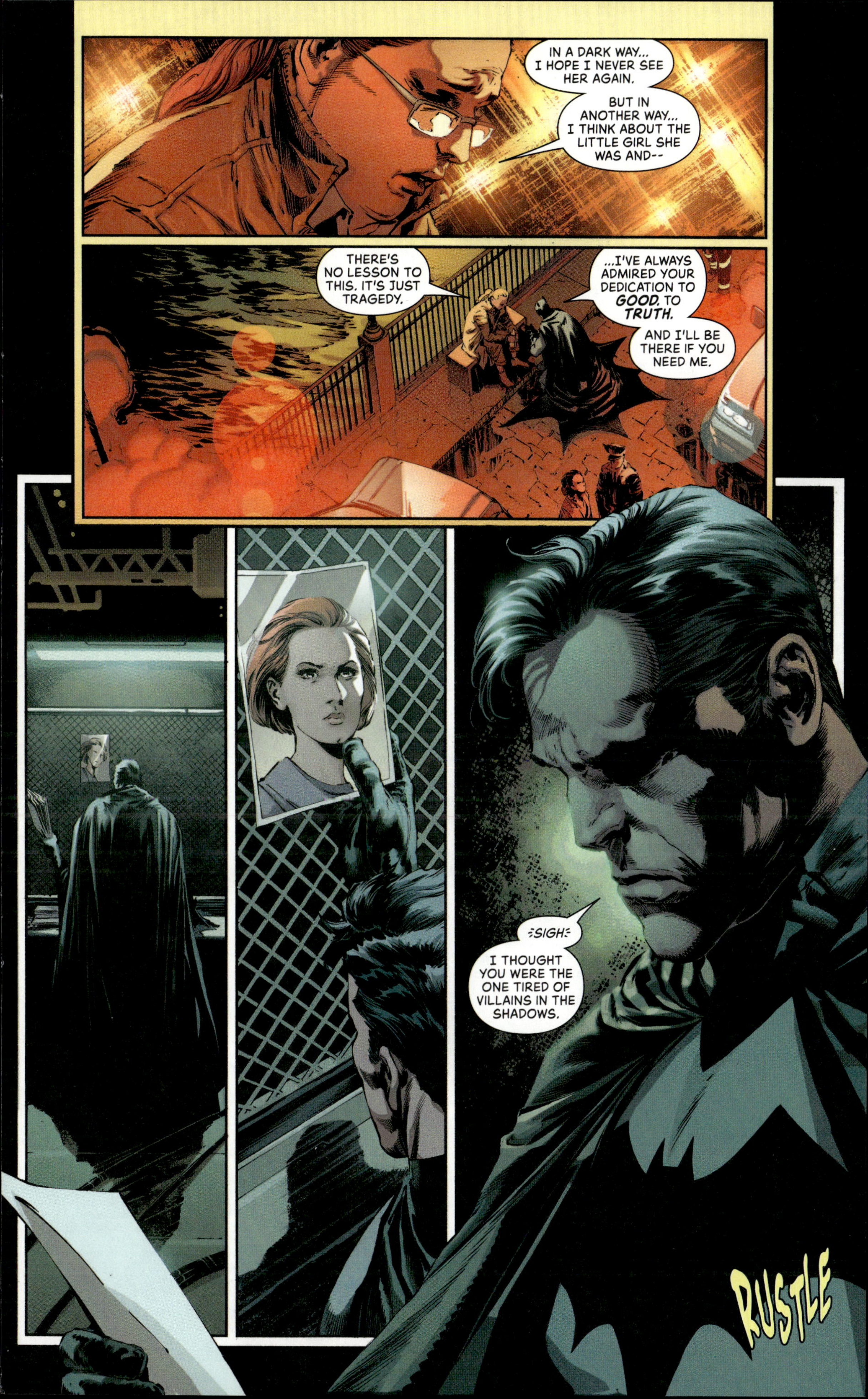
IN A DARK WAY... I HOPE I NEVER SEE HER AGAIN.
BUT IN ANOTHER WAY... I THINK ABOUT THE LITTLE GIRL SHE WAS AND--
THERE'S NO LESSON TO THIS. IT'S JUST TRAGEDY.
...I'VE ALWAYS ADMIRED YOUR DEDICATION TO GOOD, TO TRUTH.
AND I'LL BE THERE IF YOU NEED ME.
SIGH
I THOUGHT YOU WERE THE ONE TIRED OF VILLAINS IN THE SHADOWS.
RUSTLE

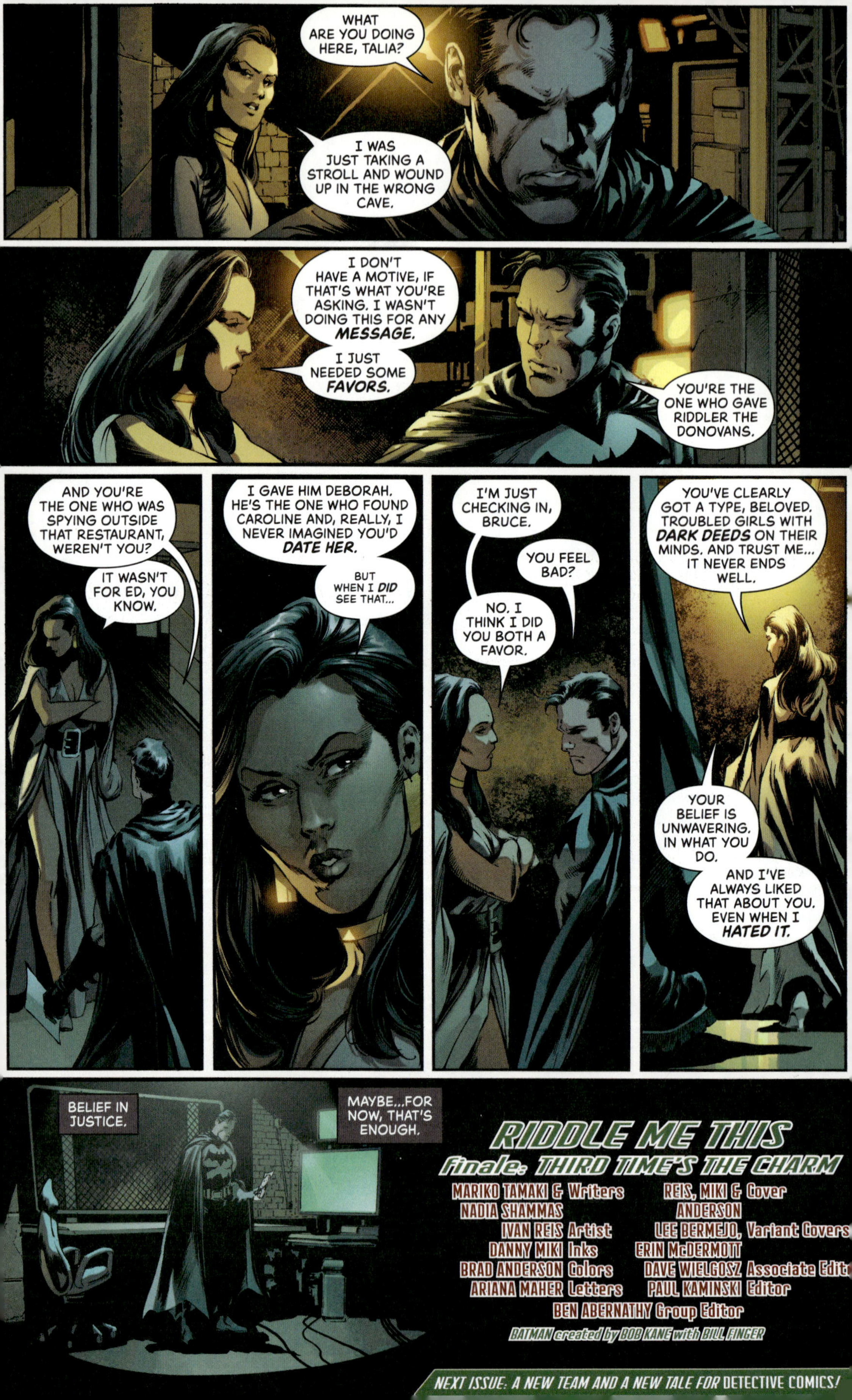

WHAT ARE YOU DOING HERE, TALIA?
I WAS JUST TAKING A STROLL AND WOUND UP IN THE WRONG CAVE.
I DON'T HAVE A MOTIVE, IF THAT'S WHAT YOU'RE ASKING. I WASN'T DOING THIS FOR ANY MESSAGE.
I JUST NEEDED SOME FAVORS.
YOU'RE THE ONE WHO GAVE RIDDLER THE DONOVANS.
AND YOU'RE THE ONE WHO WAS SPYING OUTSIDE THAT RESTAURANT, WEREN'T YOU?
IT WASN'T FOR ED, YOU KNOW.
I GAVE HIM DEBORAH. HE'S THE ONE WHO FOUND CAROLINE AND, REALLY, I NEVER IMAGINED YOU'D DATE HER.
BUT WHEN I DID SEE THAT...
I'M JUST CHECKING IN, BRUCE.
YOU FEEL BAD?
NO. I THINK I DID YOU BOTH A FAVOR.
YOU'VE CLEARLY GOT A TYPE, BELOVED. TROUBLED GIRLS WITH DARK DEEDS ON THEIR MINDS. AND TRUST ME... IT NEVER ENDS WELL.
YOUR BELIEF IS UNWAVERING. IN WHAT YOU DO.
AND I'VE ALWAYS LIKED THAT ABOUT YOU. EVEN WHEN I HATED IT.
BELIEF IN JUSTICE.
MAYBE...FOR NOW, THAT'S ENOUGH.
RIDDLE ME THIS
Finale: THIRD TIME'S THE CHARM
MARIKO TAMAKI & NADIA SHAMMAS Writers
IVAN REIS Artist
DANNY MIKI Inks
BRAD ANDERSON Colors
ARIANA MAHER Letters
REIS, MIKI & ANDERSON Cover
LEE BERMEJO, ERIN McDERMOTT Variant Covers
DAVE WIELGOSZ Associate Edit
PAUL KAMINSKI Editor
BEN ABERNATHY Group Editor
BATMAN created by BOB KANE with BILL FINGER
NEXT ISSUE: A NEW TEAM AND A NEW TALE FOR DETECTIVE COMICS!

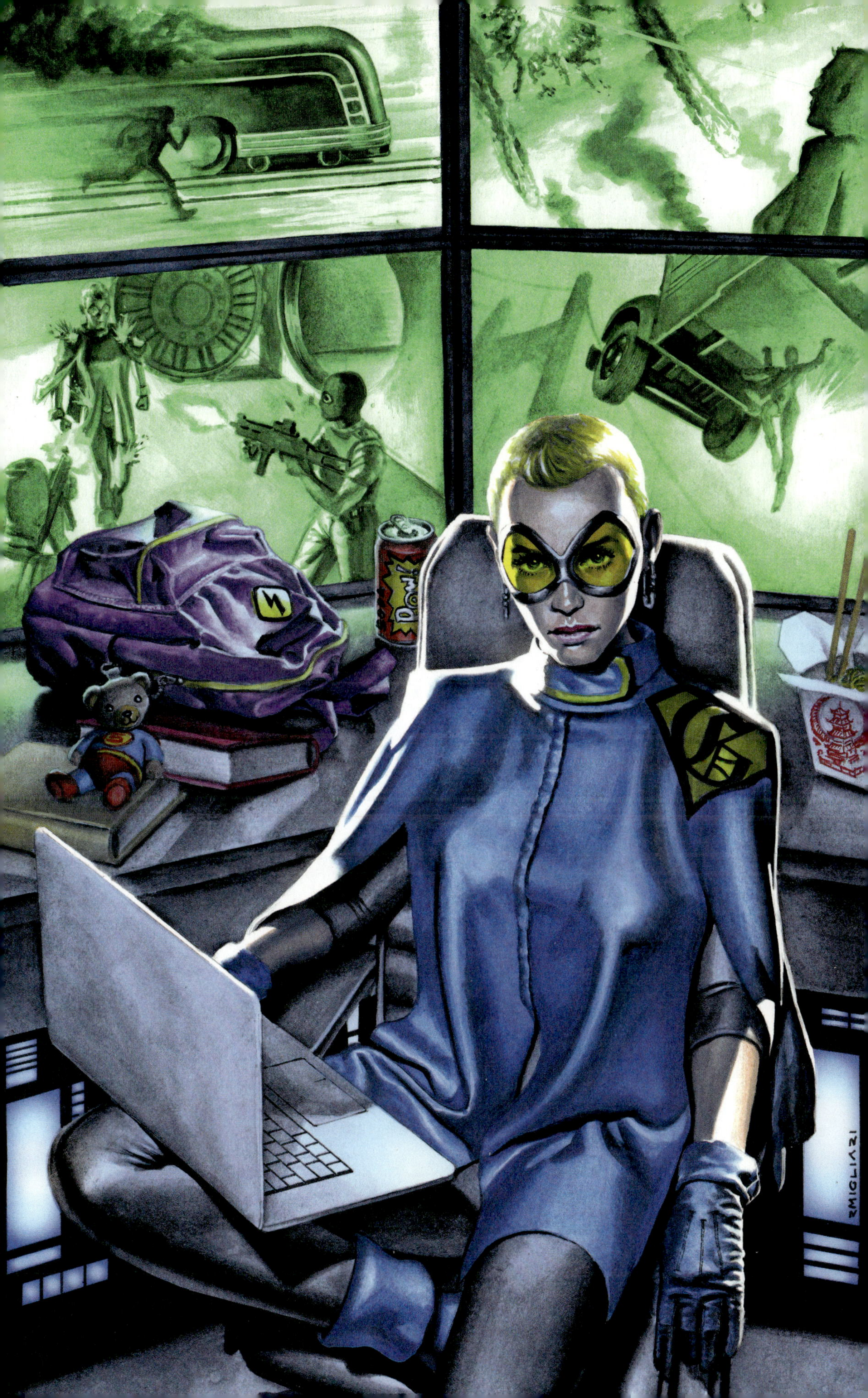
POW!
RMIGLIARI

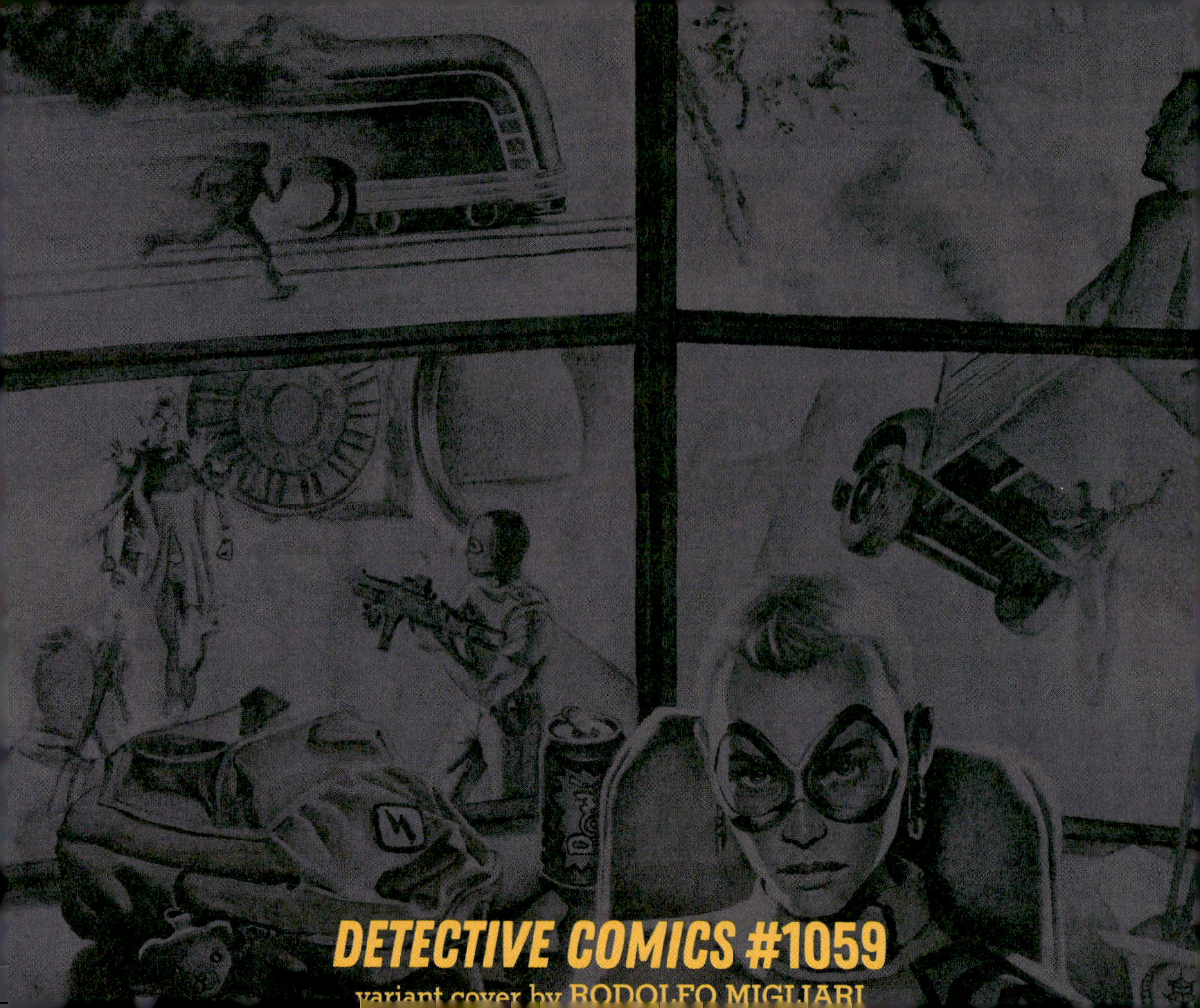

DETECTIVE COMICS #1059

variant cover by RODOLFO MIGLIARI

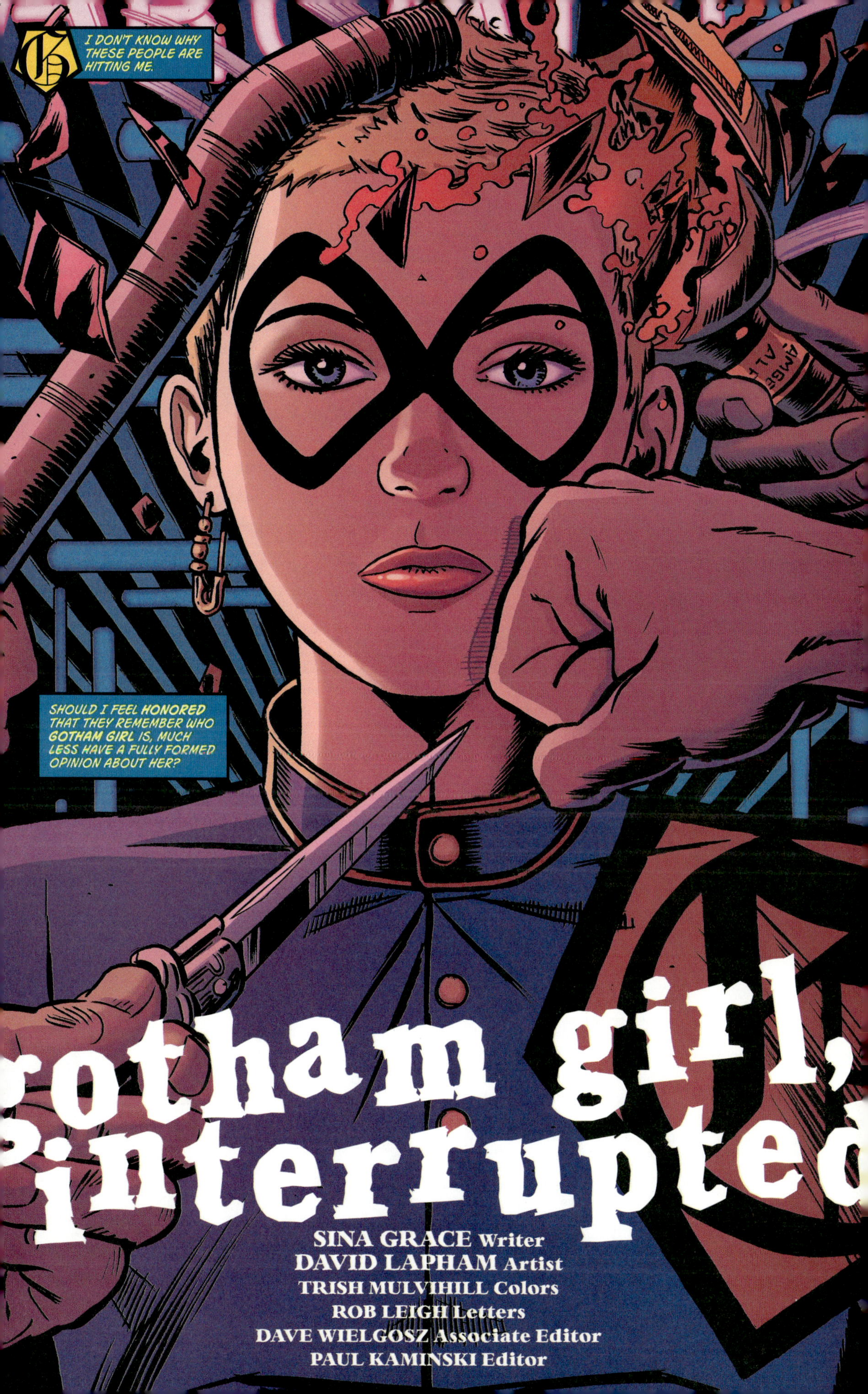
I DON'T KNOW WHY THESE PEOPLE ARE HITTING ME.
SHOULD I FEEL HONORED THAT THEY REMEMBER WHO GOTHAM GIRL IS, MUCH LESS HAVE A FULLY FORMED OPINION ABOUT HER?
otham girl,
interrupte
SINA GRACE Writer
DAVID LAPHAM Artist
TRISH MULVIHILL Colors
ROB LEIGH Letters
DAVE WIELGOSZ Associate Editor
PAUL KAMINSKI Editor

YES, BRIAN KIMURA USES HIS ARCADES TO RUN A TON OF **SUPER-SHADY** SIDE HUSTLES.

BUT I ONLY ASKED WHY THE GOTHAM GIRL WEBSITE WOULD DISH ON AN **ILLEGITIMATE DAUGHTER** HE HID FROM HIS WIFE.

'CUZ I'D REALLY LIKE TO KNOW WHO'S USING MY **NAME** FOR A GOSSIP RAG.

"DON'T DISASSOCIATE, CLAIRE," DR. MERIDIAN WOULD SAY. "STAY IN THE PRESENT TO FIND THE WAY FORWARD."

≈Sigh≈ WEREN'T WE JUST **IN AGREEMENT**, GUYS?

KINK

YOU DON'T KNOW WHO'D WANT TO AIR YOUR BOSS'S **DIRTY LAUNDRY**--

--AND I'M NOT THE ONE AIRING **SAID** LAUNDRY? I THOUGHT WE WERE GOOD.

THERE'S A SMALL DETAIL YOU ARE **OVERLOOKING**, GOTHAM GIRL.

I AM THE KIND OF PERSON WHO KEEPS **VIOLENT BODYGUARDS** WITH HIM AT ALL TIMES.

YOU'RE-- FOR LACK OF A BETTER TERM-- **CAPED.**

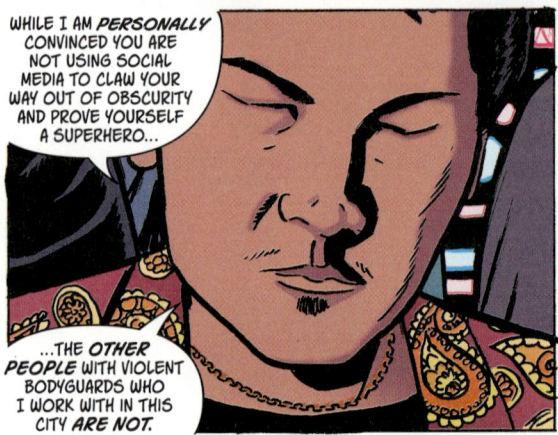

WHILE I AM **PERSONALLY** CONVINCED YOU ARE NOT USING SOCIAL MEDIA TO CLAW YOUR WAY OUT OF OBSCURITY AND PROVE YOURSELF A SUPERHERO...

...THE **OTHER** PEOPLE WITH VIOLENT BODYGUARDS WHO I WORK WITH IN THIS CITY **ARE NOT.**

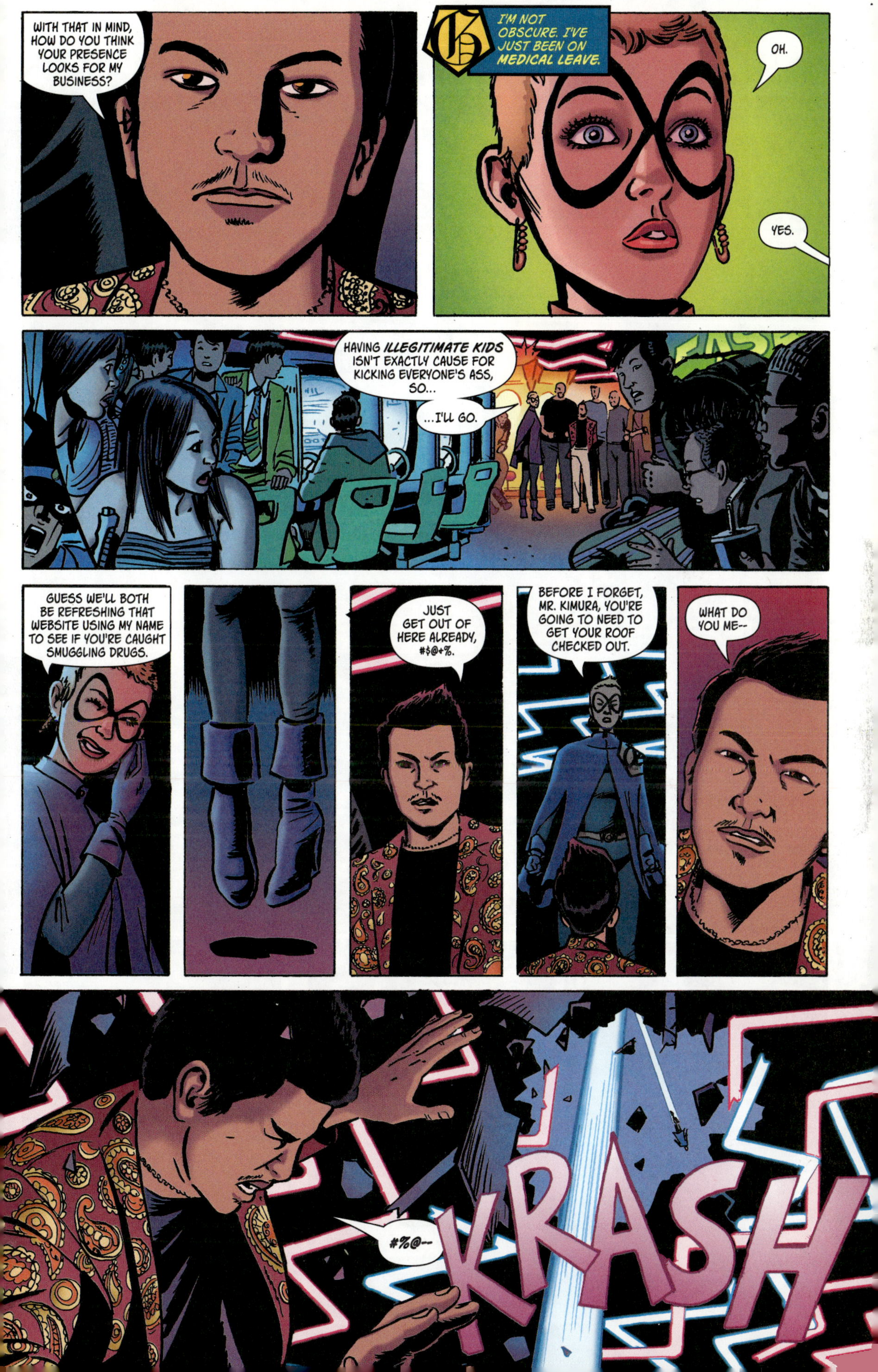
WITH THAT IN MIND, HOW DO YOU THINK YOUR PRESENCE LOOKS FOR MY BUSINESS?
I'M NOT OBSCURE. I'VE JUST BEEN ON MEDICAL LEAVE.
OH.
YES.
HAVING ILLEGITIMATE KIDS ISN'T EXACTLY CAUSE FOR KICKING EVERYONE'S ASS, SO...
...I'LL GO.
GUESS WE'LL BOTH BE REFRESHING THAT WEBSITE USING MY NAME TO SEE IF YOU'RE CAUGHT SMUGGLING DRUGS.
JUST GET OUT OF HERE ALREADY, #$@+%.
BEFORE I FORGET, MR. KIMURA, YOU'RE GOING TO NEED TO GET YOUR ROOF CHECKED OUT.
WHAT DO YOU ME--
#%@--
KRASH

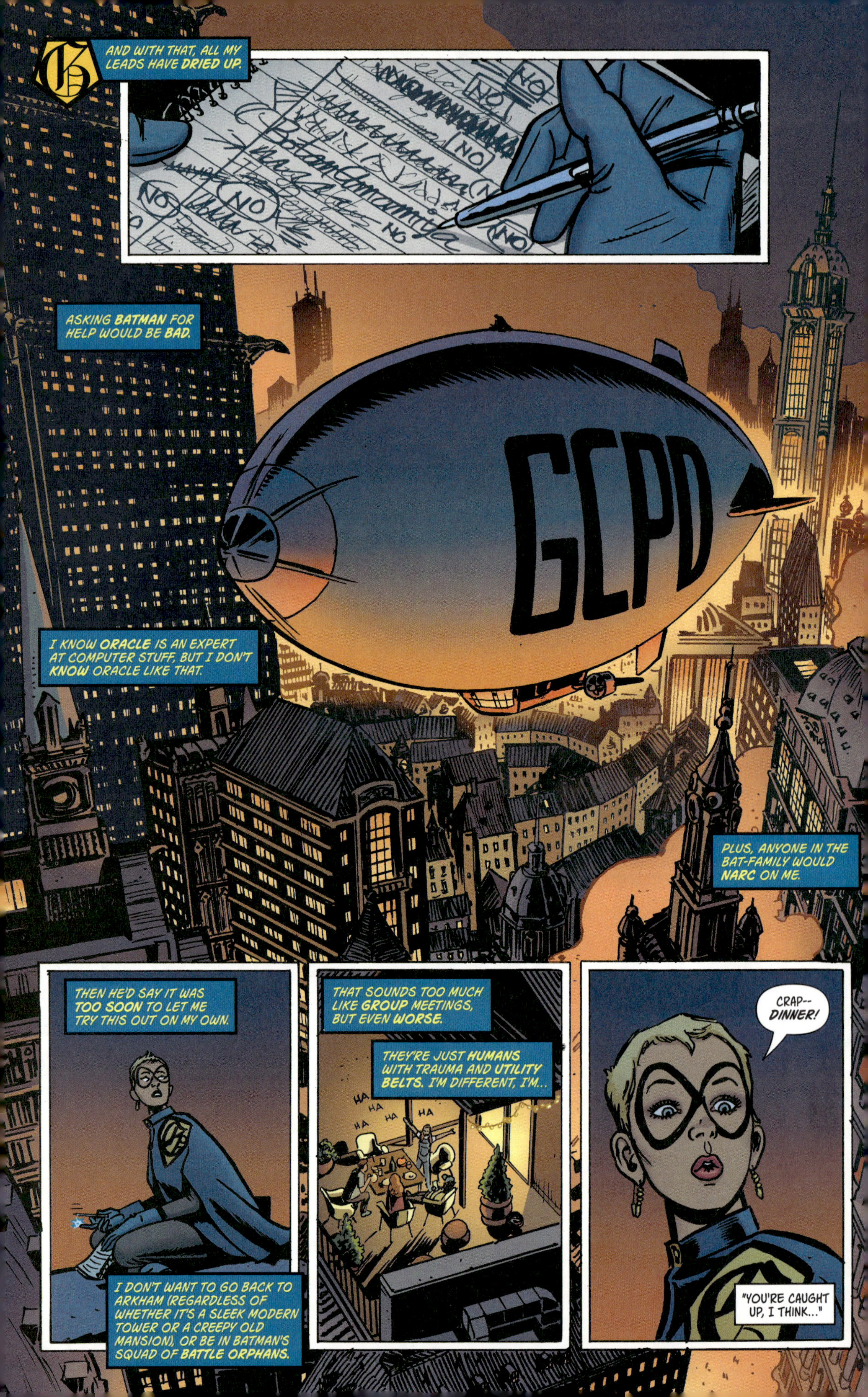
AND WITH THAT, ALL MY LEADS HAVE DRIED UP.
NO
NO
NO
NO
NO
NO
ASKING BATMAN FOR HELP WOULD BE BAD.
GCPD
I KNOW ORACLE IS AN EXPERT AT COMPUTER STUFF, BUT I DON'T KNOW ORACLE LIKE THAT.
PLUS, ANYONE IN THE BAT-FAMILY WOULD NARC ON ME.
THEN HE'D SAY IT WAS TOO SOON TO LET ME TRY THIS OUT ON MY OWN.
I DON'T WANT TO GO BACK TO ARKHAM (REGARDLESS OF WHETHER IT'S A SLEEK MODERN TOWER OR A CREEPY OLD MANSION), OR BE IN BATMAN'S SQUAD OF BATTLE ORPHANS.
THAT SOUNDS TOO MUCH LIKE GROUP MEETINGS, BUT EVEN WORSE.
THEY'RE JUST HUMANS WITH TRAUMA AND UTILITY BELTS. I'M DIFFERENT, I'M...
HA HA HA HA HA
CRAP-- DINNER!
"YOU'RE CAUGHT UP, I THINK..."

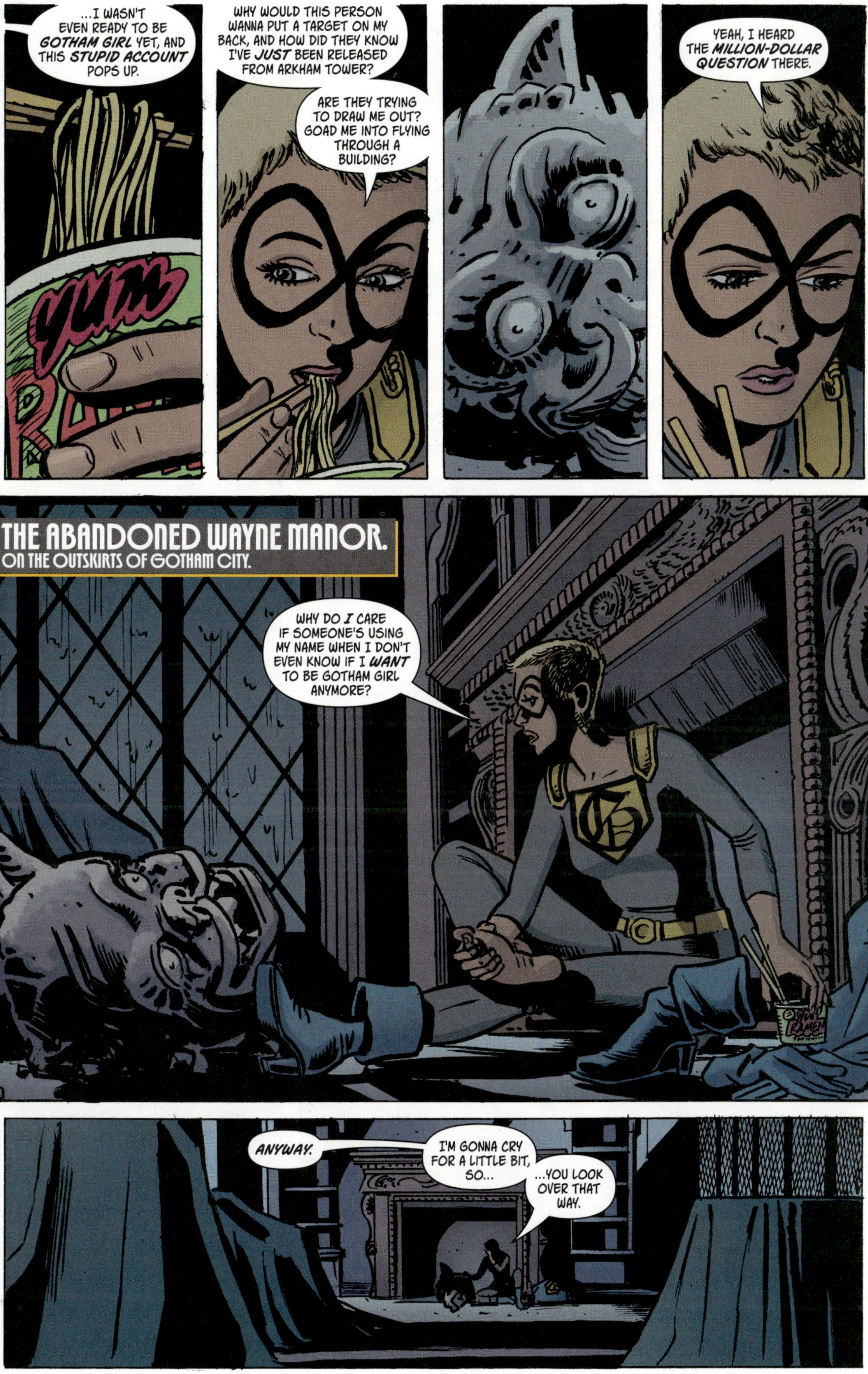
...I WASN'T EVEN READY TO BE GOTHAM GIRL YET, AND THIS STUPID ACCOUNT POPS UP.
WHY WOULD THIS PERSON WANNA PUT A TARGET ON MY BACK, AND HOW DID THEY KNOW I'VE JUST BEEN RELEASED FROM ARKHAM TOWER?
ARE THEY TRYING TO DRAW ME OUT? GOAD ME INTO FLYING THROUGH A BUILDING?
YEAH, I HEARD THE MILLION-DOLLAR QUESTION THERE.
THE ABANDONED WAYNE MANOR.
ON THE OUTSKIRTS OF GOTHAM CITY.
WHY DO I CARE IF SOMEONE'S USING MY NAME WHEN I DON'T EVEN KNOW IF I WANT TO BE GOTHAM GIRL ANYMORE?
ANYWAY.
I'M GONNA CRY FOR A LITTLE BIT, SO...
...YOU LOOK OVER THAT WAY.

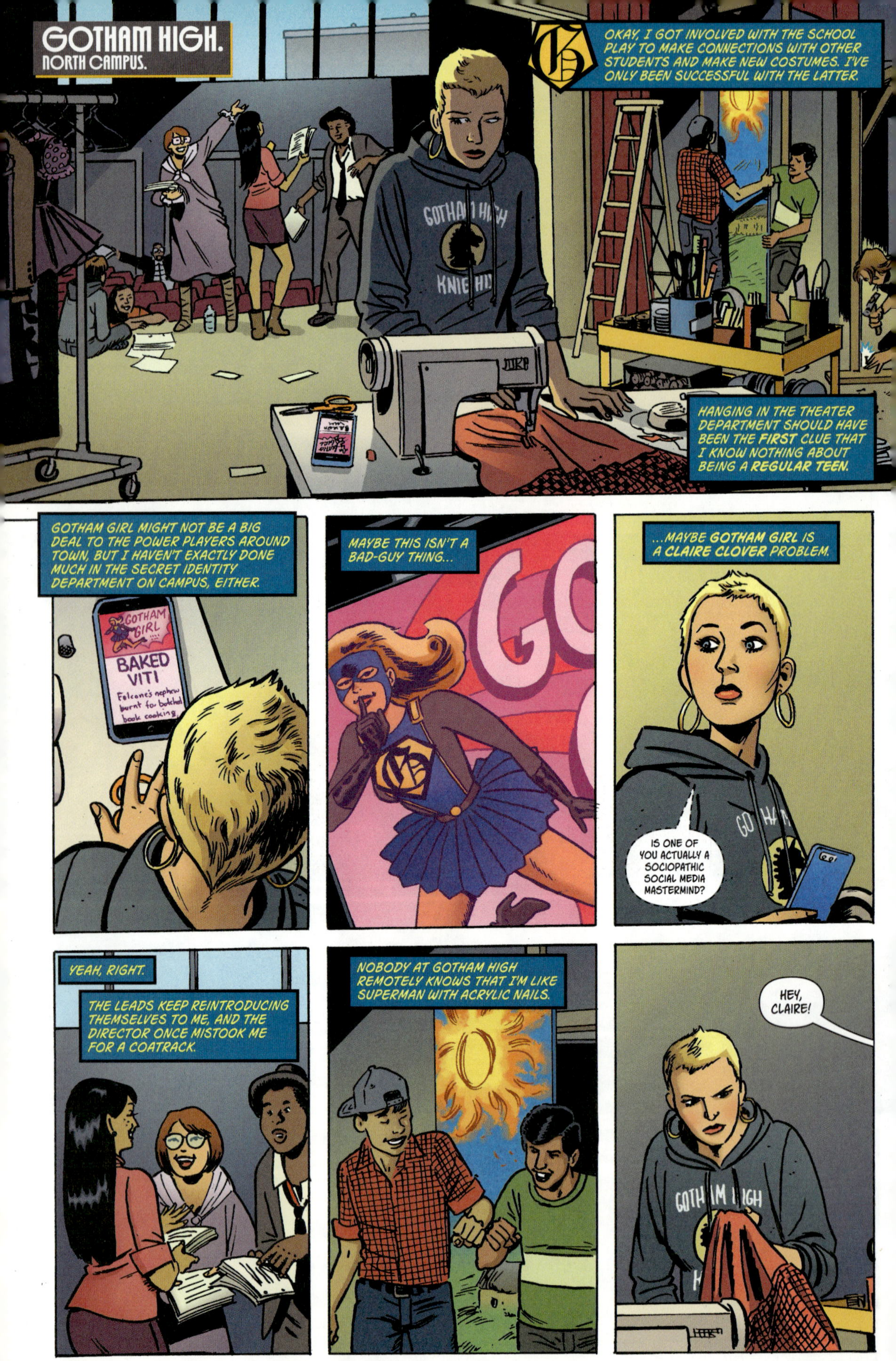
GOTHAM HIGH.
NORTH CAMPUS.
OKAY, I GOT INVOLVED WITH THE SCHOOL PLAY TO MAKE CONNECTIONS WITH OTHER STUDENTS AND MAKE NEW COSTUMES. I'VE ONLY BEEN SUCCESSFUL WITH THE LATTER.
GOTHAM HIGH KNIGHTS
HANGING IN THE THEATER DEPARTMENT SHOULD HAVE BEEN THE FIRST CLUE THAT I KNOW NOTHING ABOUT BEING A REGULAR TEEN.
GOTHAM GIRL MIGHT NOT BE A BIG DEAL TO THE POWER PLAYERS AROUND TOWN, BUT I HAVEN'T EXACTLY DONE MUCH IN THE SECRET IDENTITY DEPARTMENT ON CAMPUS, EITHER.
GOTHAM GIRL
BAKED VITI
Falcone's nephew burnt for botched book cooking
MAYBE THIS ISN'T A BAD-GUY THING...
...MAYBE GOTHAM GIRL IS A CLAIRE CLOVER PROBLEM.
IS ONE OF YOU ACTUALLY A SOCIOPATHIC SOCIAL MEDIA MASTERMIND?
YEAH, RIGHT.
THE LEADS KEEP REINTRODUCING THEMSELVES TO ME, AND THE DIRECTOR ONCE MISTOOK ME FOR A COATRACK.
NOBODY AT GOTHAM HIGH REMOTELY KNOWS THAT I'M LIKE SUPERMAN WITH ACRYLIC NAILS.
HEY, CLAIRE!

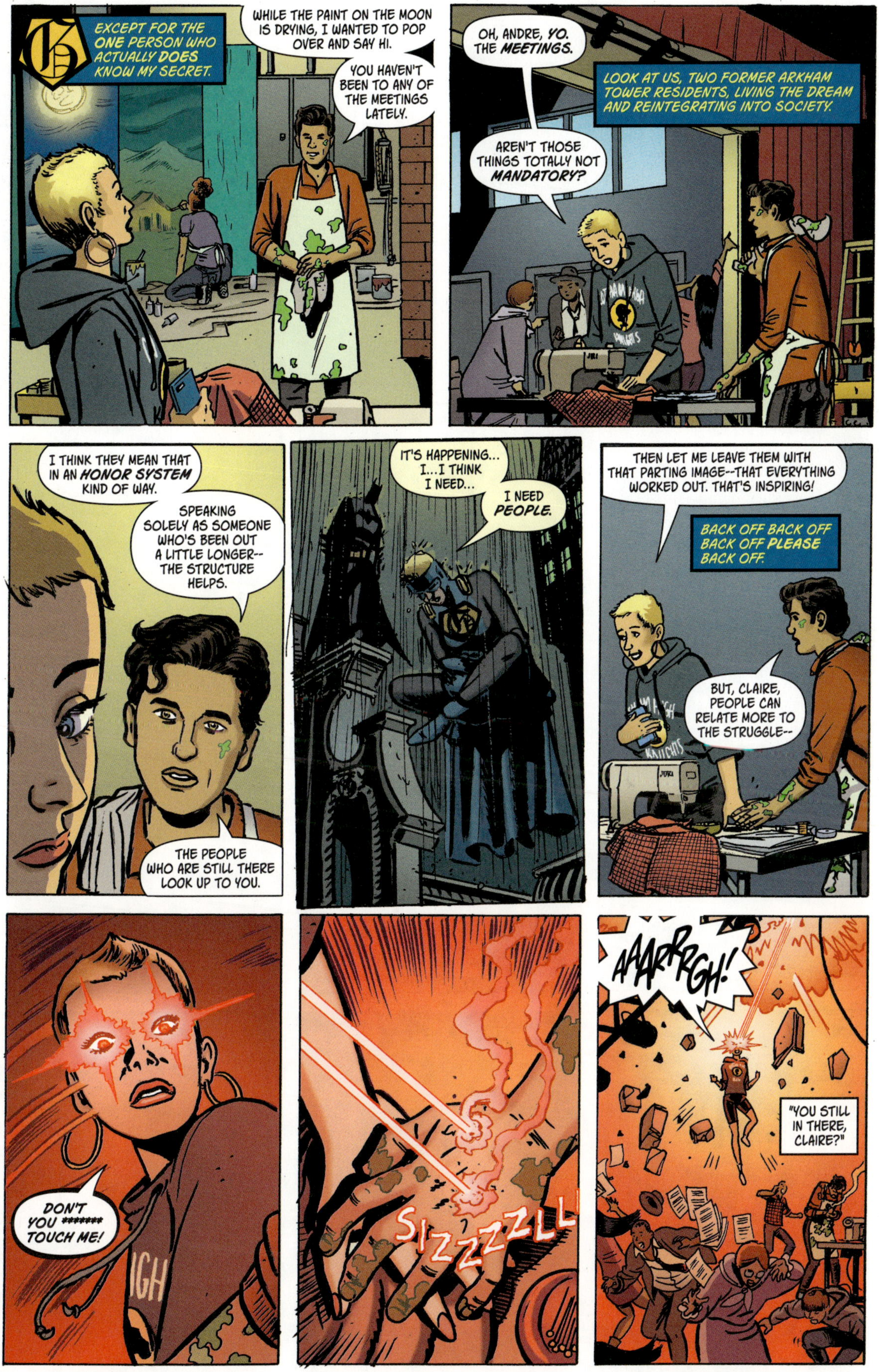

EXCEPT FOR THE ONE PERSON WHO ACTUALLY DOES KNOW MY SECRET.
WHILE THE PAINT ON THE MOON IS DRYING, I WANTED TO POP OVER AND SAY HI.
YOU HAVEN'T BEEN TO ANY OF THE MEETINGS LATELY.
OH, ANDRE, YO. THE MEETINGS.
LOOK AT US, TWO FORMER ARKHAM TOWER RESIDENTS, LIVING THE DREAM AND REINTEGRATING INTO SOCIETY.
AREN'T THOSE THINGS TOTALLY NOT MANDATORY?
I THINK THEY MEAN THAT IN AN HONOR SYSTEM KIND OF WAY.
SPEAKING SOLELY AS SOMEONE WHO'S BEEN OUT A LITTLE LONGER-- THE STRUCTURE HELPS.
THE PEOPLE WHO ARE STILL THERE LOOK UP TO YOU.
IT'S HAPPENING... I...I THINK I NEED...
I NEED PEOPLE.
THEN LET ME LEAVE THEM WITH THAT PARTING IMAGE--THAT EVERYTHING WORKED OUT. THAT'S INSPIRING!
BACK OFF BACK OFF BACK OFF PLEASE BACK OFF.
BUT, CLAIRE, PEOPLE CAN RELATE MORE TO THE STRUGGLE--
DON'T YOU ******* TOUCH ME!
SIZZZZLLL
AAARRRGH!
"YOU STILL IN THERE, CLAIRE?"

NOT visiting Arkham is what I need right now. Please respect that decision.

I APPRECIATE THE FEEDBACK AND WILL DEFINITELY CONSIDER IT.

OH. YEAH. SURE.

YOU'RE MISSED, IS ALL.

I NEED TO GO TO THE ART ROOM AND GRAB A NEW PAIR OF SCISSORS.

MINE KEEP BREAKING.

ALL RIGHT--

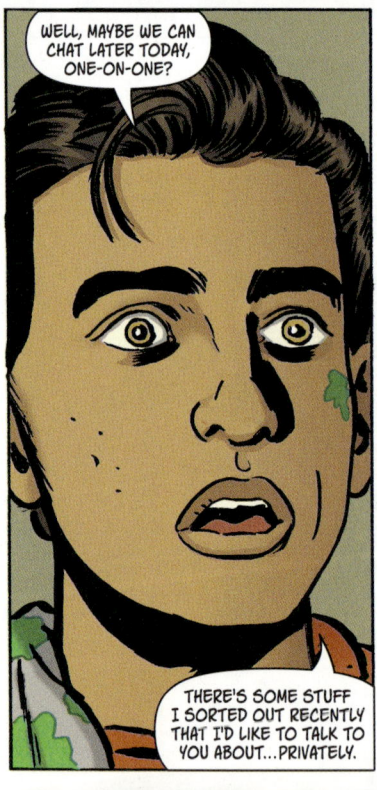

WELL, MAYBE WE CAN CHAT LATER TODAY, ONE-ON-ONE?

THERE'S SOME STUFF I SORTED OUT RECENTLY THAT I'D LIKE TO TALK TO YOU ABOUT...PRIVATELY.

WISH I COULD. I'M WASHING MY HAIR.

WELL, uhh...

...IF YOU FINISH EARLY OR WHATEVER, I'LL BE HERE PRETTY LATE.

I'M GONNA BLOW THIS GUY'S FACE OFF IF HE TRIES TO ASK ME OUT ON A DATE RIGHT NOW.

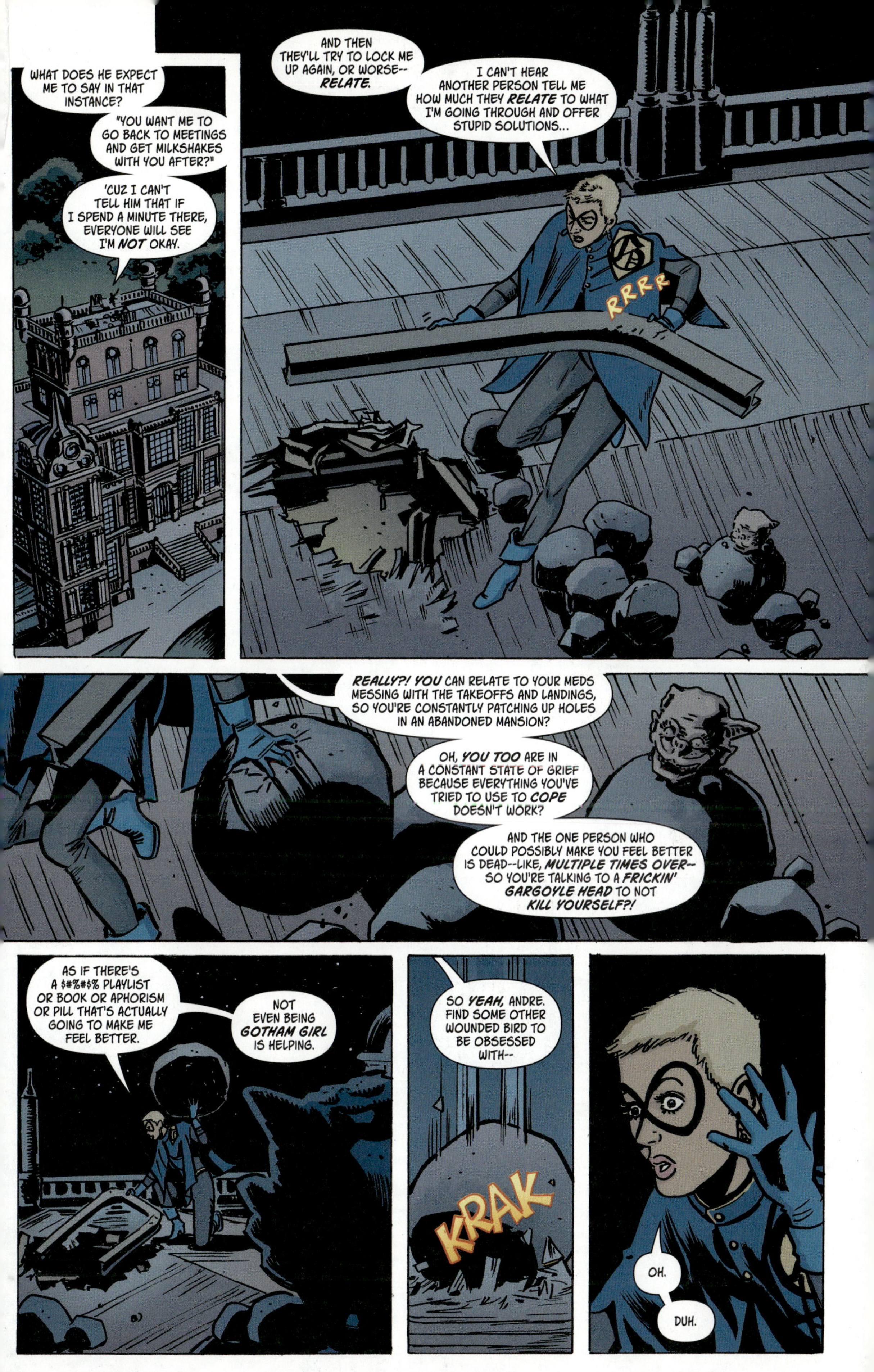
WHAT DOES HE EXPECT ME TO SAY IN THAT INSTANCE?
"YOU WANT ME TO GO BACK TO MEETINGS AND GET MILKSHAKES WITH YOU AFTER?"
'CUZ I CAN'T TELL HIM THAT IF I SPEND A MINUTE THERE, EVERYONE WILL SEE I'M NOT OKAY.
AND THEN THEY'LL TRY TO LOCK ME UP AGAIN, OR WORSE-- RELATE.
I CAN'T HEAR ANOTHER PERSON TELL ME HOW MUCH THEY RELATE TO WHAT I'M GOING THROUGH AND OFFER STUPID SOLUTIONS...
RRRR
REALLY?! YOU CAN RELATE TO YOUR MEDS MESSING WITH THE TAKEOFFS AND LANDINGS, SO YOU'RE CONSTANTLY PATCHING UP HOLES IN AN ABANDONED MANSION?
OH, YOU TOO ARE IN A CONSTANT STATE OF GRIEF BECAUSE EVERYTHING YOU'VE TRIED TO USE TO COPE DOESN'T WORK?
AND THE ONE PERSON WHO COULD POSSIBLY MAKE YOU FEEL BETTER IS DEAD--LIKE, MULTIPLE TIMES OVER-- SO YOU'RE TALKING TO A FRICKIN' GARGOYLE HEAD TO NOT KILL YOURSELF?!
AS IF THERE'S A $#%#$% PLAYLIST OR BOOK OR APHORISM OR PILL THAT'S ACTUALLY GOING TO MAKE ME FEEL BETTER.
NOT EVEN BEING GOTHAM GIRL IS HELPING.
SO YEAH, ANDRE. FIND SOME OTHER WOUNDED BIRD TO BE OBSESSED WITH--
KRAK
OH.
DUH.

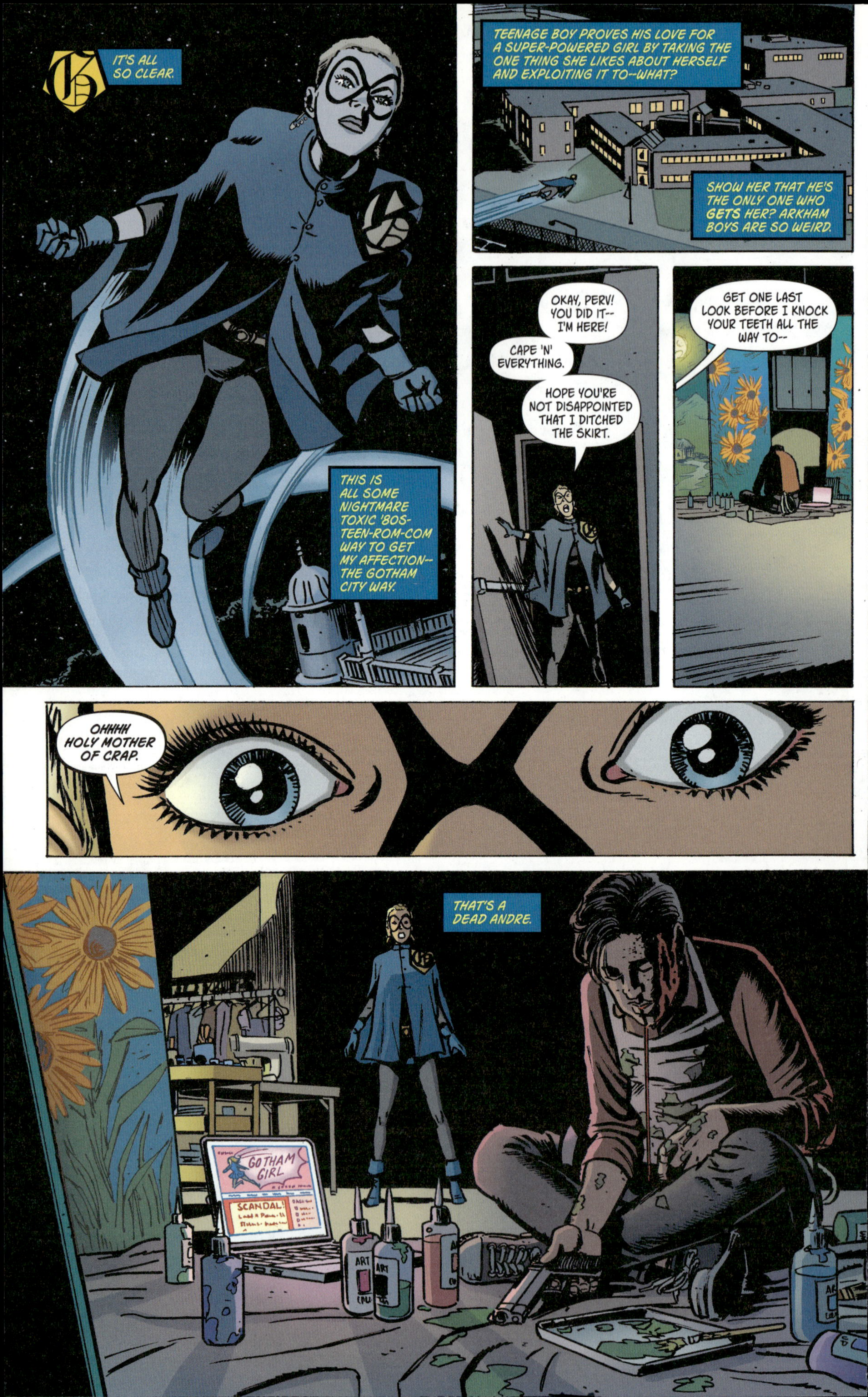
IT'S ALL SO CLEAR.
THIS IS ALL SOME NIGHTMARE TOXIC '80S-TEEN-ROM-COM WAY TO GET MY AFFECTION-- THE GOTHAM CITY WAY.
TEENAGE BOY PROVES HIS LOVE FOR A SUPER-POWERED GIRL BY TAKING THE ONE THING SHE LIKES ABOUT HERSELF AND EXPLOITING IT TO--WHAT?
SHOW HER THAT HE'S THE ONLY ONE WHO GETS HER? ARKHAM BOYS ARE SO WEIRD.
OKAY, PERV! YOU DID IT-- I'M HERE!
CAPE 'N' EVERYTHING.
HOPE YOU'RE NOT DISAPPOINTED THAT I DITCHED THE SKIRT.
GET ONE LAST LOOK BEFORE I KNOCK YOUR TEETH ALL THE WAY TO--
OHHHH HOLY MOTHER OF CRAP.
THAT'S A DEAD ANDRE.
GOTHAM GIRL
SCANDAL!
ART
ART

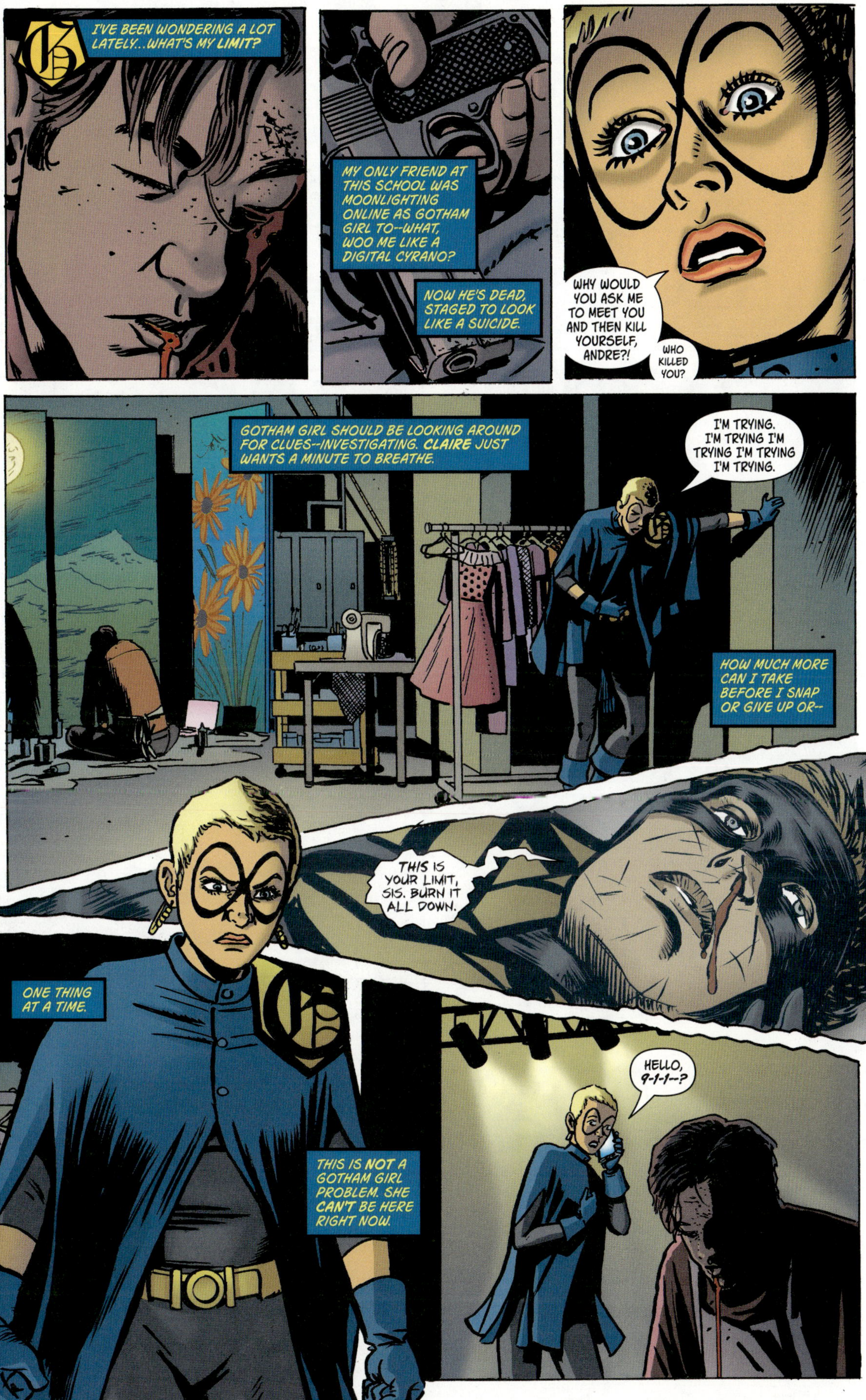

I'VE BEEN WONDERING A LOT LATELY...WHAT'S MY LIMIT?
MY ONLY FRIEND AT THIS SCHOOL WAS MOONLIGHTING ONLINE AS GOTHAM GIRL TO--WHAT, WOO ME LIKE A DIGITAL CYRANO?
NOW HE'S DEAD, STAGED TO LOOK LIKE A SUICIDE.
WHY WOULD YOU ASK ME TO MEET YOU AND THEN KILL YOURSELF, ANDRE?!
WHO KILLED YOU?
GOTHAM GIRL SHOULD BE LOOKING AROUND FOR CLUES--INVESTIGATING. CLAIRE JUST WANTS A MINUTE TO BREATHE.
I'M TRYING. I'M TRYING I'M TRYING I'M TRYING I'M TRYING.
HOW MUCH MORE CAN I TAKE BEFORE I SNAP OR GIVE UP OR--
THIS IS YOUR LIMIT, SIS. BURN IT ALL DOWN.
ONE THING AT A TIME.
THIS IS NOT A GOTHAM GIRL PROBLEM. SHE CAN'T BE HERE RIGHT NOW.
HELLO, 9-1-1--?

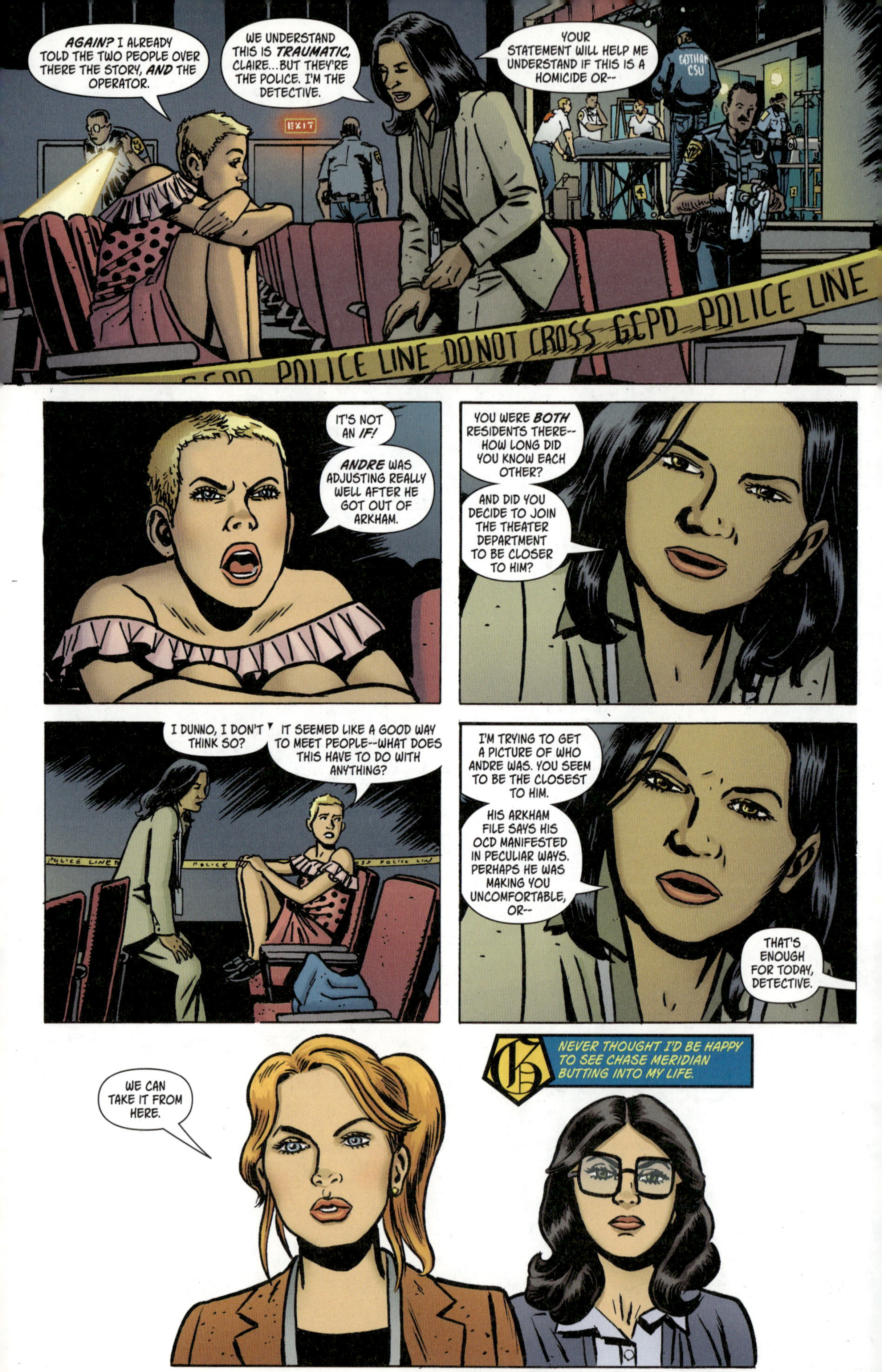

AGAIN? I ALREADY TOLD THE TWO PEOPLE OVER THERE THE STORY, AND THE OPERATOR.
WE UNDERSTAND THIS IS TRAUMATIC, CLAIRE...BUT THEY'RE THE POLICE. I'M THE DETECTIVE.
YOUR STATEMENT WILL HELP ME UNDERSTAND IF THIS IS A HOMICIDE OR--
EXIT
GOTHAM CSU
GCPD POLICE LINE DO NOT CROSS GCPD POLICE LINE
IT'S NOT AN IF!
ANDRE WAS ADJUSTING REALLY WELL AFTER HE GOT OUT OF ARKHAM.
YOU WERE BOTH RESIDENTS THERE--HOW LONG DID YOU KNOW EACH OTHER?
AND DID YOU DECIDE TO JOIN THE THEATER DEPARTMENT TO BE CLOSER TO HIM?
I DUNNO, I DON'T THINK SO?
IT SEEMED LIKE A GOOD WAY TO MEET PEOPLE--WHAT DOES THIS HAVE TO DO WITH ANYTHING?
I'M TRYING TO GET A PICTURE OF WHO ANDRE WAS. YOU SEEM TO BE THE CLOSEST TO HIM.
HIS ARKHAM FILE SAYS HIS OCD MANIFESTED IN PECULIAR WAYS. PERHAPS HE WAS MAKING YOU UNCOMFORTABLE, OR--
THAT'S ENOUGH FOR TODAY, DETECTIVE.
NEVER THOUGHT I'D BE HAPPY TO SEE CHASE MERIDIAN BUTTING INTO MY LIFE.
WE CAN TAKE IT FROM HERE.

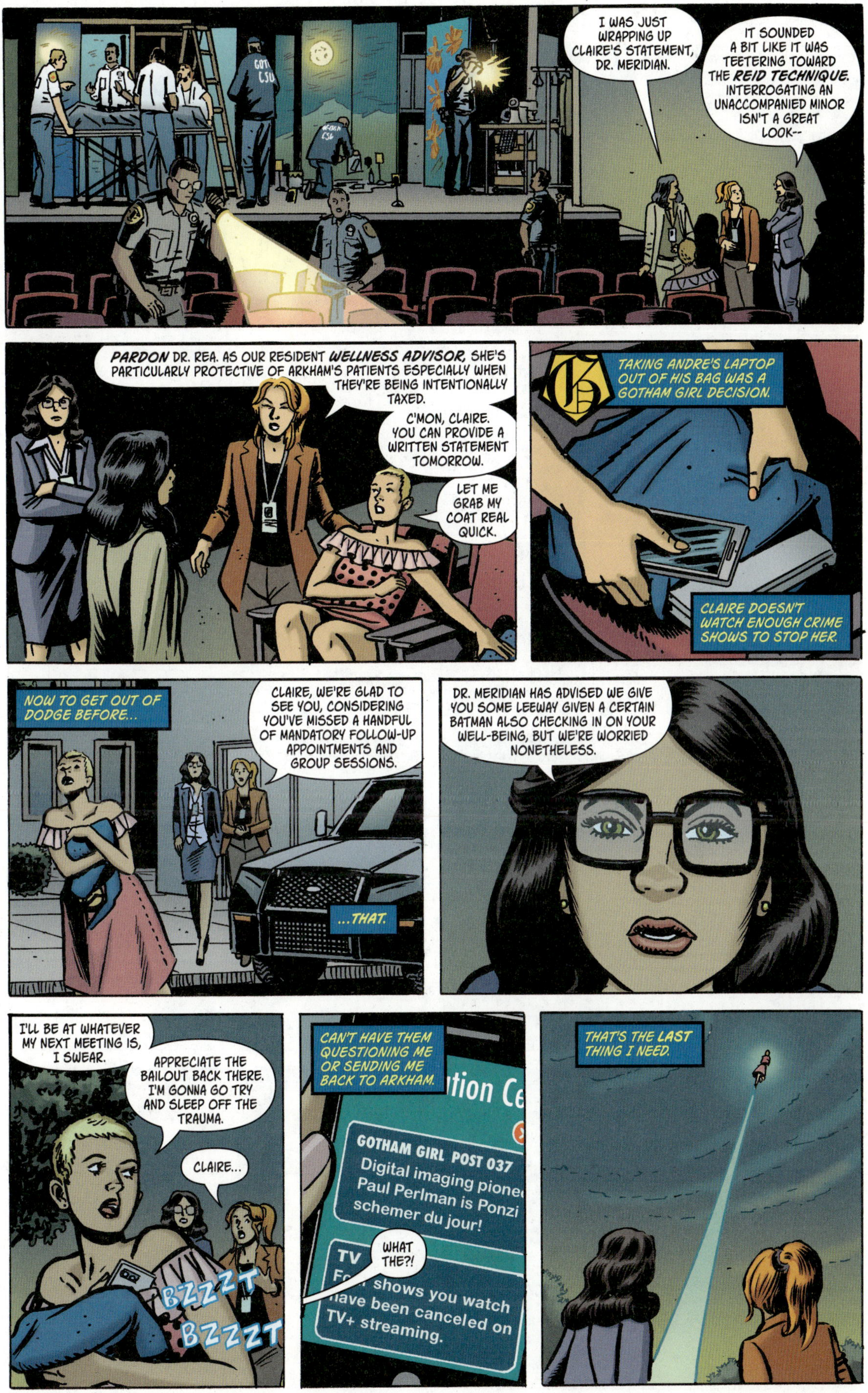

I WAS JUST WRAPPING UP CLAIRE'S STATEMENT, DR. MERIDIAN.
IT SOUNDED A BIT LIKE IT WAS TEETERING TOWARD THE REID TECHNIQUE. INTERROGATING AN UNACCOMPANIED MINOR ISN'T A GREAT LOOK--
PARDON DR. REA. AS OUR RESIDENT WELLNESS ADVISOR, SHE'S PARTICULARLY PROTECTIVE OF ARKHAM'S PATIENTS ESPECIALLY WHEN THEY'RE BEING INTENTIONALLY TAXED.
C'MON, CLAIRE. YOU CAN PROVIDE A WRITTEN STATEMENT TOMORROW.
LET ME GRAB MY COAT REAL QUICK.
TAKING ANDRE'S LAPTOP OUT OF HIS BAG WAS A GOTHAM GIRL DECISION.
CLAIRE DOESN'T WATCH ENOUGH CRIME SHOWS TO STOP HER.
NOW TO GET OUT OF DODGE BEFORE...
CLAIRE, WE'RE GLAD TO SEE YOU, CONSIDERING YOU'VE MISSED A HANDFUL OF MANDATORY FOLLOW-UP APPOINTMENTS AND GROUP SESSIONS.
...THAT.
DR. MERIDIAN HAS ADVISED WE GIVE YOU SOME LEEWAY GIVEN A CERTAIN BATMAN ALSO CHECKING IN ON YOUR WELL-BEING, BUT WE'RE WORRIED NONETHELESS.
I'LL BE AT WHATEVER MY NEXT MEETING IS, I SWEAR.
APPRECIATE THE BAILOUT BACK THERE. I'M GONNA GO TRY AND SLEEP OFF THE TRAUMA.
CLAIRE...
BZZZT
BZZZT
CAN'T HAVE THEM QUESTIONING ME OR SENDING ME BACK TO ARKHAM.
GOTHAM GIRL POST 037
Digital imaging pione
Paul Perlman is Ponzi schemer du jour!
TV
WHAT THE?!
shows you watch have been canceled on TV+ streaming.
THAT'S THE LAST THING I NEED.

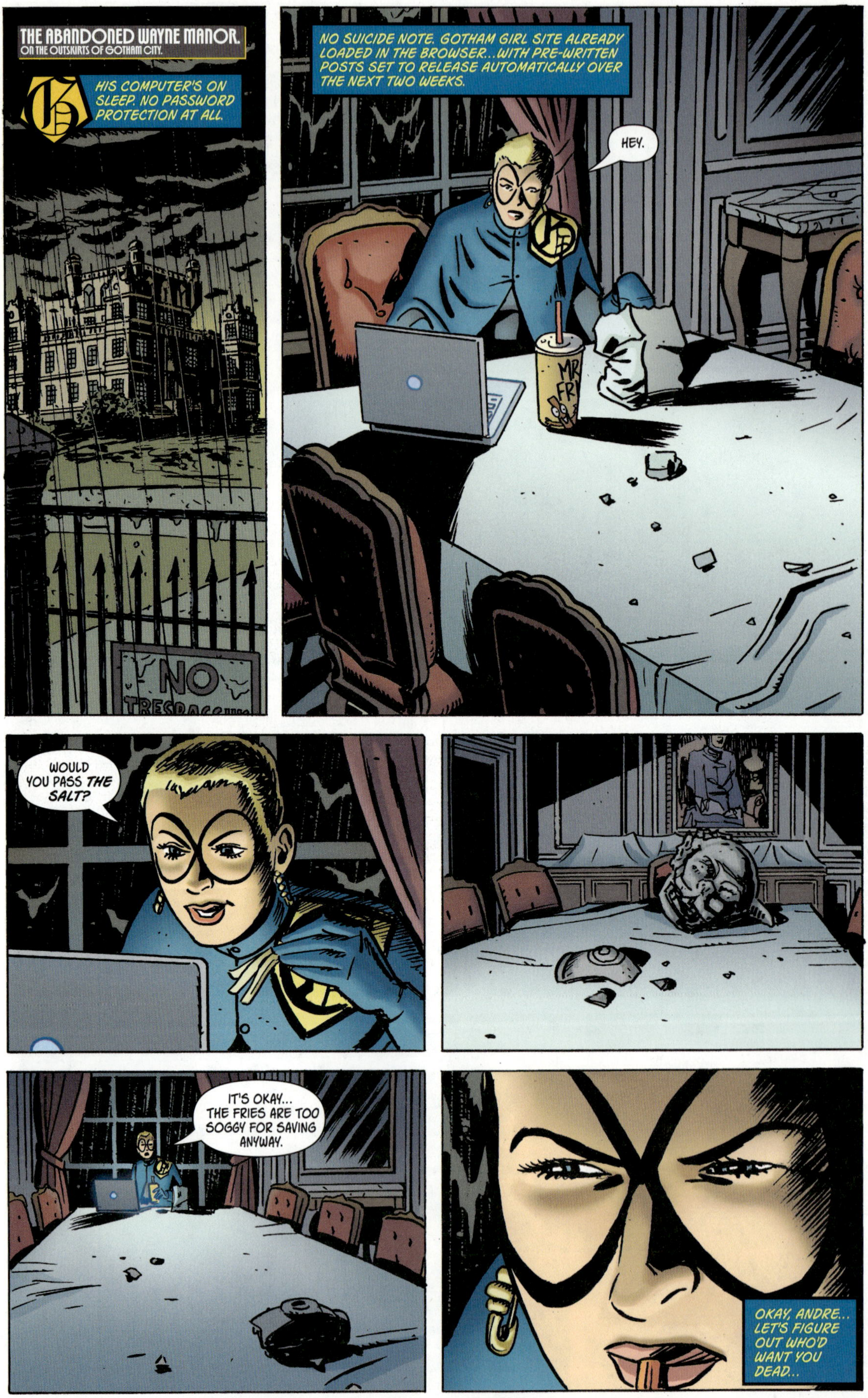
THE ABANDONED WAYNE MANOR.
ON THE OUTSKIRTS OF GOTHAM CITY.
HIS COMPUTER'S ON SLEEP. NO PASSWORD PROTECTION AT ALL.
NO TRES...
NO SUICIDE NOTE. GOTHAM GIRL SITE ALREADY LOADED IN THE BROWSER...WITH PRE-WRITTEN POSTS SET TO RELEASE AUTOMATICALLY OVER THE NEXT TWO WEEKS.
HEY.
MR FR
WOULD YOU PASS THE SALT?
IT'S OKAY... THE FRIES ARE TOO SOGGY FOR SAVING ANYWAY.
OKAY, ANDRE... LET'S FIGURE OUT WHO'D WANT YOU DEAD...

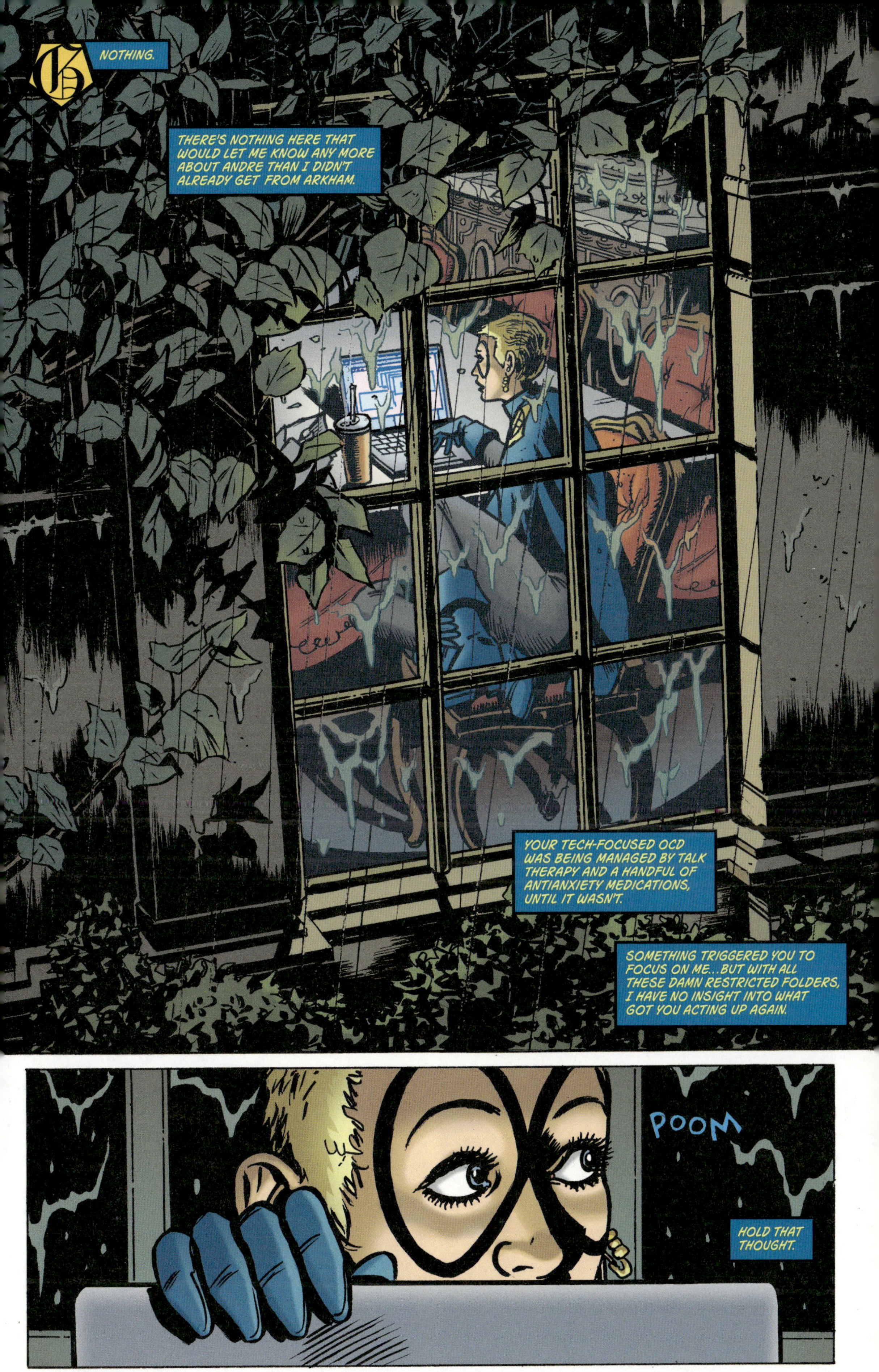
NOTHING.
THERE'S NOTHING HERE THAT WOULD LET ME KNOW ANY MORE ABOUT ANDRE THAN I DIDN'T ALREADY GET FROM ARKHAM.
YOUR TECH-FOCUSED OCD WAS BEING MANAGED BY TALK THERAPY AND A HANDFUL OF ANTIANXIETY MEDICATIONS, UNTIL IT WASN'T.
SOMETHING TRIGGERED YOU TO FOCUS ON ME...BUT WITH ALL THESE DAMN RESTRICTED FOLDERS, I HAVE NO INSIGHT INTO WHAT GOT YOU ACTING UP AGAIN.
POOM
HOLD THAT THOUGHT.

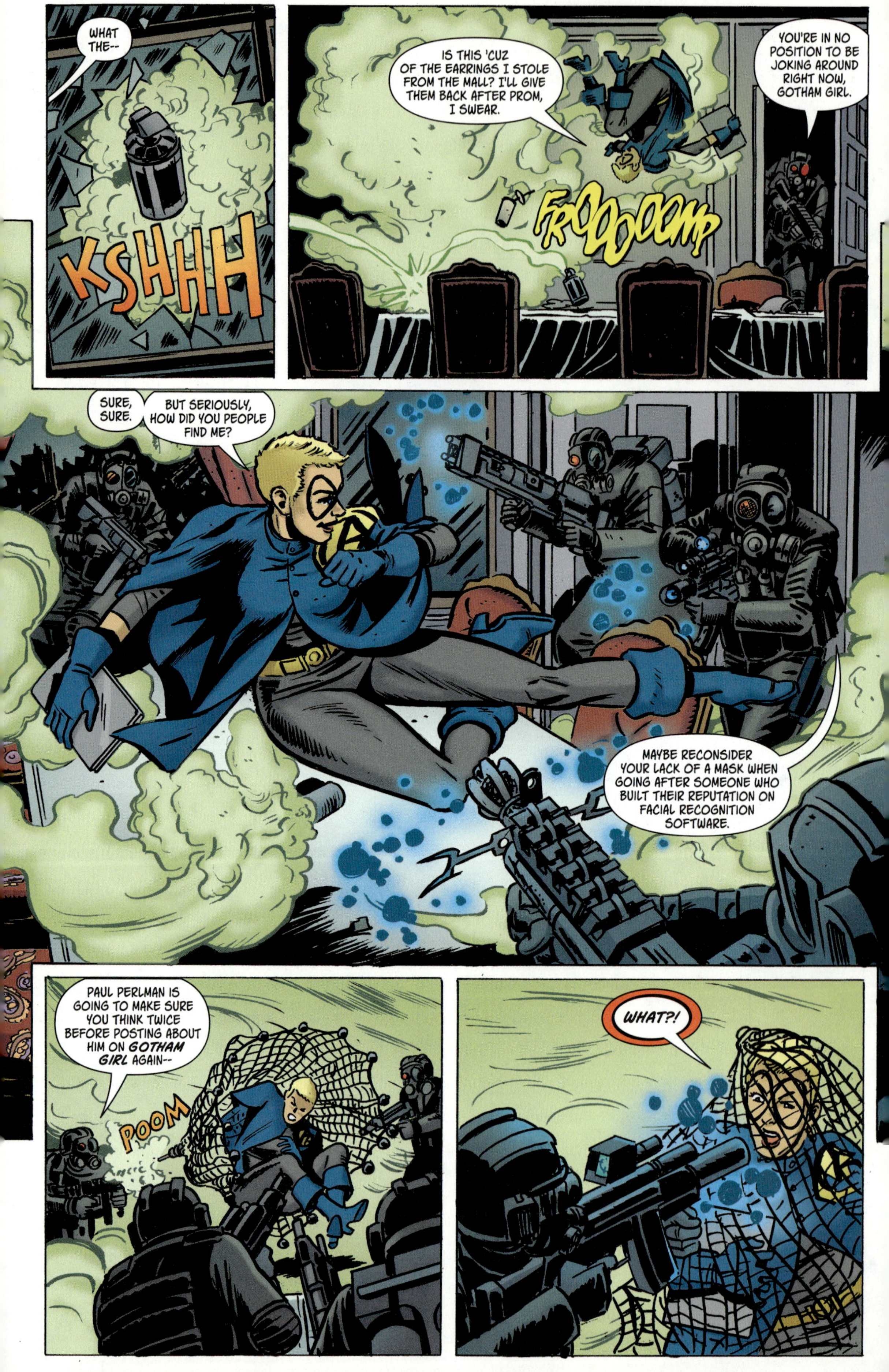
WHAT THE--
KSHHH
IS THIS 'CUZ OF THE EARRINGS I STOLE FROM THE MALL? I'LL GIVE THEM BACK AFTER PROM, I SWEAR.
FROOOOOOMP
YOU'RE IN NO POSITION TO BE JOKING AROUND RIGHT NOW, GOTHAM GIRL.
SURE, SURE.
BUT SERIOUSLY, HOW DID YOU PEOPLE FIND ME?
MAYBE RECONSIDER YOUR LACK OF A MASK WHEN GOING AFTER SOMEONE WHO BUILT THEIR REPUTATION ON FACIAL RECOGNITION SOFTWARE.
PAUL PERLMAN IS GOING TO MAKE SURE YOU THINK TWICE BEFORE POSTING ABOUT HIM ON GOTHAM GIRL AGAIN--
POOM
WHAT?!

I DIDN'T GO AFTER YOUR BOSS!

THAT STUPID SITE IS NOT ME!

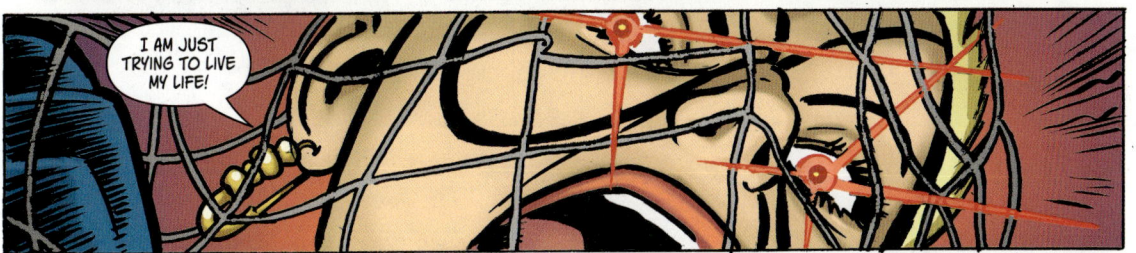

I AM JUST TRYING TO LIVE MY LIFE!

SOMEBODY ELSE WAS RUNNING THAT SITE, BUT HE'S DEAD AND ALL I'VE GOT IS HIS DUMB COMPUTER TO FIGURE OUT WHO KILLED HIM.

EXCEPT NO ONE WILL LEAVE ME ALONE AND GIVE ME ONE DAMN MINUTE TO THINK!

NOW, EITHER YOU ALL CAN HELP ME FIGURE OUT HOW TO HACK THIS STUPID LAPTOP SO I CAN STOP THE SITE FROM LEAKING *MORE* GOSSIP--

--OR YOU CAN ALL END UP IN THE HOSPITAL FOR NOT **** OFF AND MINDING YOUR BUSINESS.

SO WHAT'S IT GONNA BE?!

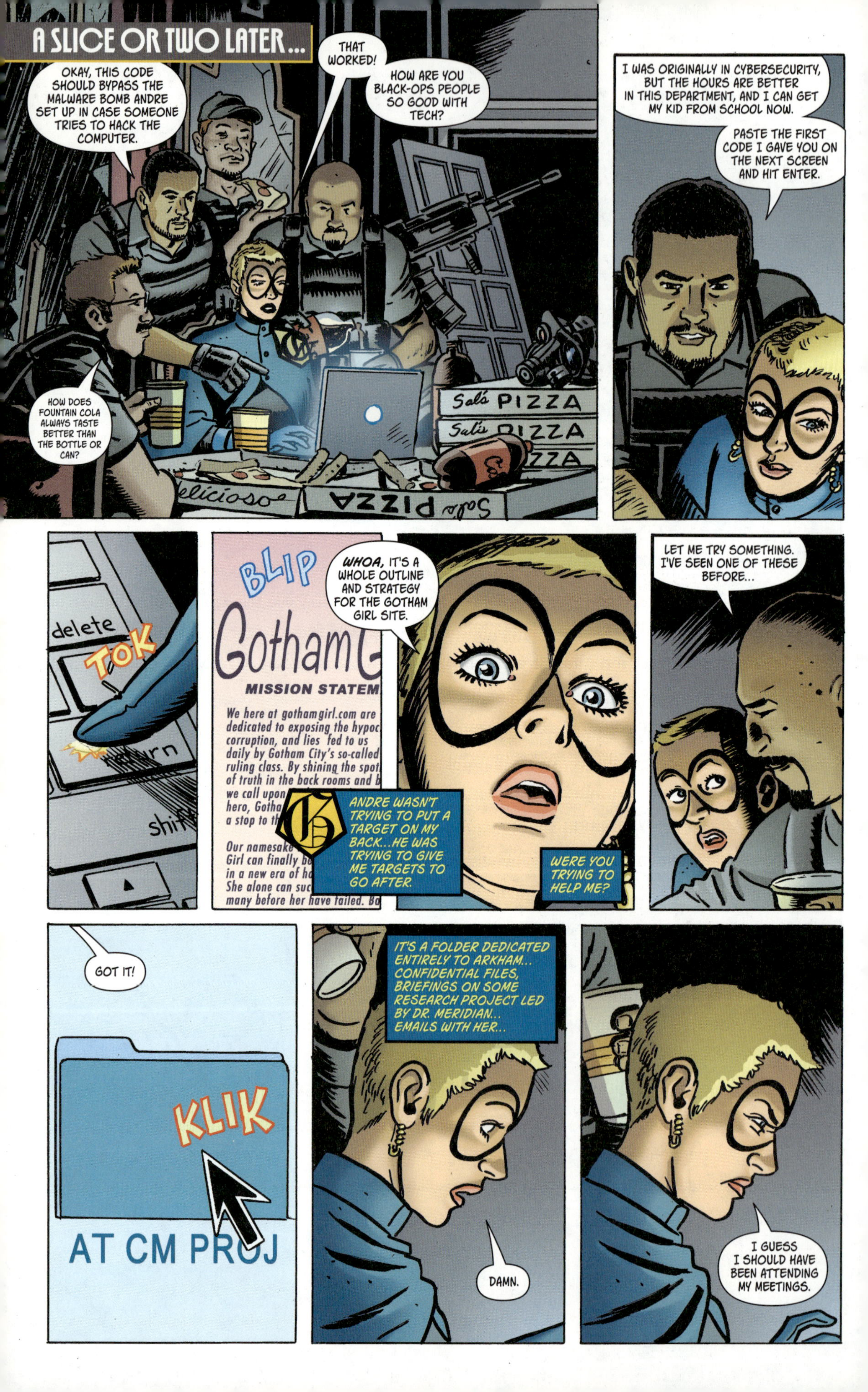

A SLICE OR TWO LATER...
OKAY, THIS CODE SHOULD BYPASS THE MALWARE BOMB ANDRE SET UP IN CASE SOMEONE TRIES TO HACK THE COMPUTER.
THAT WORKED!
HOW ARE YOU BLACK-OPS PEOPLE SO GOOD WITH TECH?
HOW DOES FOUNTAIN COLA ALWAYS TASTE BETTER THAN THE BOTTLE OR CAN?
Sal's PIZZA
Sal's PIZZA
Delicioso
Sal's PIZZA
I WAS ORIGINALLY IN CYBERSECURITY, BUT THE HOURS ARE BETTER IN THIS DEPARTMENT, AND I CAN GET MY KID FROM SCHOOL NOW.
PASTE THE FIRST CODE I GAVE YOU ON THE NEXT SCREEN AND HIT ENTER.
delete
TOK
return
shift
BLIP
GothamG
MISSION STATEM
We here at gothamgirl.com are dedicated to exposing the hypoc corruption, and lies fed to us daily by Gotham City's so-called ruling class. By shining the spot of truth in the back rooms and b we call upon hero, Gotha a stop to th
Our namesake Girl can finally be in a new era of h She alone can suc many before her have failed. Be
WHOA, IT'S A WHOLE OUTLINE AND STRATEGY FOR THE GOTHAM GIRL SITE.
ANDRE WASN'T TRYING TO PUT A TARGET ON MY BACK...HE WAS TRYING TO GIVE ME TARGETS TO GO AFTER.
WERE YOU TRYING TO HELP ME?
LET ME TRY SOMETHING. I'VE SEEN ONE OF THESE BEFORE...
GOT IT!
KLIK
AT CM PROJ
IT'S A FOLDER DEDICATED ENTIRELY TO ARKHAM... CONFIDENTIAL FILES, BRIEFINGS ON SOME RESEARCH PROJECT LED BY DR. MERIDIAN... EMAILS WITH HER...
DAMN.
I GUESS I SHOULD HAVE BEEN ATTENDING MY MEETINGS.

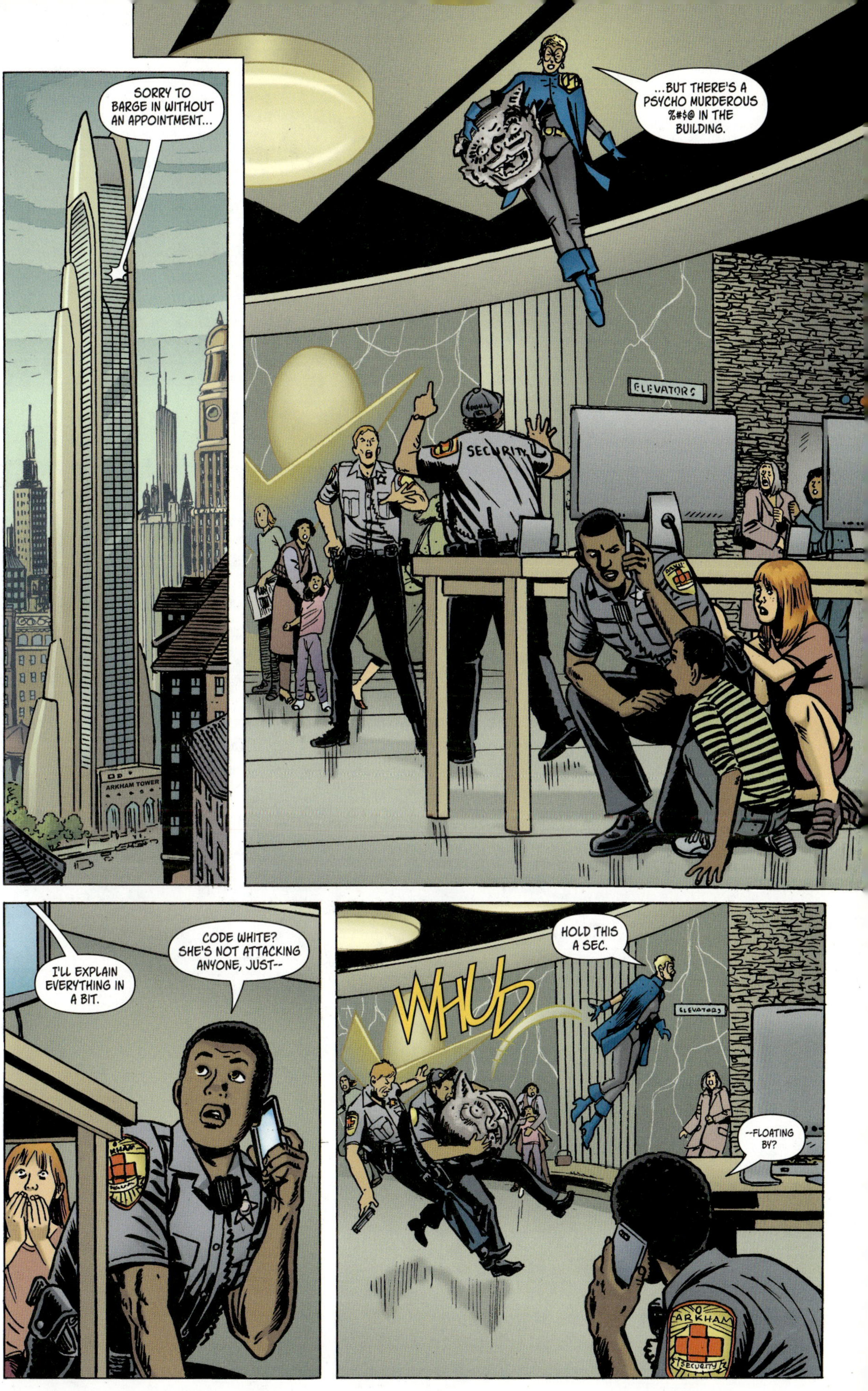
SORRY TO BARGE IN WITHOUT AN APPOINTMENT...
ARKHAM TOWER
...BUT THERE'S A PSYCHO MURDEROUS %#$@ IN THE BUILDING.
ELEVATORS
SECURITY
I'LL EXPLAIN EVERYTHING IN A BIT.
CODE WHITE? SHE'S NOT ATTACKING ANYONE, JUST--
HOLD THIS A SEC.
WHUD
ELEVATORS
--FLOATING BY?
ARKHAM
SECURITY

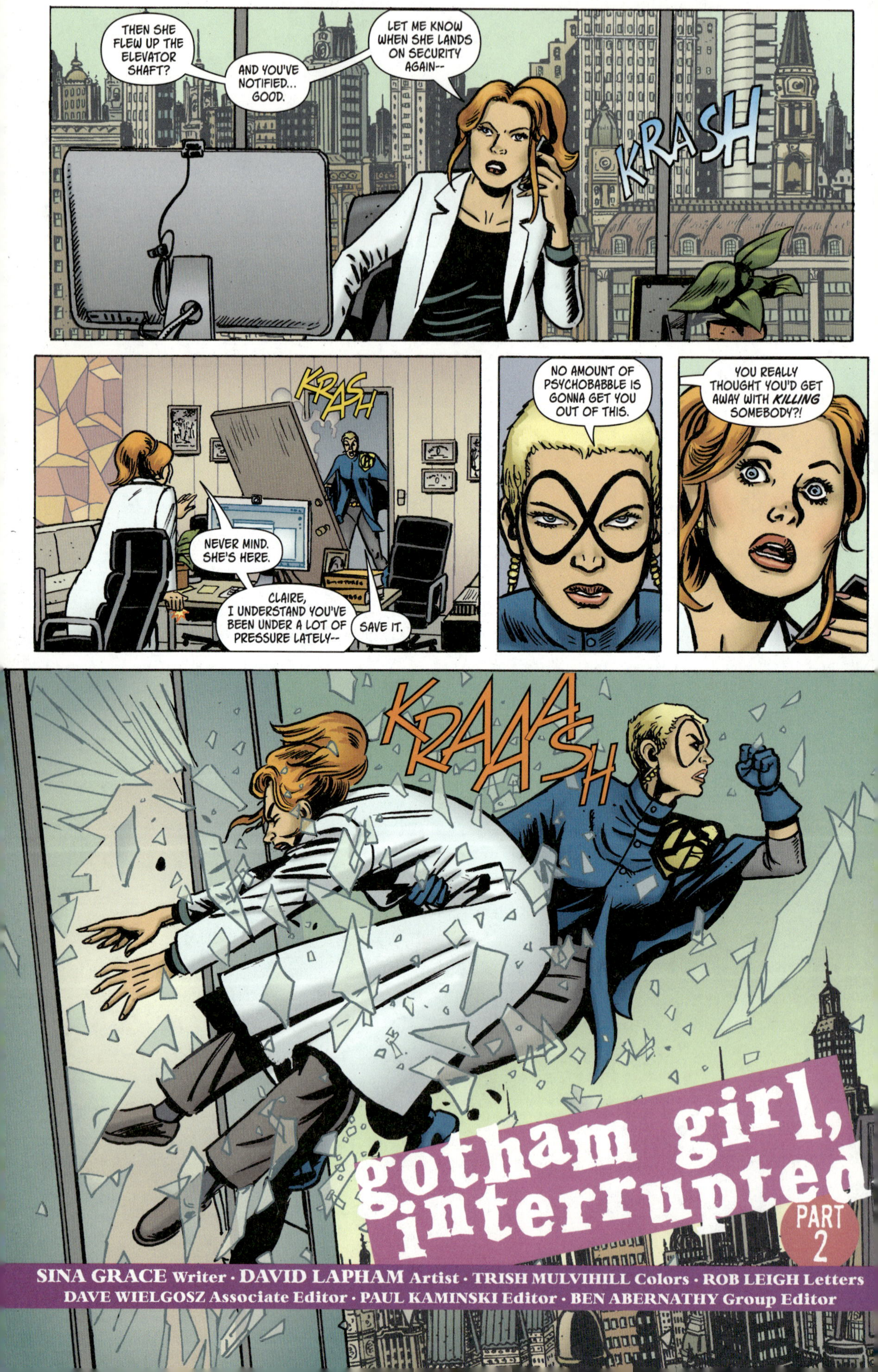
THEN SHE FLEW UP THE ELEVATOR SHAFT?
AND YOU'VE NOTIFIED... GOOD.
LET ME KNOW WHEN SHE LANDS ON SECURITY AGAIN--
KRASH
KRASH
NEVER MIND. SHE'S HERE.
CLAIRE, I UNDERSTAND YOU'VE BEEN UNDER A LOT OF PRESSURE LATELY--
SAVE IT.
NO AMOUNT OF PSYCHOBABBLE IS GONNA GET YOU OUT OF THIS.
YOU REALLY THOUGHT YOU'D GET AWAY WITH *KILLING* SOMEBODY?!
KRAAASH
gotham girl, interrupted
PART 2
SINA GRACE Writer · DAVID LAPHAM Artist · TRISH MULVIHILL Colors · ROB LEIGH Letters
DAVE WIELGOSZ Associate Editor · PAUL KAMINSKI Editor · BEN ABERNATHY Group Editor

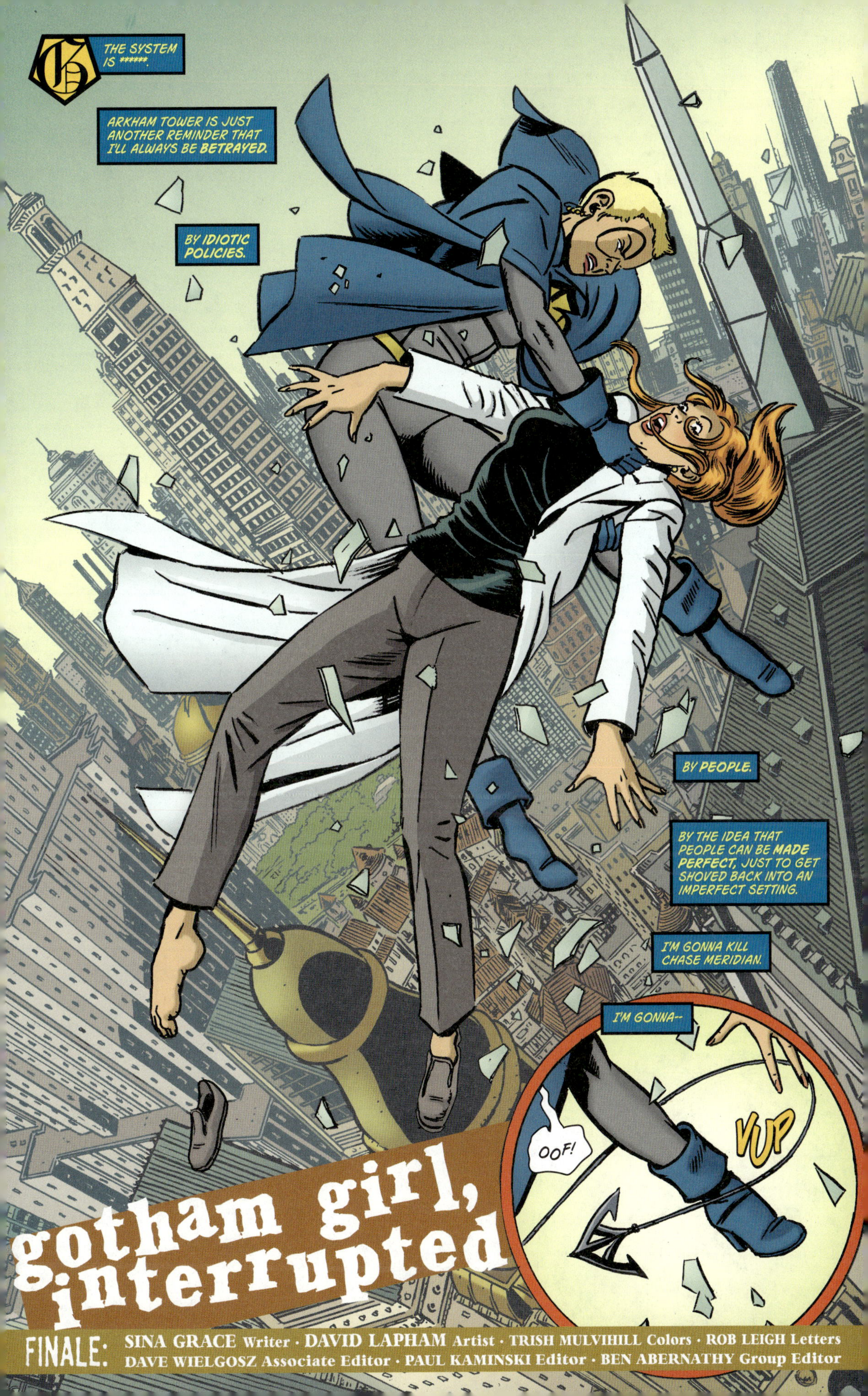
THE SYSTEM IS ******.
ARKHAM TOWER IS JUST ANOTHER REMINDER THAT I'LL ALWAYS BE BETRAYED.
BY IDIOTIC POLICIES.
BY PEOPLE.
BY THE IDEA THAT PEOPLE CAN BE MADE PERFECT, JUST TO GET SHOVED BACK INTO AN IMPERFECT SETTING.
I'M GONNA KILL CHASE MERIDIAN.
I'M GONNA--
OOF!
VUP
gotham girl, interrupted
FINALE: SINA GRACE Writer · DAVID LAPHAM Artist · TRISH MULVIHILL Colors · ROB LEIGH Letters
DAVE WIELGOSZ Associate Editor · PAUL KAMINSKI Editor · BEN ABERNATHY Group Editor

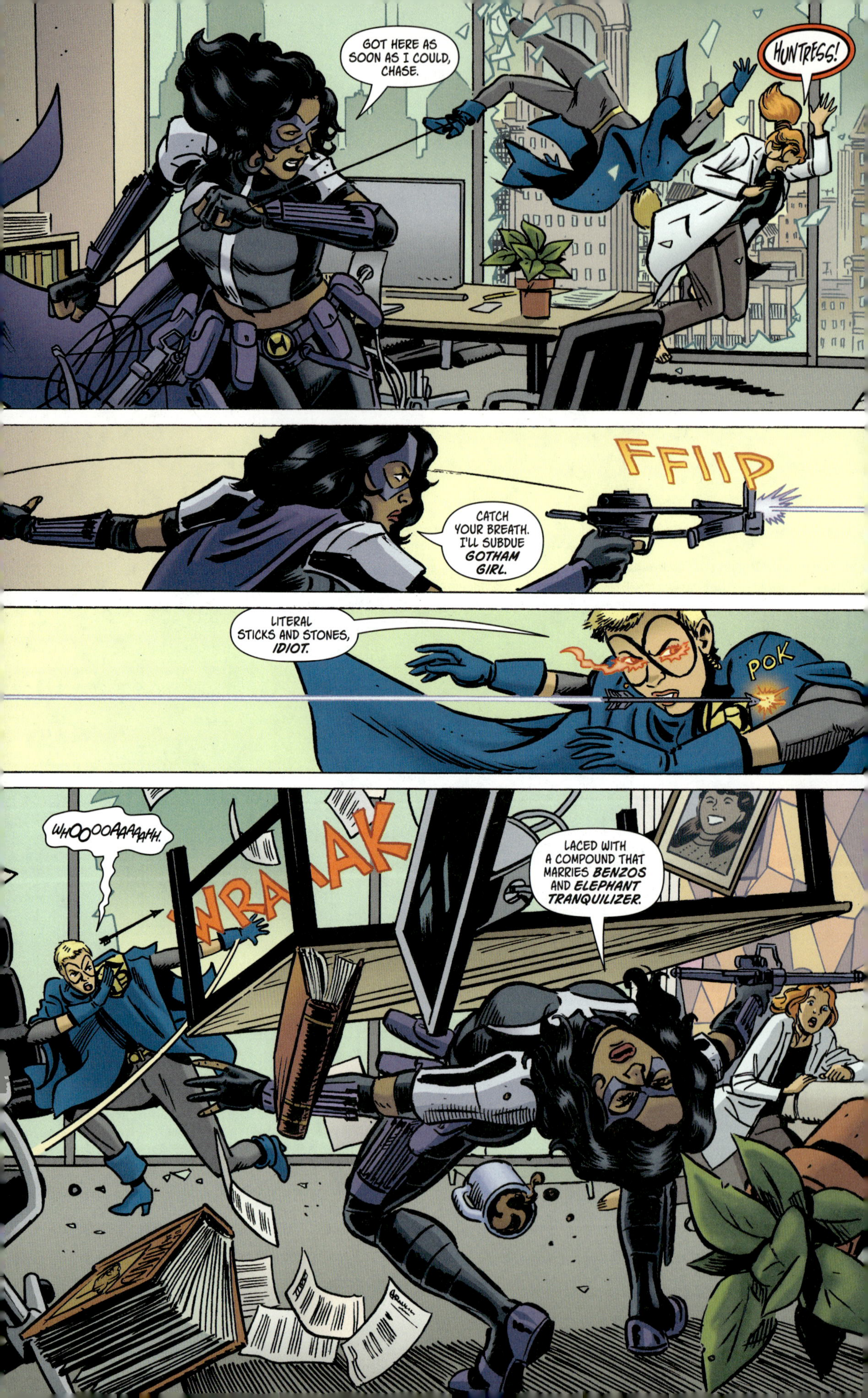

GOT HERE AS SOON AS I COULD, CHASE.
HUNTRESS!
FFIIP
CATCH YOUR BREATH. I'LL SUBDUE GOTHAM GIRL.
LITERAL STICKS AND STONES, IDIOT.
POK
WHOOOOAAAAAHH.
WRAAK
LACED WITH A COMPOUND THAT MARRIES BENZOS AND ELEPHANT TRANQUILIZER.

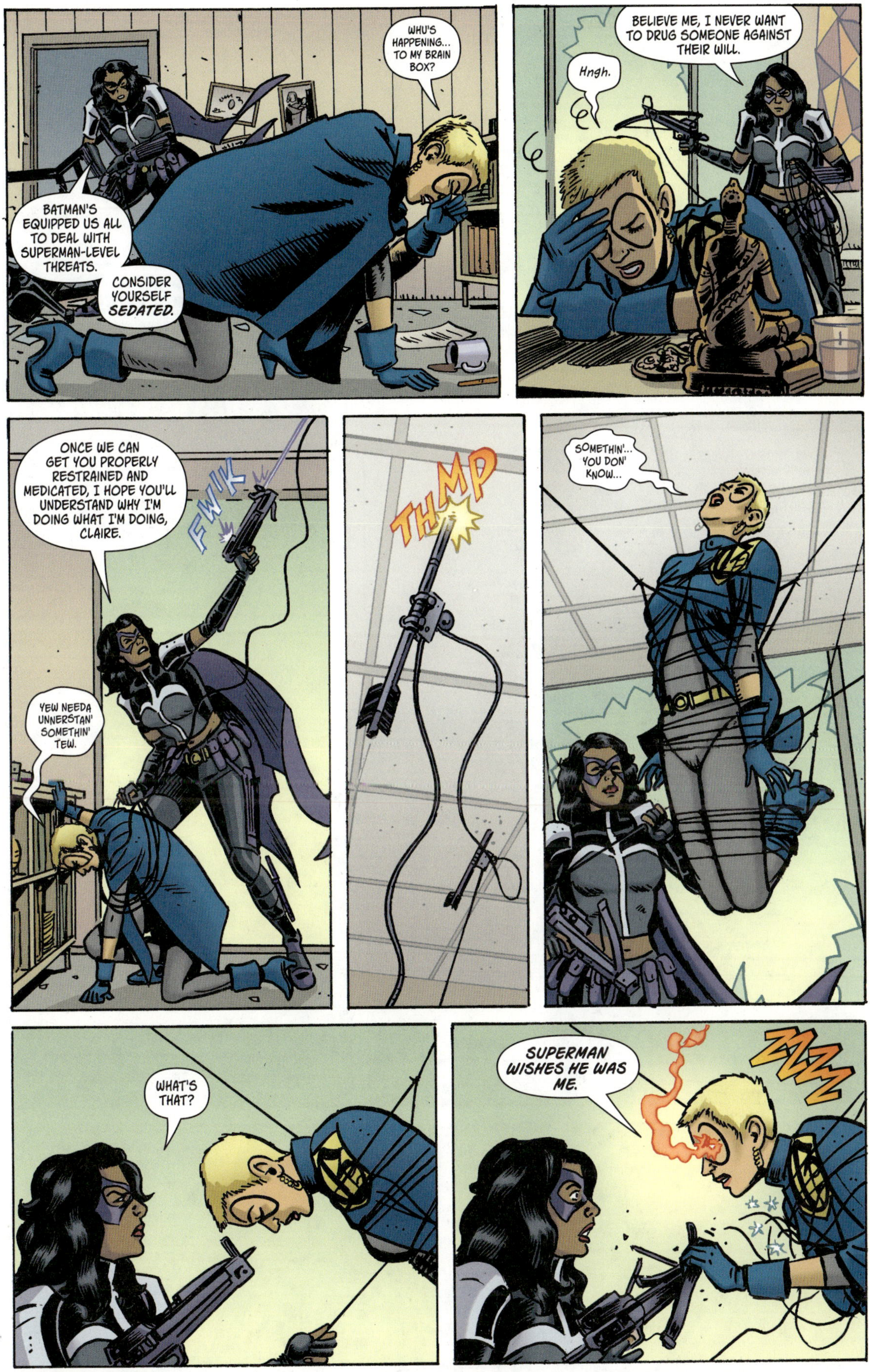
WHU'S HAPPENING... TO MY BRAIN BOX?
BATMAN'S EQUIPPED US ALL TO DEAL WITH SUPERMAN-LEVEL THREATS.
CONSIDER YOURSELF *SEDATED.*
BELIEVE ME, I NEVER WANT TO DRUG SOMEONE AGAINST THEIR WILL.
Hngh.
ONCE WE CAN GET YOU PROPERLY RESTRAINED AND MEDICATED, I HOPE YOU'LL UNDERSTAND WHY I'M DOING WHAT I'M DOING, CLAIRE.
FWIK
YEW NEEDA UNNERSTAN' SOMETHIN' TEW.
THMP
SOMETHIN'... YOU DON' KNOW...
WHAT'S THAT?
SUPERMAN WISHES HE WAS ME.
ZZZ

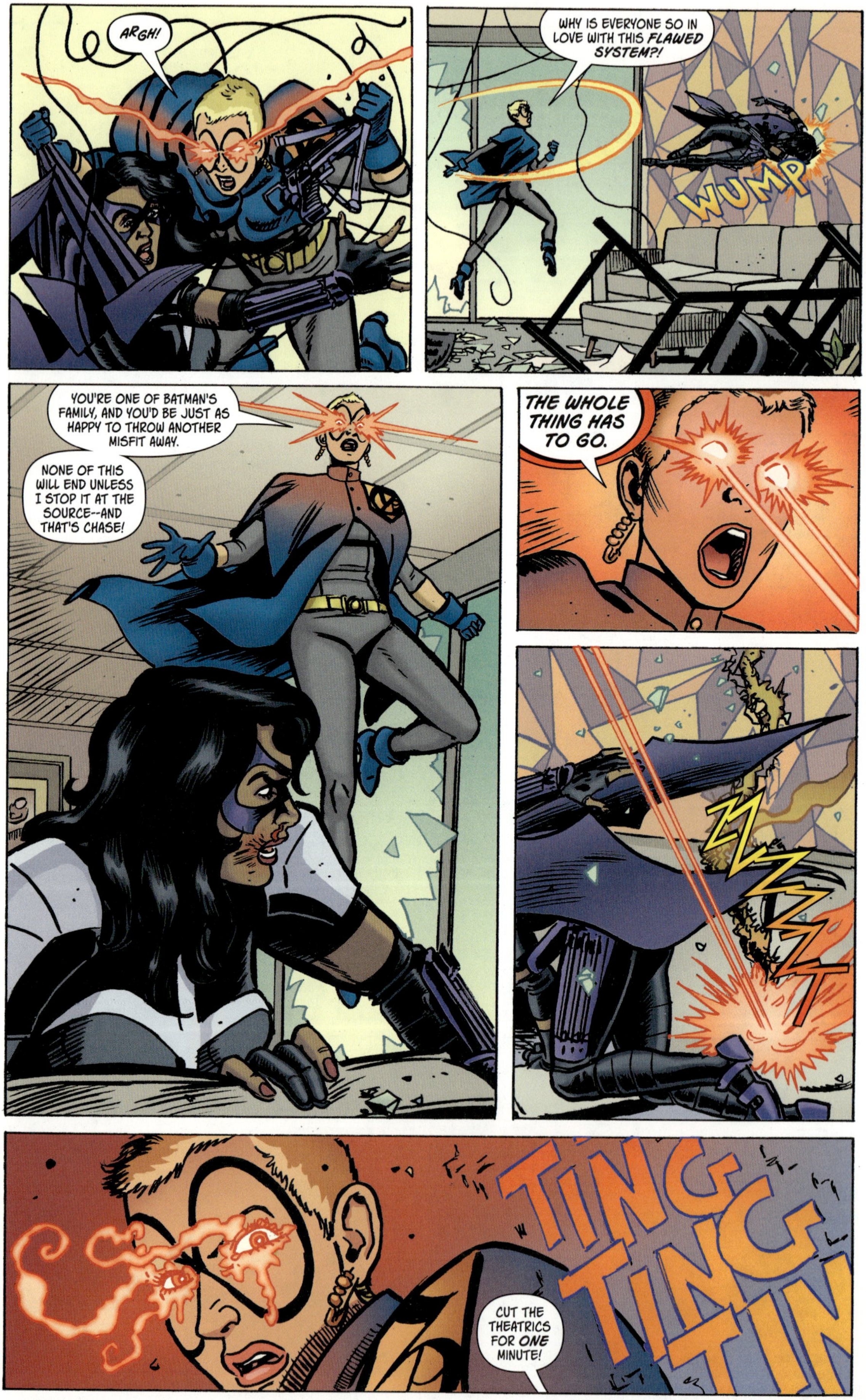

ARGH!
WHY IS EVERYONE SO IN LOVE WITH THIS FLAWED SYSTEM?!
WUMP
YOU'RE ONE OF BATMAN'S FAMILY, AND YOU'D BE JUST AS HAPPY TO THROW ANOTHER MISFIT AWAY.
NONE OF THIS WILL END UNLESS I STOP IT AT THE SOURCE--AND THAT'S CHASE!
THE WHOLE THING HAS TO GO.
ZZZAT
TING
TING
TIN
CUT THE THEATRICS FOR ONE MINUTE!

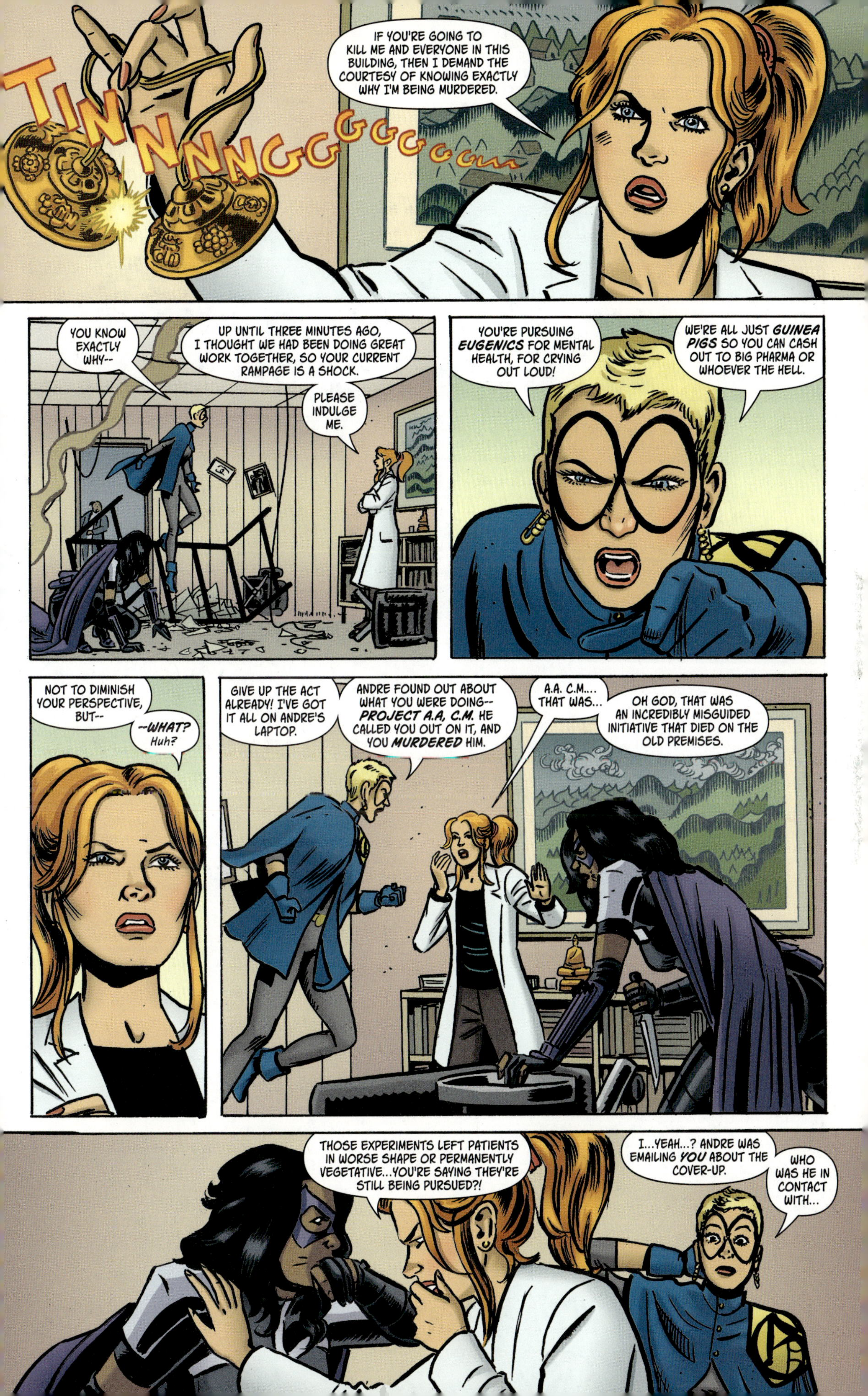
TINNNNGGGGGGGGGGGGGG
IF YOU'RE GOING TO KILL ME AND EVERYONE IN THIS BUILDING, THEN I DEMAND THE COURTESY OF KNOWING EXACTLY WHY I'M BEING MURDERED.
YOU KNOW EXACTLY WHY--
UP UNTIL THREE MINUTES AGO, I THOUGHT WE HAD BEEN DOING GREAT WORK TOGETHER, SO YOUR CURRENT RAMPAGE IS A SHOCK.
PLEASE INDULGE ME.
YOU'RE PURSUING EUGENICS FOR MENTAL HEALTH, FOR CRYING OUT LOUD!
WE'RE ALL JUST GUINEA PIGS SO YOU CAN CASH OUT TO BIG PHARMA OR WHOEVER THE HELL.
NOT TO DIMINISH YOUR PERSPECTIVE, BUT--
--WHAT? Huh?
GIVE UP THE ACT ALREADY! I'VE GOT IT ALL ON ANDRE'S LAPTOP.
ANDRE FOUND OUT ABOUT WHAT YOU WERE DOING-- PROJECT A.A, C.M. HE CALLED YOU OUT ON IT, AND YOU MURDERED HIM.
A.A. C.M.... THAT WAS...
OH GOD, THAT WAS AN INCREDIBLY MISGUIDED INITIATIVE THAT DIED ON THE OLD PREMISES.
THOSE EXPERIMENTS LEFT PATIENTS IN WORSE SHAPE OR PERMANENTLY VEGETATIVE...YOU'RE SAYING THEY'RE STILL BEING PURSUED?!
I...YEAH...? ANDRE WAS EMAILING YOU ABOUT THE COVER-UP.
WHO WAS HE IN CONTACT WITH...

"...WHO ELSE HAD ACCESS TO YOUR COMPUTER?"

IT'S A LITTLE EARLY FOR MY QUARTERLY REVIEW, DR. MERIDIAN.

PRETTY SURE YOU'RE STRAIGHT-UP *FIRED*, MARGOT.

HOW *DARE* YOU IMPLICATE ME IN REVIVING AN ARCHAIC AND BARBARIC FORM OF--

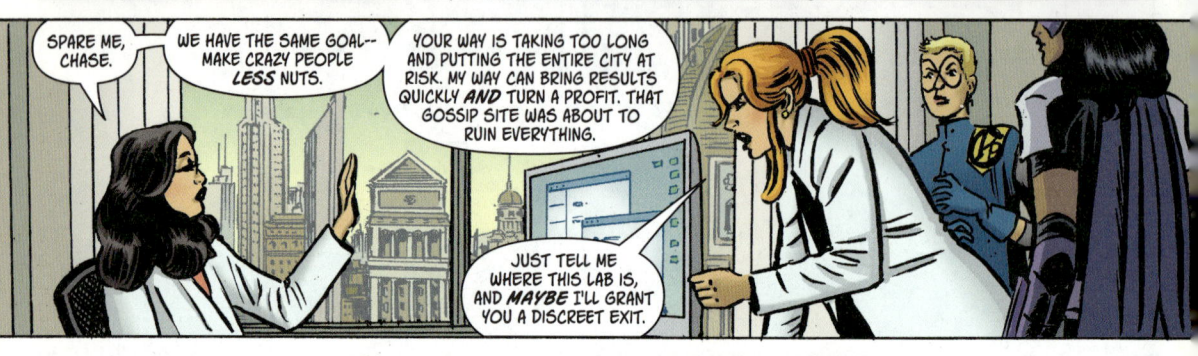

SPARE ME, CHASE.

WE HAVE THE SAME GOAL-- MAKE CRAZY PEOPLE *LESS* NUTS.

YOUR WAY IS TAKING TOO LONG AND PUTTING THE ENTIRE CITY AT RISK. MY WAY CAN BRING RESULTS QUICKLY *AND* TURN A PROFIT. THAT GOSSIP SITE WAS ABOUT TO RUIN EVERYTHING.

JUST TELL ME WHERE THIS LAB IS, AND *MAYBE* I'LL GRANT YOU A DISCREET EXIT.

"EXIT"?

IF ANY OF THIS COMES OUT, WE'RE BOTH GOING DOWN. ANDRE'S EMAILS CAME FROM YOU, AND IT'S AN UNHINGED TEENAGER'S ACCOUNT AGAINST MINE.

YOU GOT ALL THAT, ORACLE? *GREAT*. OH, WHAT ELSE?

YOUR VOICE RECOGNITION SOFTWARE UPDATE BOASTS *99.92 PERCENT ACCURACY*? WOW!

FLOOR THIRTEEN. ROOM THREE. DOOR CODE 9891.

OH, BEFORE I FORGET--

FLIK

--YOU GOT SOMETHING ON YOUR EAR.

CLAIRE!

AUGH!

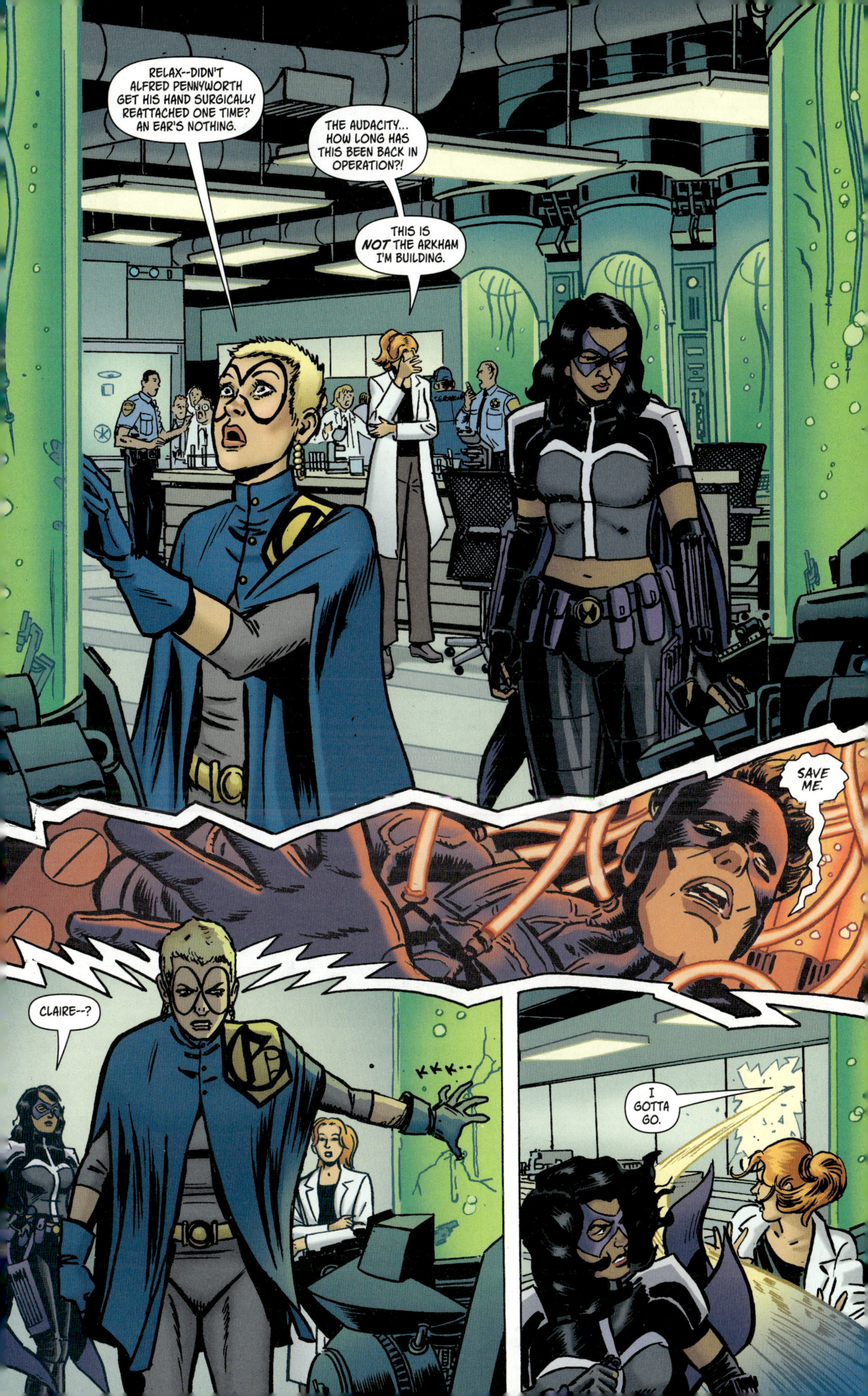
RELAX--DIDN'T ALFRED PENNYWORTH GET HIS HAND SURGICALLY REATTACHED ONE TIME? AN EAR'S NOTHING.
THE AUDACITY... HOW LONG HAS THIS BEEN BACK IN OPERATION?!
THIS IS *NOT* THE ARKHAM I'M BUILDING.
SAVE ME.
CLAIRE--?
KKK...
I GOTTA GO.

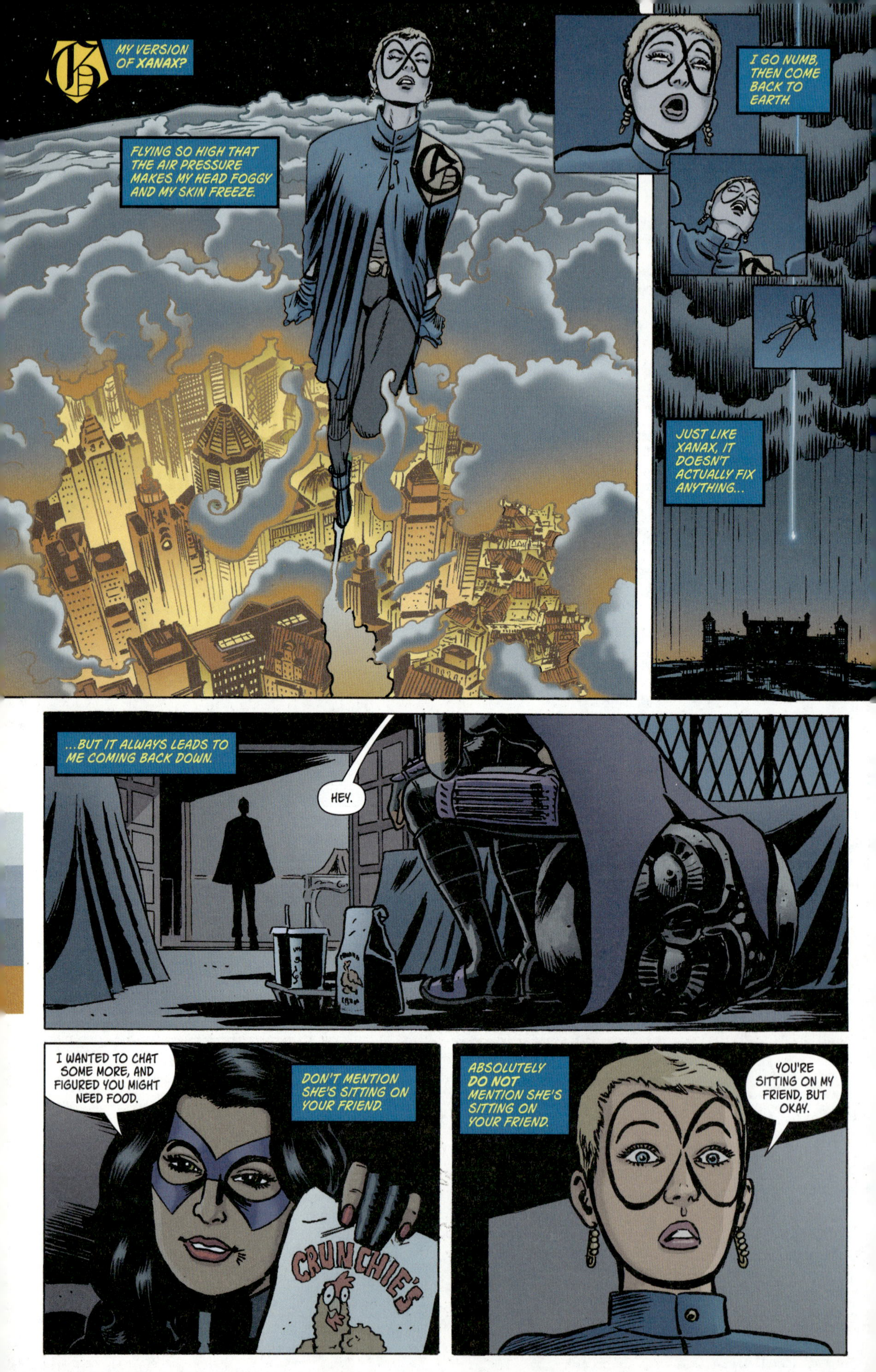
MY VERSION OF XANAX?
FLYING SO HIGH THAT THE AIR PRESSURE MAKES MY HEAD FOGGY AND MY SKIN FREEZE.
I GO NUMB, THEN COME BACK TO EARTH.
JUST LIKE XANAX, IT DOESN'T ACTUALLY FIX ANYTHING...
...BUT IT ALWAYS LEADS TO ME COMING BACK DOWN.
HEY.
I WANTED TO CHAT SOME MORE, AND FIGURED YOU MIGHT NEED FOOD.
DON'T MENTION SHE'S SITTING ON YOUR FRIEND.
CRUNCHIE'S
ABSOLUTELY DO NOT MENTION SHE'S SITTING ON YOUR FRIEND.
YOU'RE SITTING ON MY FRIEND, BUT OKAY.

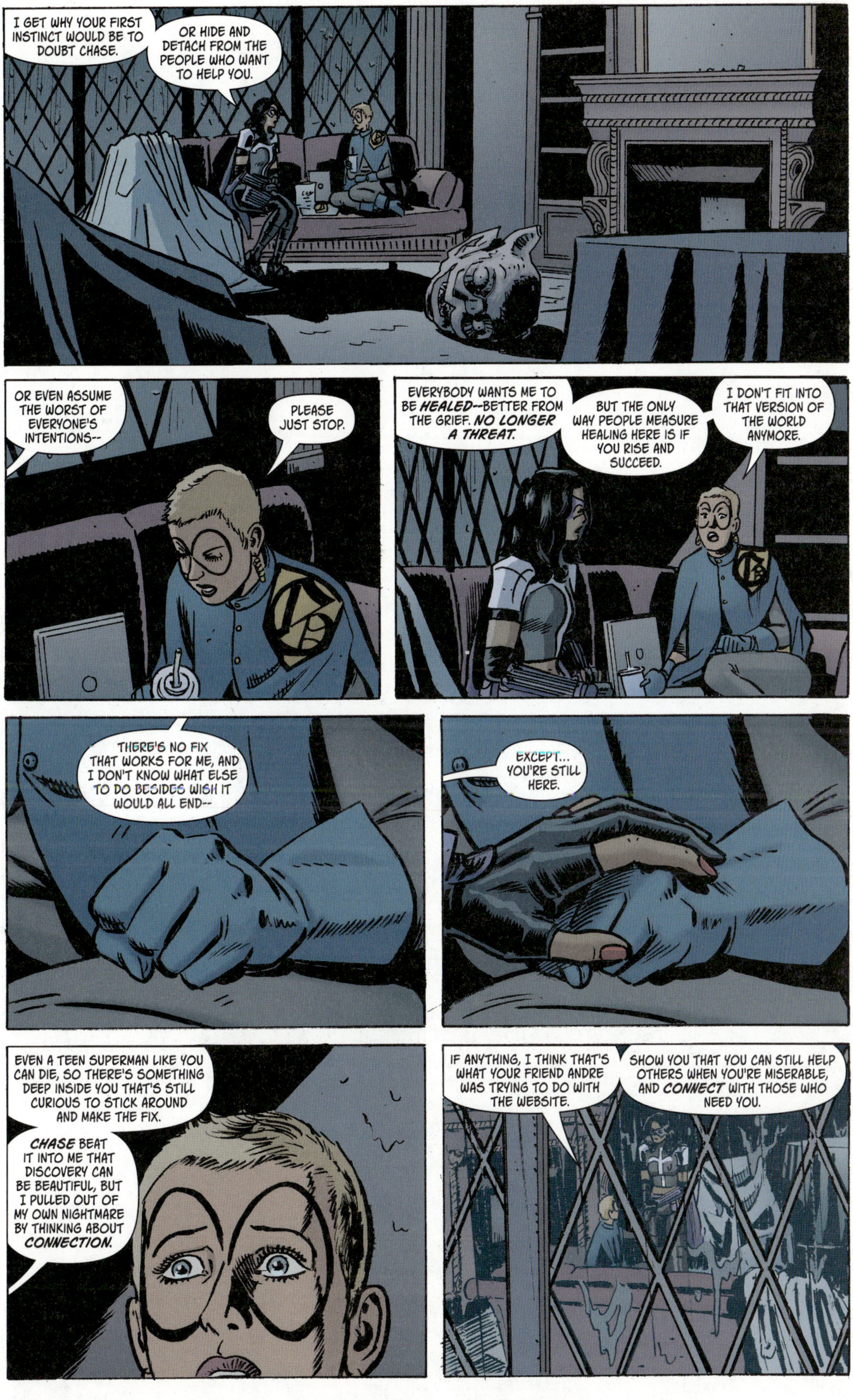
I GET WHY YOUR FIRST INSTINCT WOULD BE TO DOUBT CHASE.
OR HIDE AND DETACH FROM THE PEOPLE WHO WANT TO HELP YOU.
OR EVEN ASSUME THE WORST OF EVERYONE'S INTENTIONS--
PLEASE JUST STOP.
EVERYBODY WANTS ME TO BE *HEALED*--BETTER FROM THE GRIEF. ***NO LONGER A THREAT.***
BUT THE ONLY WAY PEOPLE MEASURE HEALING HERE IS IF YOU RISE AND SUCCEED.
I DON'T FIT INTO THAT VERSION OF THE WORLD ANYMORE.
THERE'S NO FIX THAT WORKS FOR ME, AND I DON'T KNOW WHAT ELSE TO DO BESIDES WISH IT WOULD ALL END--
EXCEPT... YOU'RE STILL HERE.
EVEN A TEEN SUPERMAN LIKE YOU CAN DIE, SO THERE'S SOMETHING DEEP INSIDE YOU THAT'S STILL CURIOUS TO STICK AROUND AND MAKE THE FIX.
CHASE BEAT IT INTO ME THAT DISCOVERY CAN BE BEAUTIFUL, BUT I PULLED OUT OF MY OWN NIGHTMARE BY THINKING ABOUT *CONNECTION.*
IF ANYTHING, I THINK THAT'S WHAT YOUR FRIEND ANDRE WAS TRYING TO DO WITH THE WEBSITE.
SHOW YOU THAT YOU CAN STILL HELP OTHERS WHEN YOU'RE MISERABLE, AND *CONNECT* WITH THOSE WHO NEED YOU.

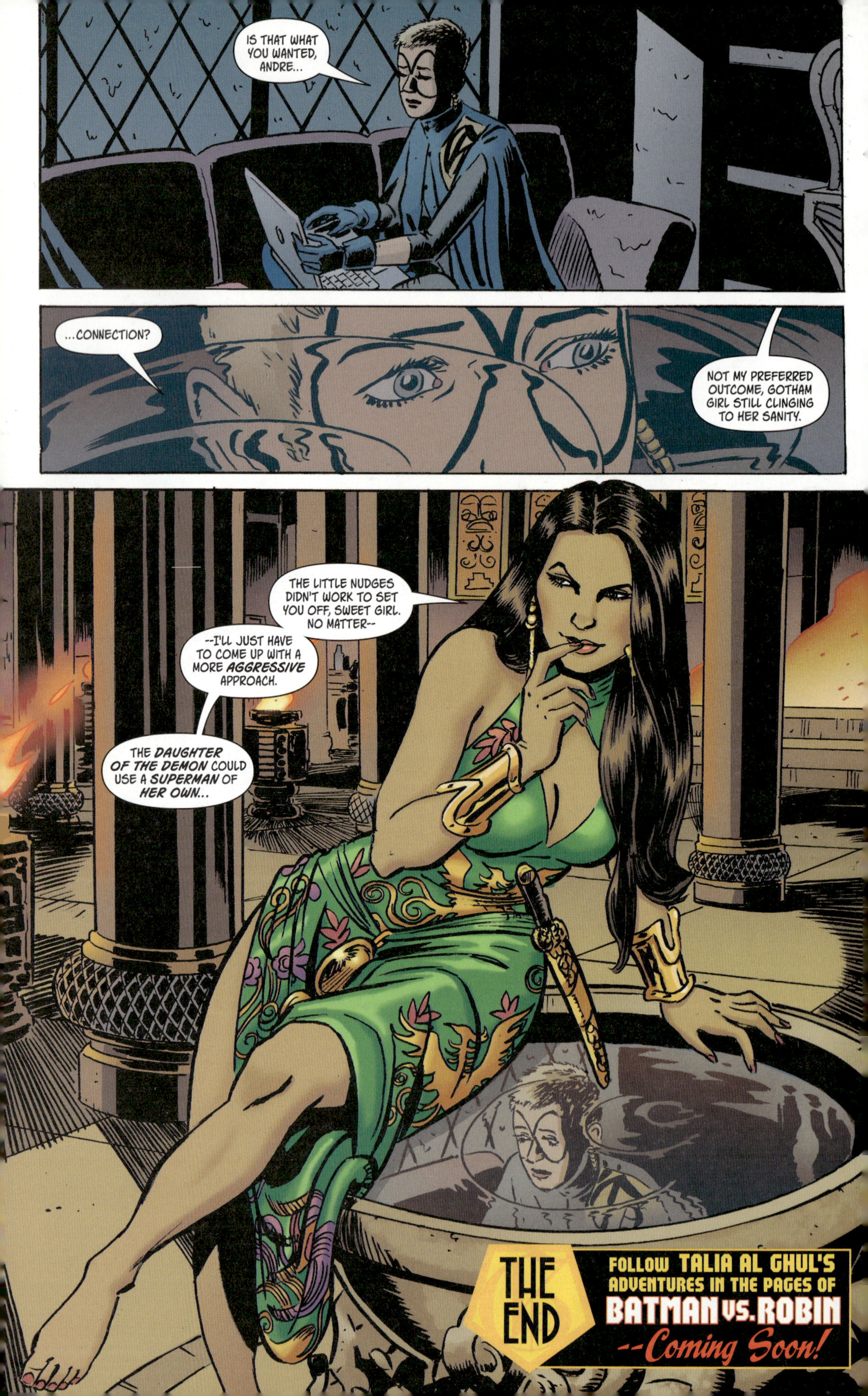
IS THAT WHAT YOU WANTED, ANDRE...
...CONNECTION?
NOT MY PREFERRED OUTCOME, GOTHAM GIRL STILL CLINGING TO HER SANITY.
THE LITTLE NUDGES DIDN'T WORK TO SET YOU OFF, SWEET GIRL. NO MATTER--
--I'LL JUST HAVE TO COME UP WITH A MORE AGGRESSIVE APPROACH.
THE DAUGHTER OF THE DEMON COULD USE A SUPERMAN OF HER OWN...
THE END
FOLLOW TALIA AL GHUL'S ADVENTURES IN THE PAGES OF
BATMAN VS. ROBIN
--Coming Soon!

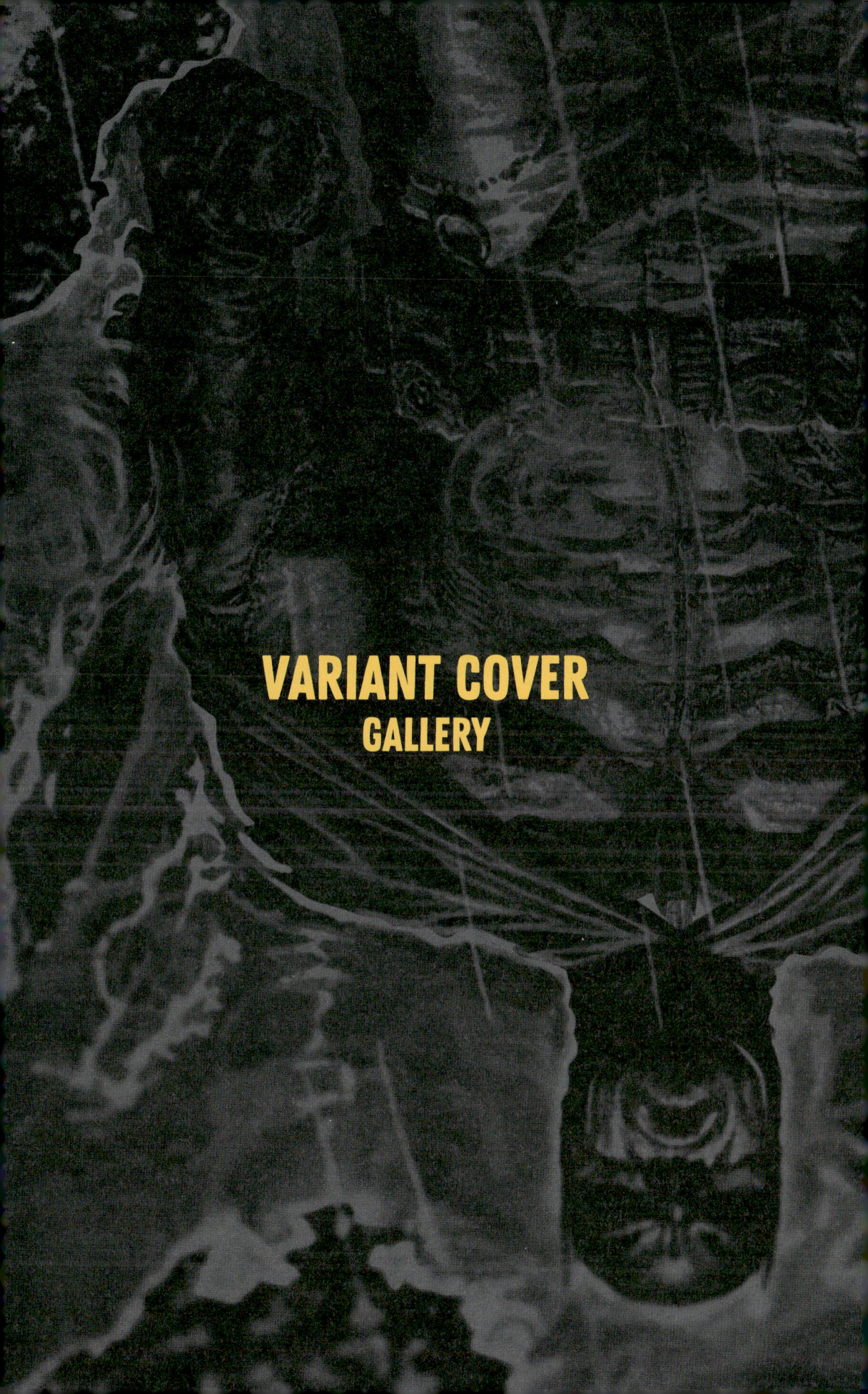

VARIANT COVER
GALLERY

***Batman: Detective Comics* #1060**
variant cover art by ERIN McDERMOTT

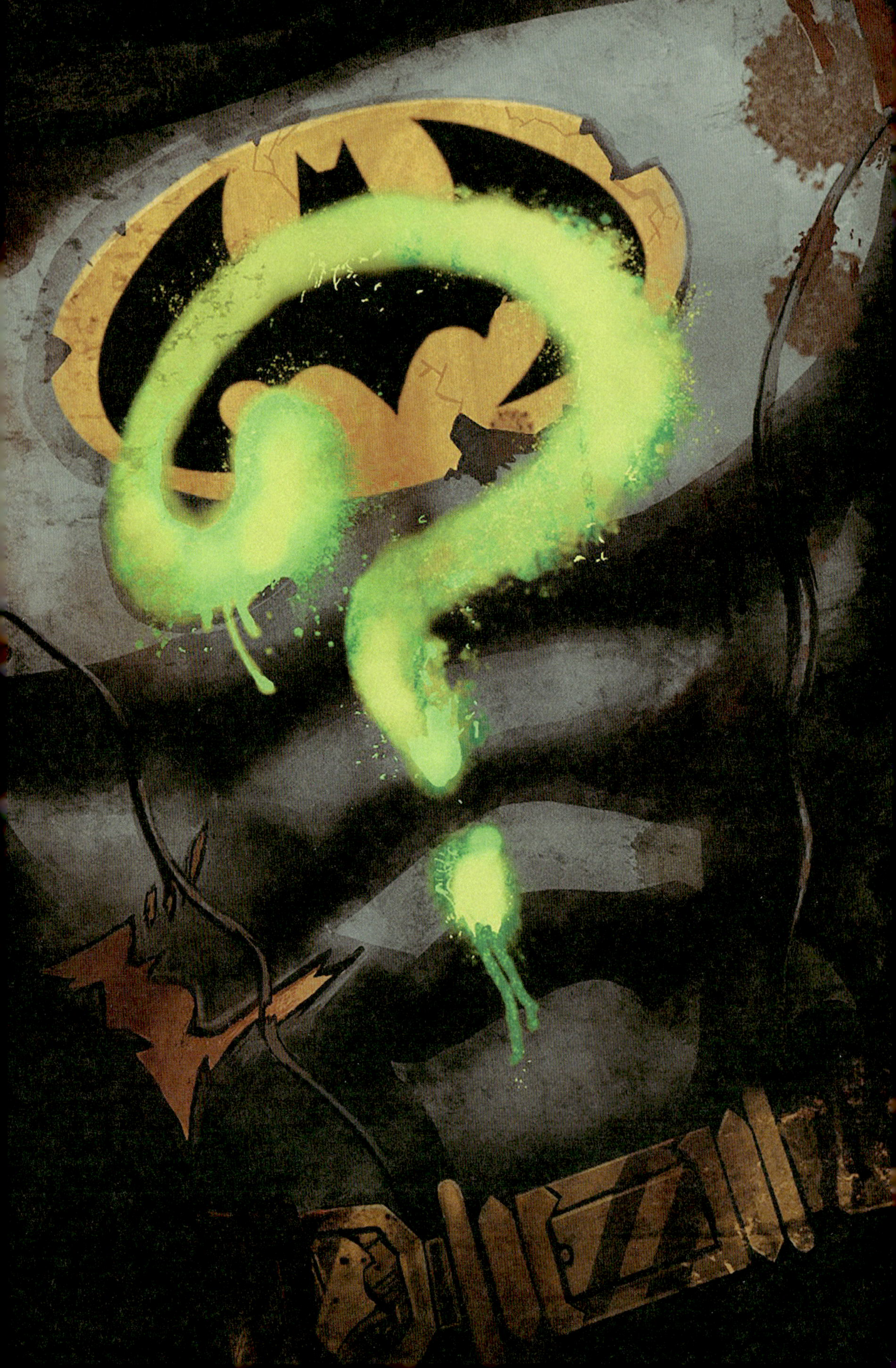

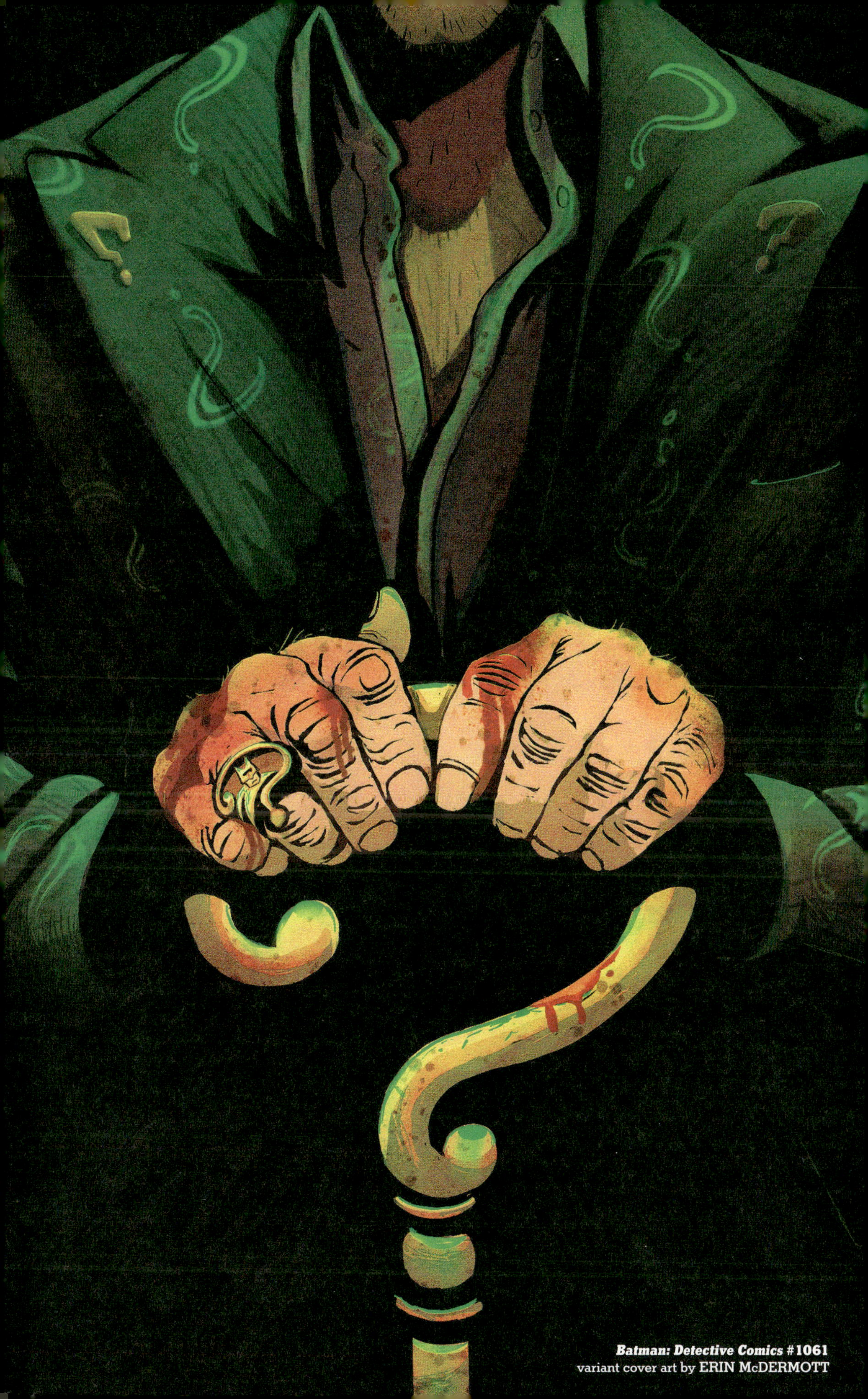

***Batman: Detective Comics* #1061**
variant cover art by ERIN McDERMOTT

Batman: Detective Comics #1059
variant cover art by LEE BERMEJO

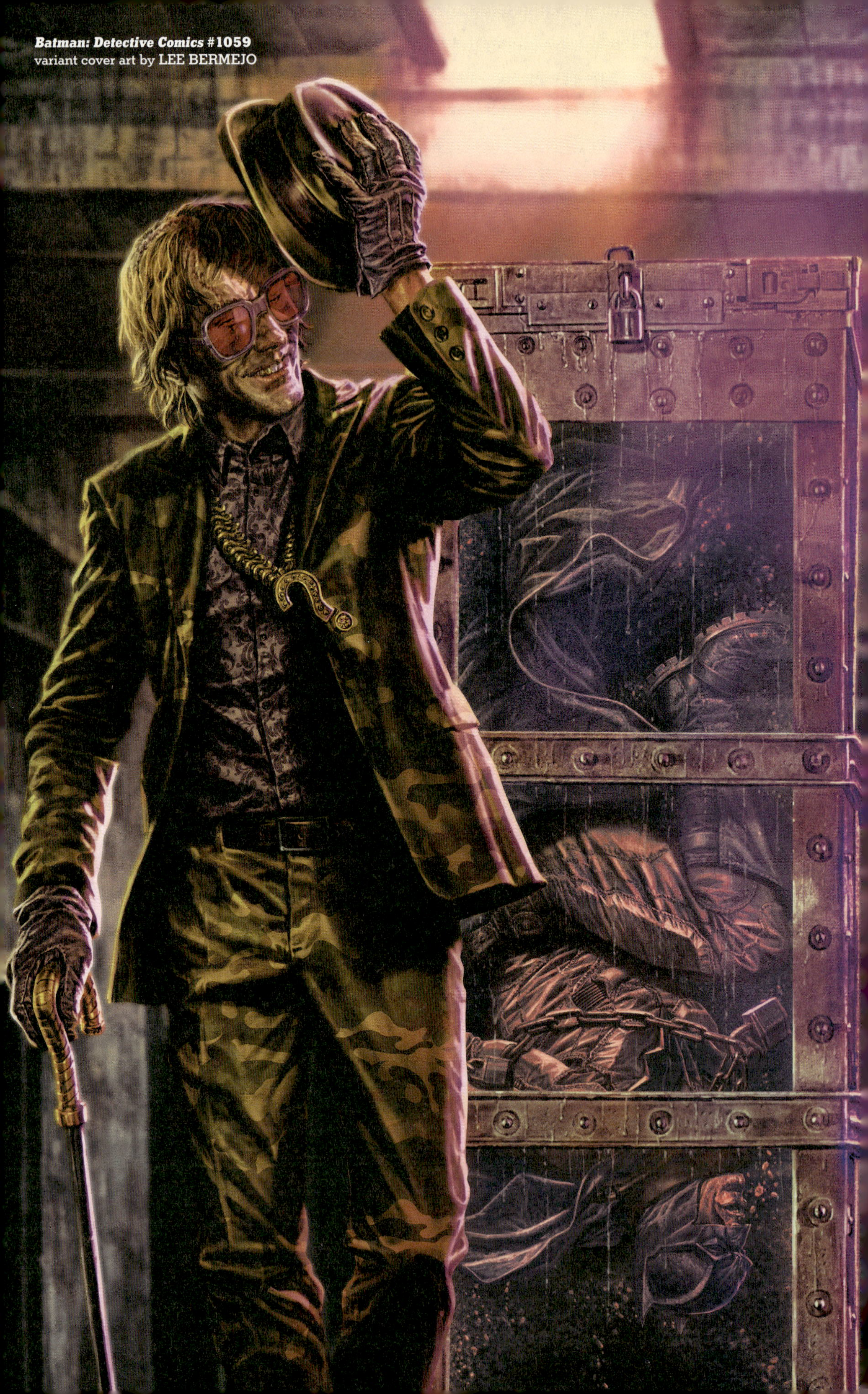

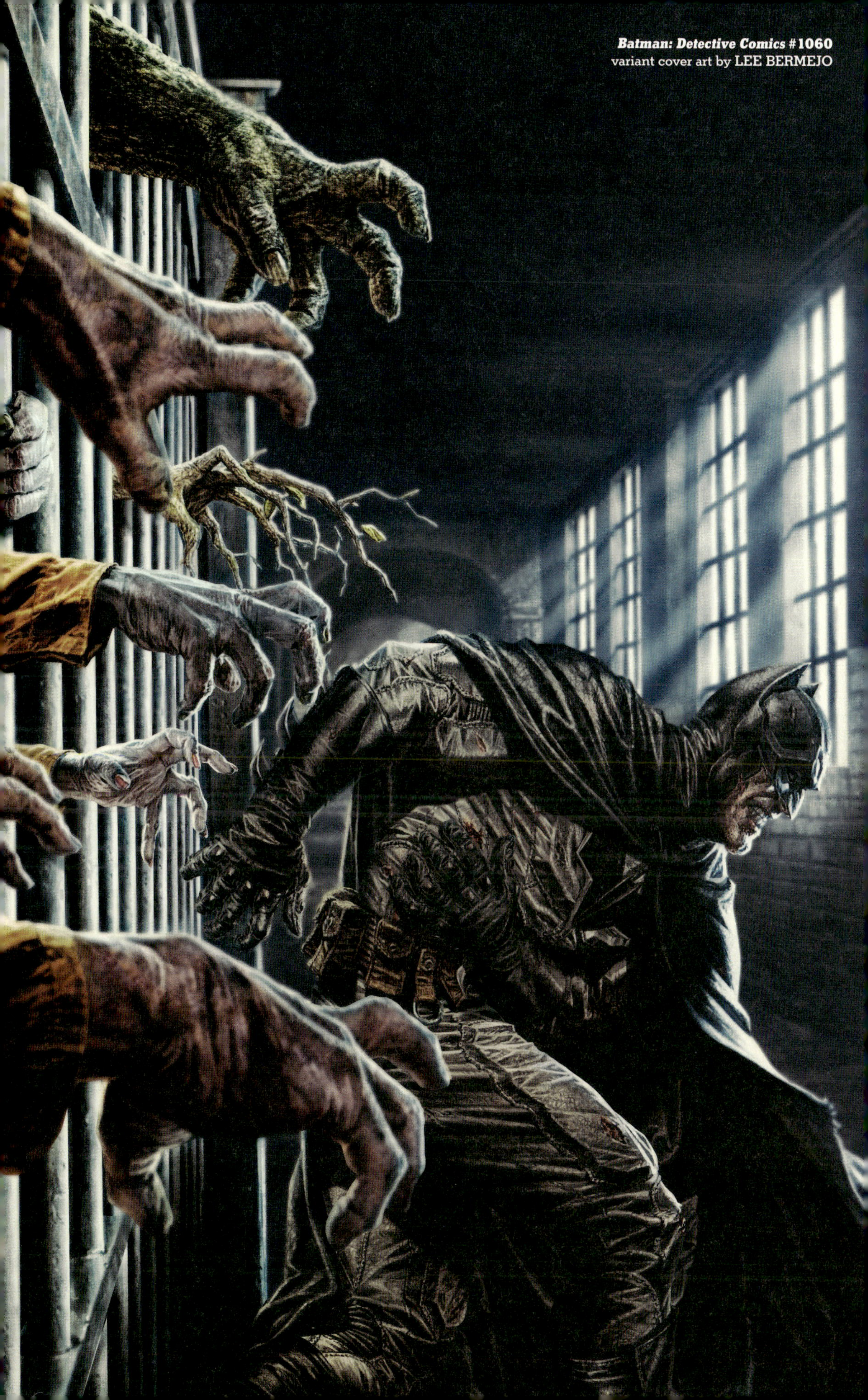

***Batman: Detective Comics* #1060**
variant cover art by LEE BERMEJO

***Batman: Detective Comics* #1061**
variant cover art by LEE BERMEJO

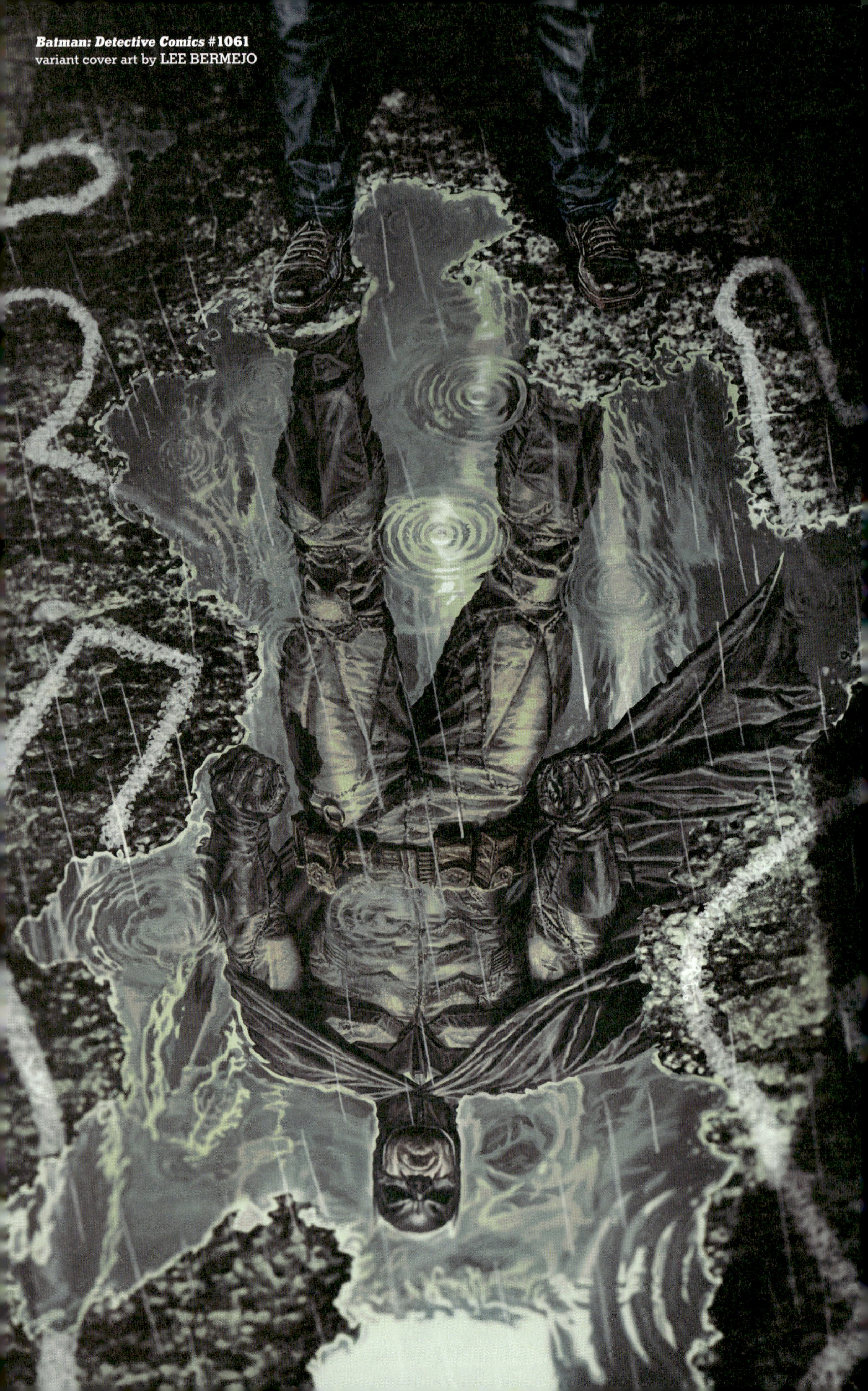

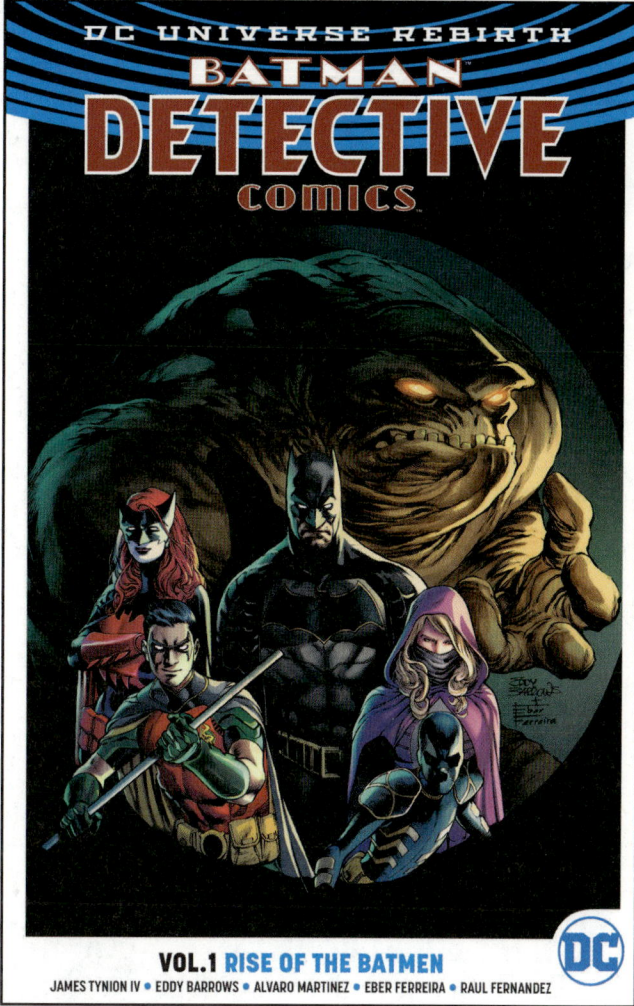
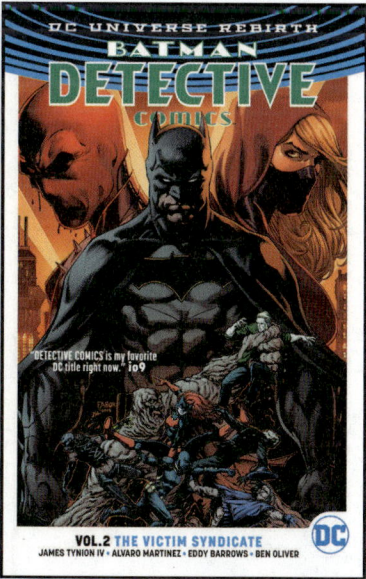
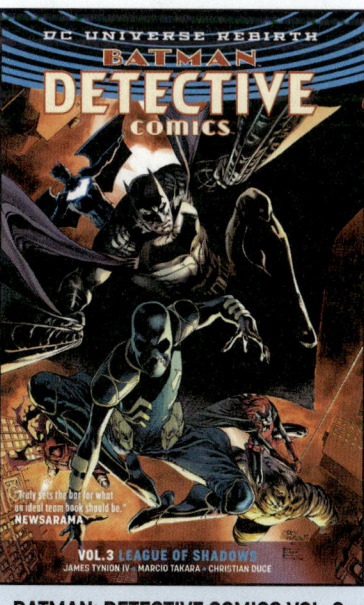

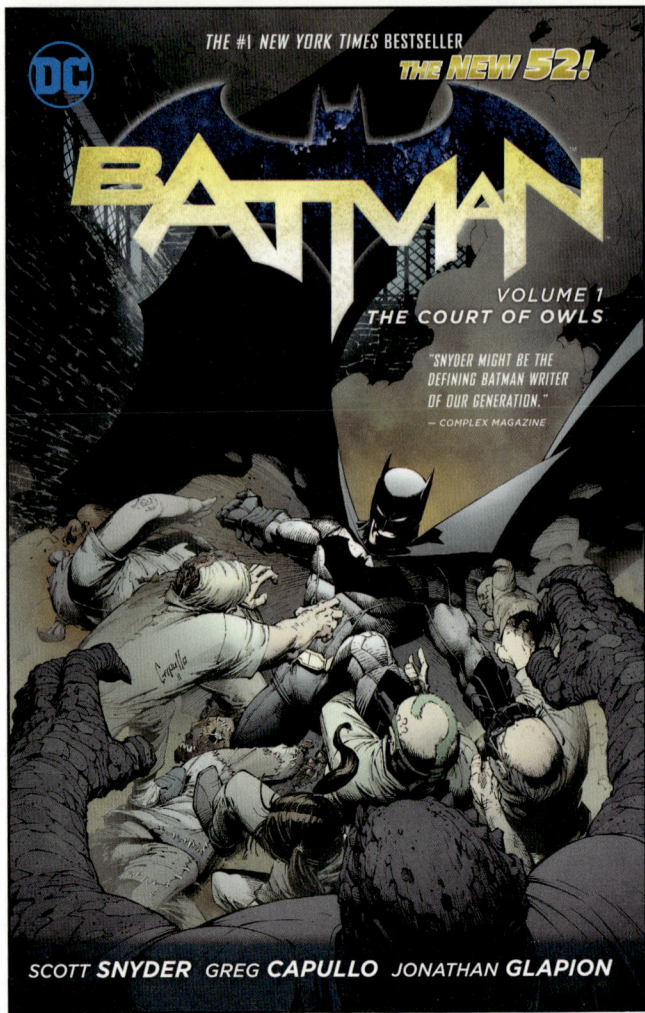

> "[Writer Scott Snyder] pulls from the oldest aspects of the Batman myth, combines it with sinister-comic elements from the series' best period, and gives the whole thing terrific forward-spin."
> **– ENTERTAINMENT WEEKLY**

START AT THE BEGINNING!
BATMAN
VOL. 1: THE COURT OF OWLS
SCOTT SNYDER with GREG CAPULLO

**BATMAN VOL. 2:
THE CITY OF OWLS**

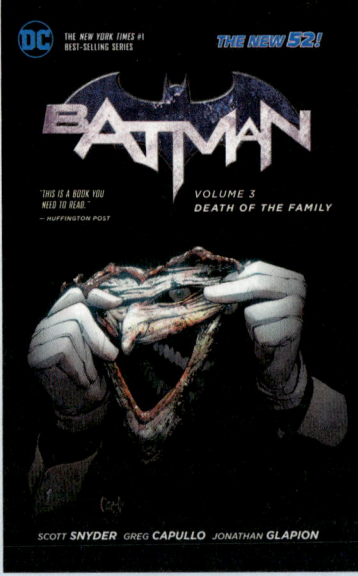

**BATMAN VOL. 3:
DEATH OF THE FAMILY**

READ THE ENTIRE EPIC!

BATMAN VOL. 4:
ZERO YEAR – SECRET CITY

BATMAN VOL. 5:
ZERO YEAR – DARK CITY

BATMAN VOL. 6:
GRAVEYARD SHIFT

BATMAN VOL. 7:
ENDGAME

BATMAN VOL. 8:
SUPERHEAVY

BATMAN VOL. 9:
BLOOM

BATMAN VOL. 10:
EPILOGUE

Get more DC graphic novels wherever comics and books are sold!

BATMAN
VOL. 1: I AM GOTHAM
TOM KING
DAVID FINCH

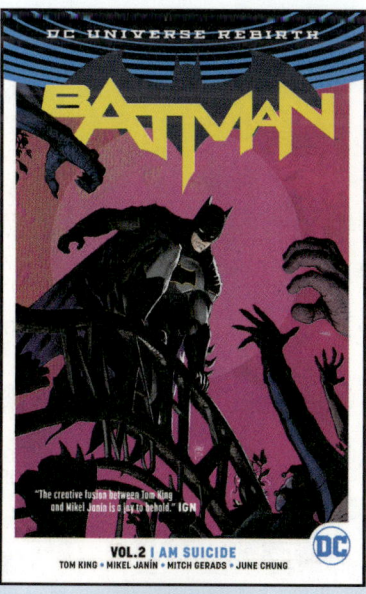

**BATMAN: VOL. 2
I AM SUICIDE**

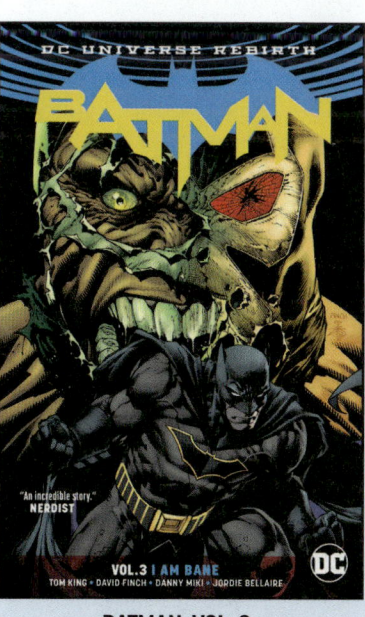

**BATMAN: VOL. 3:
I AM BANE**

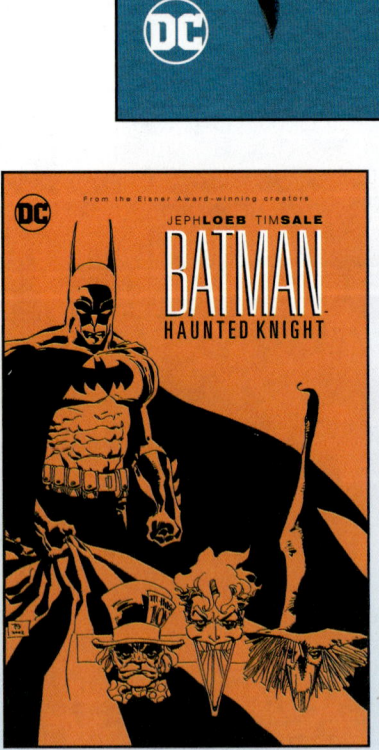

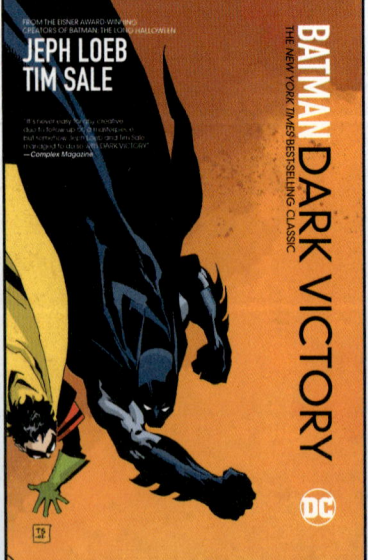
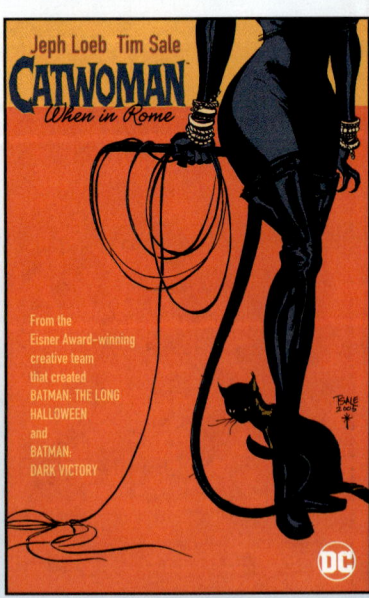

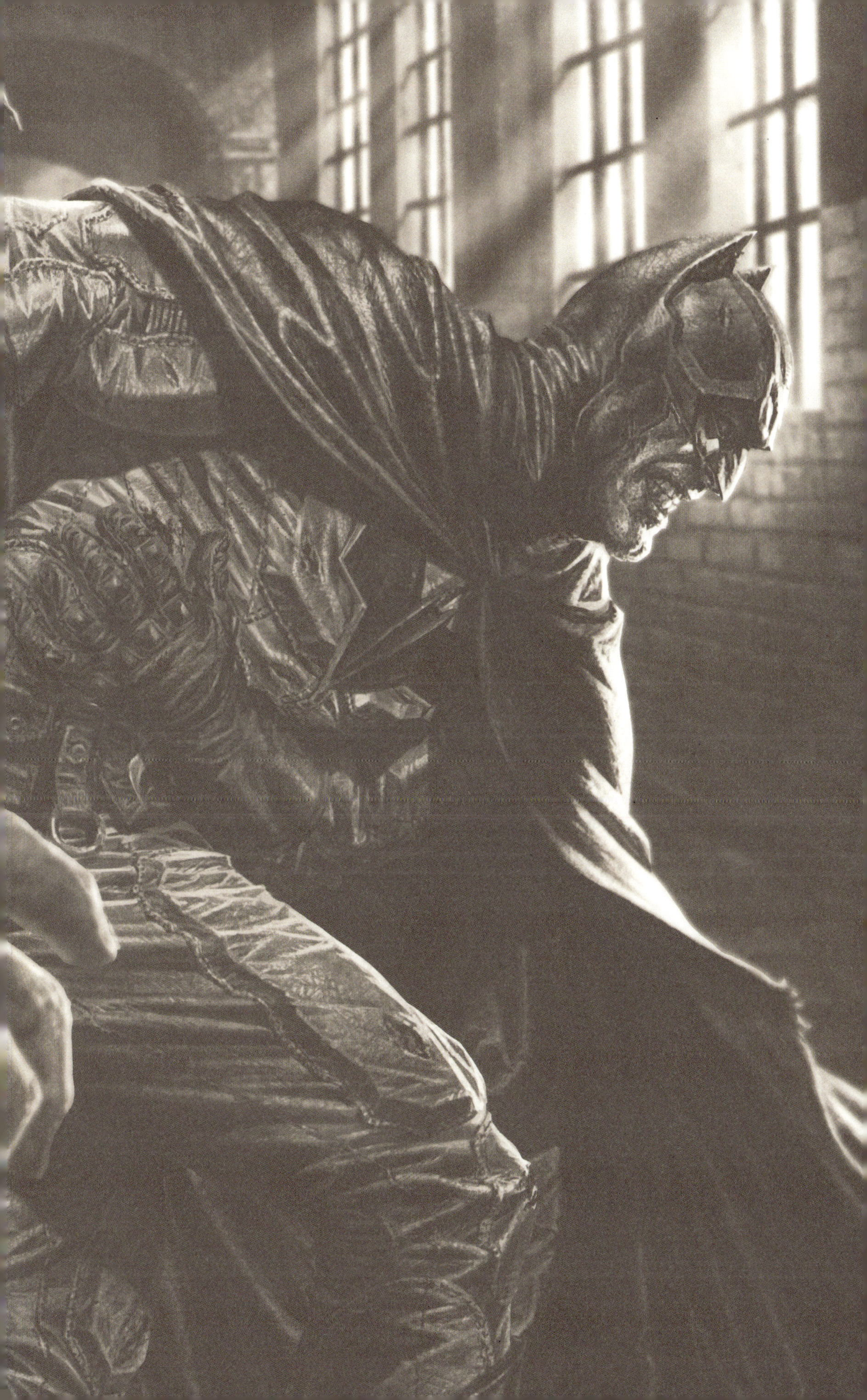

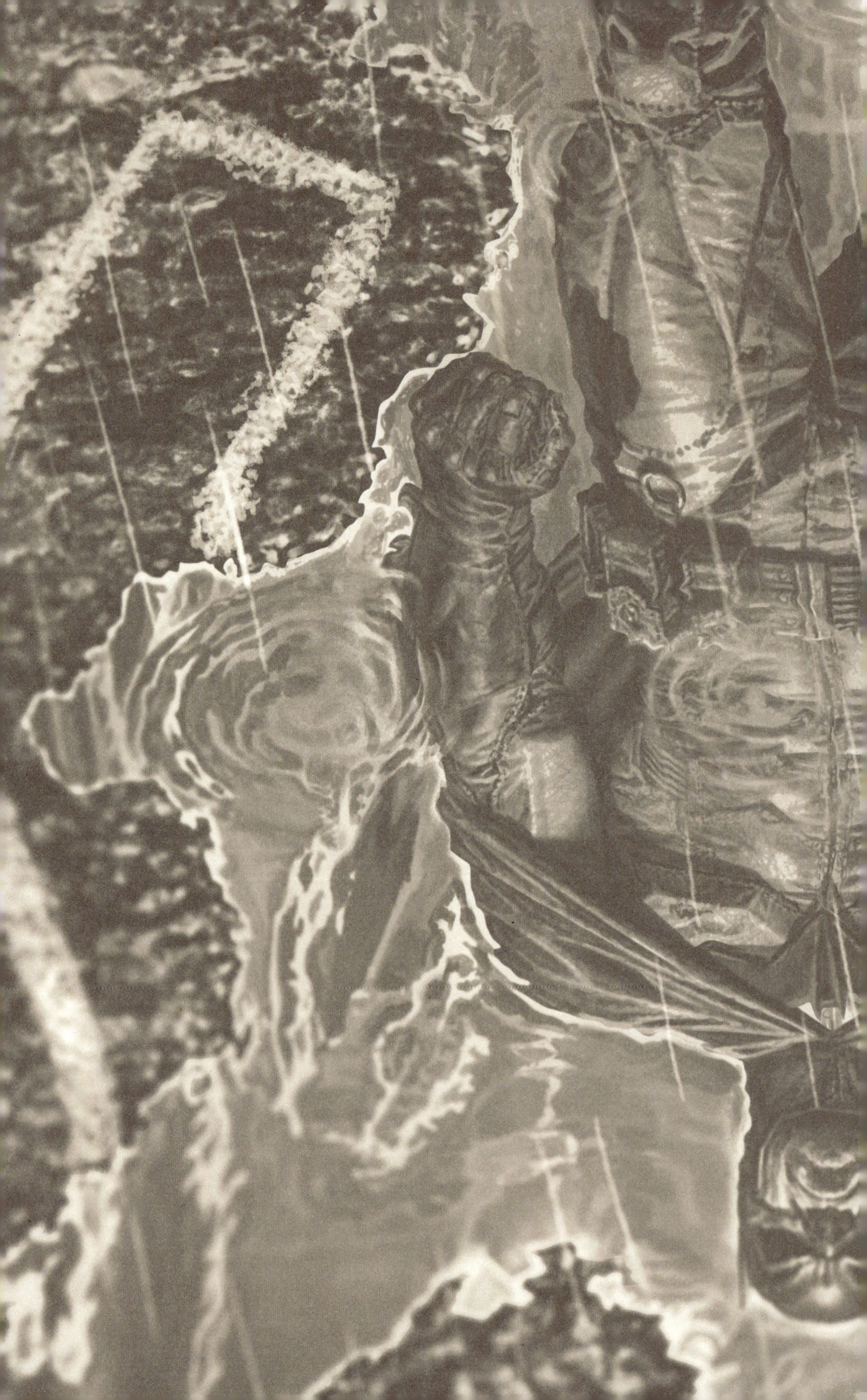